PLANNING FOR TALL BUI

In a time of recession, the challenge of building and planning for tall buildings has become even more complex; the economics of development, legislative and planning frameworks, and the local politics of development must be navigated by those wishing to design and construct new tall buildings which fit within the fabric of their host cities.

This book is a timely contribution to the debate about new tall buildings and their role and effect on our cities. In the first part of the book, the relationship between tall buildings and planning is outlined, followed by an exploration of the impacts that construction of tall buildings can have. It focuses in particular on the conservation debates that proposals for new tall buildings raise. The first part ends with an analysis of the way in which planning strategies have evolved to deal with the unique consequences of tall buildings on their urban locations. The second part of the book focuses on seven examples of medium-sized cities dealing with planning and conservation issues, and the implications that arise from tall buildings. These have been chosen to reflect a wide range of methods to either encourage or control tall buildings that cities are deploying. The case studies come from across the western world, covering the UK (Manchester, Liverpool, Newcastle and Birmingham), Norway (Oslo), Ireland (Dublin) and Canada (Vancouver) and represent a broad spectrum of approaches to dealing with this issue.

In drawing together the experiences of these varied cities, the book contributes to the ongoing debate about the role of the tall buildings in our cities, their potential impacts and the experiences of those who use and inhabit them. The conclusions outline how cities should approach the strategic planning of tall buildings, as well as how they should deal with the consequences of individual buildings, particularly on the built heritage.

Michael J. Short is a qualified planner (MRTPI) and conservation officer (IHBC) with a BSc (Hons) in Town and Regional Planning from the University of Dundee, an MA in Heritage Management from Sheffield Hallam University, and a PhD in Urban Planning and Conservation from the University of Manchester. Michael currently works as Senior Lecturer in Urban Planning and Conservation at the University of the West of England in Bristol.

Planning for Tall Buildings

Michael J. Short

Routledge
Taylor & Francis Group

LONDON AND NEW YORK

First published 2012
by Routledge
2 Park Square, Milton Park, Abingdon, Oxon OX14 4RN

Simultaneously published in the USA and Canada
by Routledge
711 Third Avenue, New York, NY 10017

Routledge is an imprint of the Taylor & Francis Group, an informa business

British Library Cataloguing in Publication Data
A catalogue record for this book is available from the British Library

Library of Congress Cataloging in Publication Data
Short, Michael J.
Planning for tall buildings / Michael J. Short.
     p. cm.
  1. Tall buildings—Social aspects. 2. City planning. I. Title.
  NA6230.S36 2012
  720′.483—dc23   2011033725

ISBN: 978–0–415–58107–3 (hbk)
ISBN: 978–0–415–58108–0 (pbk)

Typeset in Bembo
by Keystroke, Station Road, Codsall, Wolverhampton

Printed and bound in Great Britain by
TJ International Ltd, Padstow, Cornwall

CONTENTS

LIST OF TABLES

IMAGE CREDITS

The authors and the publishers would like to thank the following individuals and institutions for giving permission to reproduce material in this book. We have made every effort to contact copyright holders, but if any errors have been made we would be happy to correct them at a later printing.

Chapter 1

Figure 1.2 © Sean Pavone, Dreamstime.com
Figure 1.3 © Christian De Grandmaison | Dreamstime.com
Figure 1.5 © Anthony Wood
Figure 1.6 © Stephen Finn, Dreamstime.com
Figure 1.7 © Brandon Seidel, Dreamstime.com
Figure 1.8 © Cao Liping, Dreamstime.com

Chapter 3

Figure 3.3 © Ahdrum, Dreamstime.com
Figure 3.4 © Mauro Marzo | Dreamstime.com
Figure 3.5 © Bristol City Council

Chapter 5

Figure 5.1 © Steve Wilson, Dreamstime.com
Figure 5.2 © Mark Twedwr-Jones
Figure 5.3 © Liverpool City Council
Figure 5.4 © Liverpool City Council

Chapter 6

Figure 6.2 © Graphic79 | Dreamstime.com
Figure 6.3 © Graphic79 | Dreamstime.com

Chapter 7

Figure 7.1 © Tupungato, Dreamstime.com
Figure 7.5 © Suttonbaggies | Dreamstime.com
Figure 7.6 © Suttonbaggies | Dreamstime.com

Chapter 8

Figure 8.1 © Natalia Rumyantseva | Dreamstime.com
Figure 8.2 © Maggern | Dreamstime.com
Figure 8.3 © Joyfull | Dreamstime.com
Figure 8.4 © Oslo City Council
Figure 8.5 © Oslo City Council
Figure 8.6 © Oslo City Council
Figure 8.7 © Maggern | Dreamstime.com

Chapter 9

Figure 9.1 © Radovan Mlatec | Dreamstime.com
Figure 9.2 © Emeraldgreen | Dreamstime.com

Chapter 10

Figure 10.1 © Verity Johnson, Dreamstime.com
Figure 10.3 © Mark Tewdwr-Jones

Chapter 11

Figure 11.1 © Vismax. Dreamstime.com
Figure 11.3 © Mark Tewdwr-Jones
Figure 11.5 © Vancouver City Council

ACKNOWLEDGEMENTS

The completion of this book is, in large part, the result of the assistance and time of a large number of organisations and people who I'd like to thank.

Firstly, thanks must go to the Economic and Social Research Council and English Heritage (grant number PTA-033-2003-00023) for funding my original PhD, which this book is, in essence, based upon. Furthermore, I would like to thank the British Academy (grant number SG46047) for the award of a grant which allowed me to pursue additional material for the international chapters from 2008 to 2010. Finally I'd like to thank my employer, UWE, who have provided me with funds to assist in the completion of the work on Vancouver and, more generally, allowing me to employ Vicky Burvill, Beckie Hill and Tristan Dewhurst as proof readers. Thank you all very much, your time and energy is appreciated.

There are a large number of people who were involved in the various elements of the book, most notably those who I interviewed, chatted to and liaised with in the case study cities. I have attempted to thank you all below: in Liverpool, Christopher Young, Susan Denyer, John Hinchliffe, Jane Bennison, Jenny Douglas, Nigel Lee, John Benbow, Mike Burchnall, Martin Wright, Rob Burns and John Stonard; in Manchester, John Cooper, Andrew Martindale, Dave Roscoe, James Hubbard, Ben van Bruggen, Malcolm Cooper, Paul Butler, Ian Simpson, Richard Harvey, Marcus Shearn, Mike Sidebottom, Janet Vosper and Henry Owen-John; in Birmingham, Martin Brown, Michael Taylor, Alison Powell, Eva Ling, Peter Larkham, Nick Morton and Cordula Zeidler; in Oslo, Morten Sjaastad, Grete Horntvedt, Hogne Langset, Kevin Gallagher, Solveig Olaisen, Inger Karlberg and Arne Sødal; in Dublin, Geraldine Walsh, Kevin Nolan, Ronan Olwill, Mariam Isa Nouri, Lora Nicolaou, Angela Rolfe, Arthur Gibney, Paul Keogh, Donough Cahill, Sharon Greene, Dick Gleeson, Conor Skeen, Kieran Rose, Kevin Duff and Ian Lumley; in Newcastle, Tony Wyatt, Richard Charge, Catherine Dewar, Christopher

Harrison and Sue Cole; and in Vancouver, Sylvia Holland, Scot Hein, Gordon Price, Michael Gordon, Stan Holman and Lloyd Burritt.

Finally I would like to thank Louise Fox at Taylor and Francis for her guidance and comments during the drafting process.

Michael Short, March 2012.

INTRODUCTION

In recent years there has been increasing concern amongst built environment professionals internationally about development proposals for tall buildings and their potential impact on the fabric of our cities. Booming cities in the late twentieth and early twenty-first centuries have witnessed significant numbers of tall buildings being proposed, in part fuelled by cities' inter-urban competition (Pløger, 2010; Sklair, 2006). In many instances, planners have had to respond to these proposals using out-of-date or inadequate planning frameworks and have often worked under pressure from politicians to approve tangible symbols of economic growth. At the heart of the debate about the appropriateness of specific tall building proposals is their impact and effect on existing townscapes in general, and more specifically, protected buildings and areas; should planning frameworks encourage the siting of towers in appropriate locations, and if so, how do we decide where these locations should be? Should proposals be actively discouraged through such frameworks where they might harm the character, or distinctiveness, of a specific place, area or monument? Cities are responding to the tall building challenge on a spectrum that ranges from outright opposition to wholehearted embrace with planning as the basis for negotiation over specific proposals.

This book attempts to reflect on planning approaches to tall buildings in this time of recession, drawing on a number of cases to outline how cities are responding to this challenge. In essence it is a book about good planning: how to develop planning frameworks which encourage both a deep understanding of the character of place and how, if at all, this might be improved through the construction of tall buildings.

Planning is a multi-dimensional, multi-objective forum for the management of change in the built and natural environment that is both regulatory, in the sense that it is enshrined within a statutory system, and visionary, in the sense that future visions are promoted and implemented through it (Carmona et al., 2003). Additionally, this book reflects on instances where cities have sought to attract tall buildings with little or no attempt at good planning. It shows the broad spectrum of approaches to planning for tall buildings from outright laissez-faire un-regulated cities, to those that positively attract tall buildings as part of a coherent planning strategy.

New tall buildings assert the vision of a city that is modern, prestigious, forward-looking and open to business. They are powerful advertising tools for tourism and economic regeneration, and can project an image of the building's occupiers to the world (Abel, 2003; Strelitz, 2005; Namier, 1931). Tall buildings are being proposed and built across a wide range of cities; from Tallinn to Taipei, Santiago to St Petersburg, Bahrain to Budapest, Cairo to Chicago, Dubai to Dallas and Manchester to Melbourne. They have been defining twenty-first century urban growth by their sheer size and numbers: ". . . no other building type incorporates so many forces of the modern world, or has been so expressive of changing belief systems and so responsive to changing tastes and practices" (Huxtable, 1992: 11).

The central contention of this book is that tall buildings can "give cities identity through 'skyline', an identifiable array of icons that provide orientation" (McNeill, 2005: 46), but only if they are planned as part of a coherent strategy involving the full breadth of stakeholders and resulting from consensus. The converse, of course, is that if tall buildings are approved and built in a planning policy vacuum, their location and design being decided by the market alone, we can witness illegible, incoherent townscapes of decreasing aesthetic, physical and cultural value which show little consideration for effects on that townscape or on the people who experience it. Huxtable (1984) explains the tall building eloquently: ". . . its role in the life of the city and the individual is vexing, and its impact shattering . . ." (p. 11).

A key theme of the book is, therefore, to investigate the role and function of emerging planning frameworks and tools in dealing with the challenges of tall buildings in particular places. What can planning practice tell us about how to deal with tall buildings and their impacts? Should cities proactively plan for tall buildings and if so, how? Upon what sorts of plans should these strategies be based and how can planning authorities make effective and relevant decisions about tall buildings? Finally, what can this analysis of tall building developments and planning strategies tell us about the wider practice of planning? Using a range of case studies, including individual cities and in some instances, particular buildings, this book will seek to address these questions.

In particular the book focuses on the problems of managing proposals for tall buildings in cities where the built form reflects a palimpsest of development over time: what can be termed hybrid heritage (While and Short, 2006). In these cities the outcomes of planning decision-making processes reflect that there is little con-sensus over the type and value of the built heritage. The notion of hybridity can be used to explain the fluidity and multiplicity of "space-times generated in/by the movements and rhythms of heterogeneous associations" (Whatmore, 2002: 6). Many cities can be described as hybrid heritage cities; different ages in the evolution of those cities are reflected in their character yet there are competing values attached to those elements. This value is reflected in, amongst other things, the protection of particular built heritages. In "historic" cities with a clear and identifiable heritage – York, Amsterdam, Bruges and Krakow, for example – the character and skyline of the city often reflects consensus about the significance of that heritage amongst a wide range of interest groups, and thereby remains relatively intact through established planning frameworks. Cohen (1999) argues that the regulation of building height is critical for the conservation of the built heritage of such cities. In those cities where there is more willingness to trade conservation off against change – in Manchester, Berlin, Tokyo and Moscow, for example – judgement about the impact of tall building proposals on the built environment is less clear, especially as tall buildings might be said to improve the urban fabric. The determination of tall building proposals within such hybrid heritage contexts reflects the values attributed to different elements of the townscape, to political struggles over the future of the built heritage, its economic value and the importance of new development to cities eager to regenerate and re-image.

It is necessary to define what is meant by "tall buildings". Tall buildings are defined most readily by their height. Höweler (2003) suggests that a tall building can be one in which there is a proportional relationship of height to width. A tall building can however, be defined by ". . . some aspects of 'tallness' . . . It is a building whose height creates different conditions in the design, construction, and operation from those that exist in 'common' buildings of a certain region and period" (Beedle, 1986: 3). In other words, what may constitute tall is relational and depends upon the urban, cultural and societal context. Something tall is either "of more than average height" or "higher than surrounding objects"[1]. The dictionary definition of "tall" reflects this relational view, but it is also helpful to define what "tall" is not: "big" meaning "large in size" is unhelpful as it omits that relational view; "large" meaning "relatively great in size" reflects a relational perspective, but omits the proportional element suggested by Höweler. Height can be measured in a variety of ways. It may be expressed as height in metres (or feet), or by number of storeys. For the purposes of this book, the relational view will be adopted, and the measurement of height in either metres or storeys will depend on individual context.

Summary of book content

The book is divided into two main parts. Firstly, the relationship between tall buildings, planning and conservation is outlined focusing, in Chapter 1, on an examination of the tall building typology from the origins of the modern skyscraper in late nineteenth century North America through to the wave of tall buildings that have characterised recent urban development and growth across the world. This is followed by Chapter 2, which explores the types of impacts that construction of tall buildings might lead to. The potential impacts of a tall building can be many and may relate to the unique characteristics of the city where it is proposed, the site and the individual design of the building. Chapter 3 analyses the way in which planning strategies have evolved to deal with the impacts of tall buildings. Chapter 4 completes the first part of the book through a more detailed examination of the role of the built heritage in the evolution of our cities; its contribution to character and distinctiveness, and how decisions about impacts upon heritage are determined.

The second part of the book focuses on seven examples of medium-sized cities dealing with the planning issues and impacts that arise from tall buildings. These have been chosen to reflect the wide range of methods to either encourage or to control tall buildings that cities are deploying. They have been chosen from across the western world, covering England (Manchester, Liverpool, Newcastle and Birmingham), Norway (Oslo), Ireland (Dublin) and Canada (Vancouver) and represent a broad spectrum of approaches to dealing with this issue from a so-called laissez-faire strategy adopted by the planning authority in Manchester, to much more comprehensive strategies for encouraging tall building development in appropriate locations in both Vancouver and Newcastle. The remaining examples represent approaches to planning for tall buildings that fall somewhere between the two extremes above.

The concluding chapters will seek to draw together these experiences contributing to the ongoing debate about the role of tall buildings in our cities, their potential impact upon those cities and the experience of people that inhabit them. From this analysis, the conclusions will outline how cities should approach the strategic planning of tall buildings, as well as how they should deal with the impacts of individual buildings, particularly on the built heritage. It is hoped, therefore, that this book can demonstrate the utility of effective and robust planning frameworks in this complex area of development. Finally, the book will reflect on whether there are wider conclusions for planning practice: what do strategies for tall buildings tell us about planning complex urban systems, as well as the management of specific building projects?

1

THE TALL BUILDING TYPOLOGY

The confluence of a number of economic, social and technological innovations at the end of the nineteenth century in the USA spurred the development of the tall building. Up to that point, the tallest buildings in cities were either religious buildings such as churches or temples, palaces of the nobility or connected to defence (Kostoff, 2001). Since that time, however, a number of distinct periods of tall building development have occurred as a result of different sets of drivers. This chapter examines the challenge of tall buildings, looking specifically at the evolution of tall buildings, responses to them in particular places and the potential range of tall building impacts. It explores the evolution of the tall building using a number of cities and buildings to exemplify responses to tall buildings during specific periods and in particular locations, and is sub-divided into the following sub-sections: the emergence of the tall building; the modern movement and tall buildings; the post-modernist backlash; and the global tall building phenomenon.

The emergence of the tall building as an architectural form has been a feature of the twentieth century city (Bradford Landau and Condit, 1996). Likewise, responses to the development of tall buildings have characterised urban planning during this period. As well as the design and appearance of the buildings themselves, the urban planning implication of building tall started to be articulated from the end of the nineteenth century onwards. Goldberger (1981) outlines that at the start of the twentieth century it was beginning to be understood that tall buildings were funda-mentally different to what had been built before, and that they demanded a different set of attitudes towards the making of cities. The following sections use the examples of New York City, Paris, Houston and Shanghai to assist in understanding the drivers, impacts and responses to tall buildings during their evolution.

The emergence of the tall building

The evolution of the tall building has been punctuated by a series of technological innovations that have fuelled their development since their inception in the USA in the late nineteenth century. Webster (1959) suggests that the tall building typology would not have evolved without unique favourable conditions. Firstly, he outlines economic conditions: as the emerging cities of the USA developed, demand for land in central areas led landowners to seek to maximise their profits by demanding ever more intense development (Webster, 1959; Kostoff, 2001). This has been a characteristic of tall buildings ever since; they are a way of increasing the amount of saleable or rentable floor space of a plot in order to maximise returns to the landowner. Secondly, the nature of land ownership in many cities in the USA at that time meant that plots were small or fragmented, requiring innovative solutions for development in order to realise profits on individual sites (Bradford Landau and Condit, 1996). Finally, the availability of capital contributed to the evolution of the tall building in that it provided significant amounts of money to both experiment with built forms and to portray the wealth of individuals and corporations. Critics such as Abel (2003) and Kostoff (2001) indicate that tall buildings often represent excessive money and power and the erosion of traditional values. Furthermore, it has been argued that tall buildings can either declare to the world that there is a strong economy where tall buildings develop, or that there is economic confidence in a particular location (House of Commons, 2002). For contemporary tall building projects to come to fruition there is a requirement that an occupier for a significant amount of the internal space is found, meaning that market confidence in the location of new tall buildings is crucial to the success of such projects (Sudjic, 2005, Sudjic, 1993).

Webster outlines the technological conditions that allow tall buildings to evolve. He distinguishes these from the means (structural and material conditions) outlined above and specifically refers to the availability of suitable tools, building processes, sources of power, plumbing, heating, air conditioning and so on, as being crucial to the evolution of the tall building. The necessary synthesis of these technological developments is often overlooked as they are not readily visible yet are crucial to the successful completion of tall buildings.

The evolution of this new built form at the beginning of the twentieth century resulted in a new set of challenges for planning, regarding the impacts of tall building in particular places, how the impact of such buildings could be managed through existing or new regulatory mechanisms, and finally, how this regulation could be incorporated within decision-making processes. Furthermore, the unique challenges posed by building tall were magnified in situations where built heritage and character of place were relevant, necessitating the evolution of regulatory tools designed to protect buildings and townscapes of historic or architectural significance.

The first quarter of the twentieth century saw the evolution of the skyscraper as a distinctly American invention, providing much needed office space to over-crowded and rapidly growing cities. The debates around the impacts of such

FIGURE 1.1 The Chicago skyline

buildings related mainly to the concerns of light and shadow, impact on neigh-bouring buildings, the health and safety of occupants, and the transport of large numbers of workers to and from such buildings.

This phase of the evolution of tall buildings, and responses to them, was distinctive to North America (Goldberger, 1981) (see Figure 1.1). At that time unique conditions in the USA saw the invention of the iron frame that proved pivotal in assisting buildings to grow taller. This displaced solid, load-bearing walls with an interior metal frame utilising technology borrowed from bridge building (Hall, 1998). Furthermore, when used with the iron frame structure, a curtain wall could be made of thinly-cut stone, glass or metal thereby opening up opportunities for dressing buildings. Finally, the development of the Otis mechanical lift, in 1880, facilitated a great range of building heights (Abel, 2003). Other innovations – from the replacement of the iron frame in the early twentieth century by the use of both rolled steel and reinforced concrete (which expand and contract at the same rates and bond to steel extremely well), to current technological innovations in sustainable building forms – are resulting in the potential for taller buildings with unique forms (Webster, 1959; Yeang, 2002).

New York City and the zoning response to skyscrapers

The example of New York City, regarding the emergence of the tall building, is useful in seeking to articulate responses to this new form of building at a certain point in time. A palpable rivalry developed between Chicago and New York City at the turn of the twentieth century, which manifested itself in competitive battles for the tallest building in the world. The beginning of the new century saw New York City predominate for many years, as the city absorbed expanding corporations requiring more efficient workspace and more prestigious headquarters (Hall, 1998). Goldberger (1981) defines two forms of skyscraper that evolved in New York City separate from the Chicago skyscraper style: those which were theatrical, built for sheer visual pleasure and those which were conduits for making money, "systems for building rentable floors in the air" (p. 26). The development of the skyscraper in New York City was, however, ten years behind Chicago, and it borrowed from the techniques that were pioneered and employed there (Watkins, 2000). The city was a more conservative environment than Chicago in which a rigid building code operated, limiting the height and massing of buildings on a tight grid-iron street pattern. Only after building techniques had been tried and tested in Chicago were they utilised in New York City. Hall (1998) postulates that the tall buildings built in the city were mostly commissions from particular corporations, rather than speculative developments like those in Chicago. New York City skyscrapers were the result of two great periods of building, one from 1892 to 1914 and the other in the 1920s (Hall, 1998). The first period brought together the new technologies pioneered in Chicago whilst the second period reflected the burgeoning commercial role of the city in the USA. Artistic expression flourished in the city and the new skyscrapers borrowed strongly from existing architectural genres. The skyline of the city began to rise as a result of growth in the city's economy (see Figure 1.2). Tall buildings were the new symbols of corporate power and were built "to be seen" (Domosh in Hall, 1998: 774).

As a result of the increasing height of building in the city, a group of concerned citizens formed calling themselves the *Committee on Congestion of Population in New York* to lobby the City Building Commission about the perceived impacts of these buildings. A report issued in 1913 by the Committee has been recognised as the blueprint for the zoning regulations of 1916. Namier (1931) indicates that in the USA skyscrapers had, up to this point, related to and reflected human form, representing "vertical streets that have risen to their feet and stand upright like human beings" (p. 7). The erection of the Equitable Building in 1916 (see Figure 1.3) however, showed how such buildings could dominate the environment and negatively impact upon the way in which people lived. The neo-Renaissance building occupying the whole block, rising in two masses above the base and connected by a wing for the building's whole height, forms a giant letter "H" when viewed from above (Abel, 2003). The building is tall but not slender like many of its contemporaries (Kitt-Chappell, 1990).

The Equitable Building had a profound impact upon the way in which people viewed tall buildings in the city, it was said to block ventilation of the surrounding streets, deposit 13,000 workers onto already overloaded pavements, roads and subways, and create a problem for fire-fighting. Furthermore, the building was said to cast a shadow six times the size of itself at noon and it visually dominated the

FIGURE 1.2 The Flatiron building, New York City

FIGURE 1.3 The Equitable building, New York City

surrounding streets (Kitt-Chappell, 1990). The Equitable Building, in essence, became a whipping-boy for the political lobby which supported some sort of building height control in the city, even though it was not one of the tallest buildings in the city at that time. It is apparent, in hindsight, that the building did pioneer both lift design and building management, but also that it became a necessary scapegoat in the passing of the zoning regulations in 1916.

The 1916 zoning regulations, drafted in advance of the completion of the Equitable Building, required tall buildings to be set-back to allow sufficient daylight to reach the streets and adjacent buildings. Many subsequent landmark buildings such as the Chrysler Building and the Empire State Building owe their distinctive shape to the impact of this building and these zoning laws, although the new style could be seen to be an evolution of the type exemplified by the Singer Building.

The modern movement and tall buildings

The development of the American skyscraper in the early twentieth century was followed by the development of a distinct phase of tall building promoted by the modern movement. Also known as the International Style, modernism was a major architectural trend in the 1920s, mainly influenced by German and Dutch movements such as Bauhaus, de Stijl and Deutscher Werkbund, which all rejected tradition and revelled in radicalised ideas of the future (Webster, 1959). The movement's goal was a rational, even scientific, approach to art and architecture, informed in part by a popular view of evolution, namely that progress toward a perfected world was inevitable, making the past obsolete (Lampugnani, 1983). The particular importance of tall buildings in the modern movement was evident from the initial ideas of architects who believed that the form of buildings should follow their function. Lampugnani (1983) outlines a number of attributes of this movement which can be termed the "machine aesthetic": a radical simplification of built form; the rejection of ornament; the use of "modern" materials such as glass, concrete and steel; the literal transparency of buildings (reflecting an open public view of traditionally private space); the rationalisation of space and a reliance on industrial mass production in buildings (see Figure 1.4). Architects such as Le Corbusier and van der Rohe experimented with new styles for housing and offices at this time.

Le Corbusier's "*Plan Voisin*" for Paris, for example, took the removal of historicism from architecture to new lengths, proposing an urban planning solution to the perceived chaos of the old city on the right bank (see Figure 1.5). Instead of the beauty of the city of Paris, he proposed row after row of identical skyscrapers to replace the historic fabric of the city, a veritable skyscraper park. Interestingly, the main impacts of this movement were felt after the Second World War when the legacy of Le Corbusier's work and the production of new iconic buildings by van der Rohe, amongst others, stimulated the wholesale adoption of modernist principles in architecture and urban planning. Modern movement ideas represented the "bold . . . mystical rationality of a generation that was eager to accept the scientific spirit of the twentieth century on its own terms and to throw off all pre-existing ties

FIGURE 1.4 Lake Point Tower, Chicago

– political, cultural, conceptual – with what was considered an exhausted, outmoded past" (LeGates and Stout, 2003: 317). Furthermore, for the first time, other uses apart from offices were suggested for tall buildings, most notably as dwellings. The main impacts of this movement were felt after the Second World War, when its legacy stimulated the wholesale adoption of modernist principles in architecture and urban planning. Buildings inspired by modernist ideas were built across the globe.

FIGURE 1.5 Le Corbusier's "*Plan Voisin*"

The towers of glass proposed by the modern movement were both radical and contemporary, reflecting advances in tall building engineering that created new pressures to build upwards. The regulation of built form in general, and height in particular, spread rapidly during this time as a means of controlling the worst excesses of modernism, particularly the impact of tall buildings on the built heritage of cities (Vickers, 1999). The impact of the modern movement in tall building design was significant in Europe as well as the USA, the home of the movement. However, there was no gentle easing into the introduction of tall buildings in Europe, such as was the case in the USA. For Europe particularly, the case was traumatic (Kostoff, 2001) with very few examples of existing tall buildings in cities. The fabric of European cities was much older than in the USA, so that the sudden contrast with tall buildings was one of shock. The impact of tall buildings on the grid system in American downtowns was radically different from their impact on complex urban networks such as in Paris or London. In Europe, tall buildings gave ammunition to conservationists who were appalled at the destruction of the historic fabric of their cities by inappropriately sited and designed towers (Tung, 2001; Kain, 1981).

The debate surrounding the modernisation of Paris in the immediate post-war period offers a useful insight into the perceived threats to the historic city from tall buildings. A number of factors led to the adoption of a modernist solution to the city's needs; a large number of obsolete dwellings, particularly in the historic centre of the city, the need to provide accommodation for an expanding population, an increase in urban traffic, the realisation that historic districts required some sort of positive protection, the need for modernisation after the trauma of the Second World War and finally, the influence of Corbusian ideas on planning and architectural thought and practice (Kain, 1981; Tung, 2001; Evenson, 1979). Concern over the erection of tall buildings in the city contributed to a siege mentality of Parisians during the 1960s in particular, which was centred on the proposed Tour

Montparnasse, the zoning of a growth centre at La Défense and the protection of the historic core of the city.

The dominance of the central city by tall buildings has, by and large, been avoided in Paris through prudent planning with only a small number of exceptions puncturing the romantic rhythm (Evenson, 1979) of the skyline, such as the Tour Montparnasse. The project for modifying the Montparnasse area was finalised by the urban development authorities in 1956, confirming the relocation of the railway station around which the entire area was to be restructured. Commencing in 1958, the development was undertaken by a semi-public company and involved the demolition of a number of particularly run-down streets. It was deemed appropriate that the development required a monumental landmark, namely the Tour Montparnasse. The tower, 210 metres high, was visible from all parts of the city and was completed in 1973. The city architects believed that the tower design had ". . . been minutely studied so that it [could] be inserted without any fault of taste into the Parisian landscape" (Evenson, 1979: 194). In reality, however, the looming tower has been attacked, on the one hand, as an assault on the visual harmony of the city and, on the other, welcomed as an addition to the city in keeping with the radicalism for which the city is famous, particularly with reference to the Tour Eiffel, initially despised for its blighting effects yet now admired as an important landmark (Evenson, 1981). It has been criticised for destroying views of the city when looking south and is visible from many of the main monuments of the city. Recognised as a building of high quality in its own right by commentators such as Evenson (1979) and Sudjic (1993), it has nevertheless had a major impact upon the historic skyline and rhythm of the city. Furthermore, it has impacted upon the way in which planning and conservation policy in the city has subsequently developed with President Pompidou banning tall buildings completely in the historic centre of the city in 1974. Strong political support for the protection of the historic centre of Paris as a cultural resource was crucial to the retention, in the main, of the historic skyline.

A new and comprehensive building code, put in place in 1967 through the city's development plan, attempted to prevent further destruction of the townscape, partly as a result of the increase in building height in the city (Evenson, 1979; Pickard, 2001; Tung, 2001). Office construction was restricted within the historic city and the height of new buildings was controlled to maintain the texture of the city fabric. As a result, in approximately two-thirds of the city the height of buildings could not be increased beyond the existing heights to any great degree (Evenson, 1981). Large parts of the city were, however, exempt from any control which led to high-rise development in areas of the city such as Place d'Italie on the suburban rim of the historic city (Evenson, 1981; Tung, 2001). The 1974 development plan for Paris envisaged tall buildings outside the historic centre of the city in a proactive bid to attract investment in the burgeoning service sector. It was soon realised that these buildings could have a visual impact far beyond their immediate surroundings. The development of a new commercial district to the west of the historic city at La Défense, beyond the Bois de Boulogne, was designated as conscious effort to build a European Manhattan (Sudjic, 2005) (see Figure 1.6). La Défense was identified as

FIGURE 1.6 La Défense, Paris

the place in which to develop not just France's premier commerce and financial centre, but also a business district that would make Paris a major business centre in Europe and one that would rival cities such as London and Frankfurt. In more recent times the mayor of Paris, Bertrand Delanoë, has sought to relax the city's rigid building code to allow tall buildings within the Rue Péripherique, much to the horror of the city's intelligensia (Millard, 2010).

The modernist principles of urban planning and architecture have been widespread across the globe and have elicited a significant amount of anger and distress by local populations who perceive that modernism does not respect or reflect local culture and the uniqueness of particular places (Vickers, 1999). The experience of modernist tall buildings by the general population has been varied with the wholesale adoption of this solution to housing shortages across the continent being implemented in various ways in different countries (Harwood et al., 2002; Watkins, 2000). In eastern Europe, modernist residential areas provided housing solutions that were managed directly by the communist state and were an instrument of control (Watkins, 2000). Similarly, in France and the UK tall buildings were built in inner and outer cities to provide for a housing shortage in the post-war period, particularly for working class housing. In France the initial use of a concierge in such buildings continued the French tradition of apartment block management whereas in the UK no such tradition had existed, resulting in neglect and disrepair on a huge scale (Watkins, 2000).

In many instances the standard of construction and poor materials often resulted in maintenance issues from an early stage post-construction (Evenson, 1981).

However, in more recent times modernist residential tall buildings in the inner and outer cities of Europe are either being demolished or revamped into public or private housing to meet a demand for housing by population groups unable or unwilling to seek housing solutions in the traditional suburbs.

The post-modernist backlash and tall buildings

In the 1970s, a backlash against the perception of modernist architecture as "poorly built and aesthetically dull" (Abel, 2003: 34) led to a new post-modern movement in architecture. Post-modernism can be defined as a "populist language scattered with playful classical quotations" (Vickers, 1999: 167) that is both "camp and kitsch" (Watkins, 2000: 661). To the dictum of van der Rohe, "less is more", American architect and leading post-modernist Venturi replied, "less is a bore". Arguing that the modernist aesthetic was stifling to creativity, disliked by the masses, and uninteresting to design, post-modern architects celebrated diversity, colour and historical references in their designs. Huxtable (1984) and Cobb (2003) have argued that this effort to humanise the tall building and give it the demeanour of a good citizen has preoccupied architects. To critics however, post-modernism has borrowed past styles and motifs distorting them for rhetorical effect and went no deeper than mere cladding (Goldberger, 1983; Kostoff, 2001; Abel, 2003). Furthermore, there has been criticism of post-modernism in the sense that the context for new architecture has been wilfully ignored leading to, amongst other things, urban skylines of little coherence or integrity where private interests are valued over public good.

The city of Houston in America's south is one of the country's most intriguing cities and a useful example of a city which attracted large numbers of tall buildings during the post-war period, and one which could be viewed through a post-modern lense. It has grown exponentially with its population increasing from 1.36 million to 4.17 million between 1960 and 2000 (see Table 1.1). It is a place where "growth is something of a religion and yet planning is something of an anathema" (Goldberger, 1981: 83) and therefore provides a useful way of examining how tall buildings are viewed in a context quite different from that of the historic cities of Europe. Alone amongst major cities on the continent, Houston has no zoning laws. In fact, zoning is seen as "a violation of private property and personal liberty" (Qian, 2010: 31). At the same time, however, the city has a system of development control which is entirely in the hands of private developers in the shape of restrictive covenants in the title deeds of individual parcels of land. These covenants relate to issues such as use, size of development, cost and height and are administered by approximately 630 civic clubs. This frontier city is exceedingly wealthy, built upon the oil industry and has ridden a number of recessions of the economy well. As a result the buildings of the city reflect both the unrestricted capitalism of wealth and the lack of any meaningful control on building height or density by the city authorities.

As the city has grown in height, corporations have had to employ fashionable architects to identify their buildings and products on the Houston skyline (Höweler, 2003). The role of prestigious architects in creating schemes that are visionary for

TABLE 1.1 Houston's population growth in millions, 1960–2000

1960	1970	1980	1990	2000
1.36	1.90	2.75	3.32	4.17

Source: www.censusscope.org (accessed 17 May 2010)

the city authorities recurs in the debate about tall buildings. Due to a lack of any form of planning, the buildings themselves don't relate to one another and are entirely dependent upon car traffic to feed workers and goods to them (Höweler, 2003). The result is a lack of any cohesive urban form combined with the abandonment of the area around the centre of the city to scrub: an archetypal post-modern city. Sudjic (1993) asserts that it is misleading even to call the central business district a city centre in the conventional meaning of the term. He suggests that the tall buildings in the centre exist as a visual signal that Houston is a city and that it exists, but nothing more; nobody lives in the centre and the only way to traverse the centre is by car. Tall buildings provide a visual focus for the city even while there is often little or no public space or function to that centre. Houston itself has developed a visually defined city centre in the absence of any form of planning control over the height of buildings. At the same time, the city has grown exponentially outwards into the surrounding countryside over the past thirty years. Evidence in the 1980s and 1990s that the edge of the city was so difficult to commute from, and that apartments and other dwellings were being built in the centre of the city for the first time attracted considerable attention (Huxtable, 1984; Goldberger, 1981). Furthermore, there is little work for the few citizens interested in historic preservation to undertake. The laissez-faire attitude of the city authorities has literally led to the wholesale removal of most of the historic fabric of the city.

Houston has been described as a laboratory of skyscrapers by a number of commentators (Huxtable, 1984; Goldberger, 1981) (see Figure 1.7) reflecting the experimentation in tall building form which has occurred as a result of the lack of control of building. The post-modernist additions to the Houston skyline are particularly celebrated. The Nationsbank Center (built 1983) has been one of the most popular post-modern designs in the city, light-heartedly borrowing from German secular Gothic style, whilst creating a distinctive and instantly recognisable piece of art. The building's bold silhouette is "a larger than life advertisement of the ascendancy of the corporation in the twentieth century" (Dupré, 1996: 87).

In conclusion, the example of Houston points not only to the stylistic developments of the post-modern movement in tall building architecture but also indicates the impact of a laissez-faire regime in which urban planning is subsumed under broader economic and corporate interests. The resultant urban form, whilst producing single tall buildings of architectural and artistic merit, has little resemblance to the accepted notion of a city. Whilst tall buildings in Houston have a clear function to act as landmarks for orientation purpose and as markers of city identity, they have resulted in the privatisation of the central city and of the skyline (Qian, 2010).

FIGURE 1.7 The Houston skyline

The contemporary global tall building phenomenon in Shanghai and London

In the last twenty years, there has been a noticeable re-engagement with the tall building as a symbol of economic and cultural ascendancy characterised by pressure for land in global cities, the emergence of new forms of building and a need for cities to assert themselves as unique in a global world. As part of the rapid spread of global-isation as an economic system, the forces of "communication, migration, business, and technology are rapidly erasing borders, eroding former geographic and cultural divides, and creating urban conditions that are common to many cities" (Höweler, 2003: 16). The tall building therefore is becoming a common solution, as it was during the modernist period, in diverse locations (LSE, 2002). As such, the early twenty-first century is witnessing a vast increase in the number of tall buildings being built, as global symbols of prosperity, confidence and culture. Again, this phase of building tall is distinctive; many of the buildings being proposed are for offices, residential, hotel or a mix of uses (Wood, 2004). In the closing decade of the twen-tieth century, the global centre of economic and cultural change was shifting inex-orably from the countries bordering the Atlantic, to those bordering the Pacific (Abel, 2003). The rise of the Pacific mega-cities has reflected, amongst other things, the globalising nature of world business, with corporations relocating to developing countries in order to reduce costs through cheap overheads including labour. Cities absorbed and continue to absorb huge numbers of rural migrant workers in the "unauthorised metropolis" (Tung, 2001) of squatter settlements that surround the city proper.

Just as there is a noticeable engagement with tall buildings on the Pacific Rim and across much of the rest of the world, in Europe, a renaissance in design and construction of tall buildings is occurring. Cities as diverse as London, Amsterdam, Paris, Berlin, Frankfurt and Rotterdam are experiencing a rush to build tall and are responding to this in locally distinctive ways. In Amsterdam for example, there is a strong regulatory framework that protects the historic city centre and directs large new development to the edge city, whilst in Berlin, tall buildings are being planned in the new central area around Potsdamer-Platz. In Frankfurt, adjacent to the historic city centre, tall buildings are positively encouraged in the central business district so that the city can accommodate financial services. In London, the picture appears somewhat more complex. The Mayor of London and the New Labour Government have been keen to promote tall buildings to retain and promote world city status whilst a diverse range of other interest groups have either welcomed them or sought to combat them due to their real or perceived impact on the form of the city.

The economically and culturally vibrant central business districts of mega-cities are witnessing an explosion in the number and scale of new tall buildings. Cities as diverse as Jakarta, Tokyo, Los Angeles, Osaka, Shanghai, Beijing, Bangkok, Manila, Singapore, Seoul, and Taipei are growing at an enormous rate (see Table 1.2). This new wave of tall buildings "demonstrate [their] symbolic power . . . and the explicit role they can play in establishing a national and cultural identity" (Höweler, 2003: 28). In tall building design and construction, Pacific Rim cities currently reflect "attempts to mediate and articulate the complex negotiations between universal building type and local cultural associations" (Höweler, 2003: 17). Regionalist-inspired tall building design is becoming common. The case of Shanghai is useful in that it is a city that has an identifiable history and culture and is developing at a massive rate. This will be followed by a review of the phenomenon in London, where several tall buildings are under construction.

TABLE 1.2 Projected growth in population of mega-cities in millions

City	1995	2015
Tokyo, Japan	26.96	28.89
Mexico City, Mexico	16.56	19.18
São Paulo, Brazil	16.53	20.32
New York, USA	16.33	17.60
Bombay, India	15.14	26.22
Shanghai, China	13.58	17.97
Los Angeles, USA	12.41	14.22
Calcutta, India	11.92	17.31
Buenos Aires, Argentina	11.80	13.86
Seoul, Korea	11.61	12.98
Beijing, China	11.30	15.57
Osaka, Japan	10.61	10.61
Rio de Janeiro, Brazil	10.18	11.86

Source: United Nations Population Division, *Urban Agglomerations, 1950–2015* (UN, 1996)

Shanghai, the biggest and most cosmopolitan of China's cities (Tan and Low, 1999) is at the forefront of China's entry into the capitalist world economy. The city is gradually transforming itself from a self-sufficient economy to an open economy; from an industrial city to a post-industrial city, from low-rise to a high-rise city. The city, with a population approaching 17 million, has implemented a growth strategy centreing on the development of the Pu-dong area. In common with many other mega-cities, Shanghai envisages itself as a world economic, financial and trade centre, and has identified Pu-dong as the hub of this activity. The traditional urban fabric is undergoing a rapid transformation, and there are fears that the city is gradually losing its distinctive identity.

Pu-dong, located opposite the historic Bund area, is witnessing the rise of large numbers of tall buildings, representing the robustness and power of the Chinese economy. The skyline of the city has been transformed in recent years into a seething mass of unrelated towers representing a worldly "sophistication with a touch of vulgarity" (Tan and Low, 1999: 149). Variously described as both Paris of the East and the Whore of Asia, Shanghai's vocation as a money-making city par excellence is reasserting itself after many years of constraint under the communist system. Lee (1999), Tan and Low (1999) and Shiling (2002) indicate that the Shanghai tall building has symbolic meaning in this burgeoning metropolis; the tall building as urban experiment, as a symbol of economic and cultural openness, and as a symbol of ascendancy of China as a nation.

In Shanghai, the tall building as urban experiment is plainly evident in the skyline of Pu-dong (Oldfield and Wood, 2009) (see Figure 1.8). It has adopted, moulded and improved the tall building typology for its own unique set of circumstances.

FIGURE 1.8 The Shanghai skyline

There is, however, growing concern about both the loss of historical landmarks amongst the sea of tall buildings, and the style of contemporary Shanghai architecture. A superficial tall building style is evolving which fatuously seeks to create impressive, unique, and above all, increasingly tall, skyscrapers for their own good. The result is a chaotic grab for the sky which bears little relation to the former historic city (Höweler, 2003).

The tall buildings of Shanghai project the ascendancy of China as a nation on the global stage as a symbol of both economic and cultural power (Oldfield and Wood, 2009; Francis-Jones et al., 2009). Commentators such as Lee (1999) and Shiling (2002) have expressed concern that as a visible sign of the rise of industrial capitalism, these tall buildings could also be regarded as the most intrusive addition to the Shanghai landscape, as they not only tower over the regular residential buildings in the old city, but offer a sharp contrast to the general principles of Chinese architecture in which height was never a crucial factor, especially in the case of houses for everyday living. It is suggested that to the average Chinese person, most of these tall buildings are, both literally and figuratively, beyond their reach.

London has a long history of height regulation, often focused on particular views of key monuments and palaces throughout the city. This tradition has been reflected in more recent times through various studies of the role of tall buildings in the metropolitan area: Tim Catchpole's *London Skylines* (1987); Roger Simon's *Skyscrapers and the New London Skyline* (1996); the London Planning Advisory Committee's *High Buildings and Strategic Views in London* (1998); and DEGW's *London's Skyline, Views and High Buildings* (2002). Each of these studies attempts to characterise the impact of existing towers on the London landscape and set out key considerations in the assessment of future proposals and is useful in setting a baseline dataset. Many of the recent tall buildings which have been built, or are under construction, have, however, been assessed against a clear set of planning policy frameworks starting with the Commission on Architecture and the Built Environment (CABE) and English Heritage *Guidance on Tall Buildings* (2003 and 2007).

The *London View Management Framework* Supplementary Planning Guidance (SPG) (ML, 2010) provides guidance on the policies in the London Plan for the protection of strategically important views in London and complements the tall building policies of the plan. Firstly, it recognises that the preserving views of key monuments, whilst encouraging development which will allow London to retain its international presence, is a fine balance and one which needs to rely on highly skilled architects, urban designers and conservation planners. Secondly, the proposed view corridors in the SPG actually reduce the width of existing corridors set in previous Regional Planning Guidance. Finally, the SPG has been crucial in the consideration, by UNESCO, of the impact of tall building proposals on the World Heritage Sites in London. As such the national government has been particularly interested in how implementation of the SPG is being played out.

The response of individual London Boroughs to the emerging planning framework for tall buildings particularly (and more generally to the wide changes to planning in England) has been diverse with the City of London, for example, embracing tall building proposals as a way of perpetuating London's pre-eminent economic position in the world, and to compete with neighbouring Tower Hamlets for jobs and investment (Canary Wharf is situated in this Borough) whilst balancing a need to protect some of the nation's finest architectural and archaeological treasures (St Paul's Cathedral, the Tower of London). As such it has been particularly positive about proposals such as the "Walkie Talkie" (a Viñoly designed 39-storey building on Fenchurch Street), the Heron Tower (a 46-storey building on Bishopsgate) and the Cheese-grater (or Leadenhall Building, a 48-storey tower) all of which will have a major impact upon the London skyline and which English Heritage, amongst others, objected to.

The City of Westminster, by way of comparison, has been noted in its opposition to tall building development and there have been frequent clashes between it and the Mayor over specific proposals in recent times. It has been particularly concerned about the proposed 50-storey building at Victoria (Victoria Interchange) and the potential to destroy key views of the Palace of Westminster. Other London Boroughs such as Hammersmith and Fulham and the Royal Borough of Kensington and Chelsea are selectively encouraging tall buildings along the River Thames, coming in for much criticism from the general population and amenity groups of the perceived privatisation of the river's views and the over-intensification of development.

The United Nations Educational, Scientific and Cultural Organization (UNESCO) has been concerned with the approval and construction of a range of towers which might impact negatively on the character of the World Heritage Sites of London. A mission was sent to London to consider the appropriateness of tall building development proposals near to the Tower of London and World Heritage Sites in Westminster in 2006 as a result of increasing concern over what type of development was taking place and within the context of UNESCO action over similar issues in cities such as Cologne, Vienna and Tallinn.

At the heart of the debates about the implementation of planning policies and development management frameworks for tall buildings in London are the issues of the protection and enhancement of the built heritage, the multi-scaled nature of tall building management characterised by a diverse and expansive list of interested parties, and the politics of the world city and the promotion of tall buildings as visual and economic symbols of London's power and status.

One of the key tensions related to assessing proposals relates specifically to the multi-scaled nature of tall building management characterised by a diverse and expansive list of interested parties. If one considers the long list of interested parties who are mandated to implement and reflect upon planning policy in relation to tall buildings (UNESCO, the International Council on Monuments and Sites (ICOMOS), the Department for Culture, Media and Sport (DCMS), the Department of Communities and Local Government (CLG), London Assembly, Mayor of London, London Boroughs) covering international–national–regional –local policy interests combined with conservation based interests (English Heritage, heritage bodies such as the Victorian Society, Twentieth Century Society for example), developers, landowners, local groups, concerned citizens and politicians, a picture is drawn of the difficulty planning authorities have in implementing a coherent set of principles in assessing tall building proposals. Adding to this the unique international profile of London, with landmarks which are instantly recognisable across the globe, a set of unique circumstances emerge which place tall building proposals at the centre of the debate about the future of London.

Conclusions

It is apparent that each phase of tall buildings is distinctive in a number of ways. Firstly, the form of tall buildings reflects the particular drivers for development of a specific time and place. Secondly, the city examples utilised above have shown how the uniqueness of place (country–city–neighbourhood–site) and the dynamics of local planning regimes and actor–network relationships affect the form of the city through the decisions taken on tall building proposals. Thirdly, that the particularity of place combined with the characteristics of the local planning regime result in complex decision-making processes that require the benefits of tall building pro- posals to be weighed against impacts and the desire to regenerate and re-image. Fourthly, the examples outlined above have shown, however, that there is potential to actively manage tall building proposals in a way that positively contributes to a sense of place and evolution of the city. In each of the examples there is evidence that regulatory mechanisms have evolved in order to try and actively manage tall building proposals once the impacts of those buildings have become known. Mechanisms which limit the form of tall buildings (such as in New York), which direct them to specific nodes (such as in Shanghai and Paris), or which combine the two with a desire to protect important elements of the townscape (such as in London) are still evolving. As such, the new wave of tall buildings sweeping the globe means that a period of reflection on the potential regulatory and assessment frameworks is underway. The following chapter will examine the ways in which tall buildings might impact specifically upon the built environment around it.

2

THE POTENTIAL IMPACTS
OF TALL BUILDINGS

Tall buildings are likely to have significant impacts on cities that will vary between places depending on a wide range of factors. This chapter will examine the potential impacts of tall buildings in relation to the unique characteristics of both the place where they are proposed and the individual design of the building. These have been summarised in Table 2.1. This table outlines eight categories of potential impacts of a tall building covering both visual and spatial impacts as well as potential for improvement to be made to both as a result of such development. The list of potential impacts is long, yet proposals for tall buildings would normally be expected to address all of them. Whilst this categorisation is useful in understanding how tall buildings can impact upon the surrounding environment, they are not mutually exclusive. Each is discussed in more detail below.

Context

The relationship of a tall building to, and its potential impact on, local topography is crucial. Topography is the "physical arrangement of the physical features of an area", in other words the natural environment that forms the backdrop for the evolution of the city. Kostoff (2001) indicates that it is impossible to separate the form of human settlement from the natural landscape. Specific topographic features, such as rivers, hills and valleys form the basis of settlement either through incorporation into the settlement or their avoidance (Kostoff, 2001; Lynch, 1960). Tall buildings can impact upon the topography of a city both positively or negatively. They can interrupt the rhythm of the natural setting of place (Attoe, 1981), block access or views of a particular feature or erase that feature by the scale of buildings. Conversely, tall buildings might enhance a particular topographical feature through appropriate siting or enhance access to a particular place (Lynch, 1960). Likewise, the relationship of a tall building to, and its potential impact on, local morphology

TABLE 2.1 Tall buildings impacts and issues

Category	Impact upon	Explanation	Conservation planning context
Context	Topography Morphology Site Urban grain Skyline Streetscape Scale Height	Unique form of the local landscape Unique urban form Unique attributes Pattern of existing urban area Outline of land and buildings against sky Pattern of existing street Relative size Number of storeys	Contextual elements give character of place which is recognised both through statutory protection and recognition of importance of everyday street
Effect on historic environment	Built heritage Open space Views Panoramas	Protected elements in the townscape Parks, gardens, rivers, waterways, etc. Of particular buildings View of wider area	On protected elements of townscape
Effect on local environment	Microclimate Sunlight, daylight and shadowing Night time appearance	Climate of the immediate area around the tower Casting of a shadow Form of building at night including casting of shadow, amount of light, etc.	Can impact upon the experiential element of character of place
Relationship to transport	Infrastructure Capacity Feasibility of improvement Aviation	Existing transport Existing capacity for all methods of transport affected Potential created by tower to improve transport options and capacity Flight paths and signal issues	How building integrates into surrounding transport systems and changes the way in which the city is used and navigated

TABLE 2.1 Continued

Category	Impact upon	Explanation	Conservation planning context
Permeability	Site	Improve access into and through site	How city is navigated and experienced by the user
	Legibility	Allows improved reading of site and wider area	
	Wider area	Improve access into and through area	
	Linkages	Opportunities for improved linkages of site and wider area for pedestrians	
Architectural quality	Form	Expression of tower through shape	What the tall building adds to the existing townscape and how this relates to context
	Massing	Form and shape of tower and its expression	
	Proportion	Of elements of tower as a coherent whole	
	Silhouette	Outline of individual tower on skyline	
	Materials	Facing of tower	
	Relationships	How tower relates to neighbouring sites and the wider city	
Contributions	External space	Opportunity to improve external space	What are the benefits of the building; what can tall building add to existing townscape
	Internal space	Opportunity to improve internal space	
	New facilities	Opportunity to provide new facilities	
	Mix of uses	Particularly at ground floor	
Sustainability	Physical	Through broad physical sustainability	Do tall buildings contribute to sustainability and how does this relate to the existing townscape
	Social	Through new facilities or social housing	
	Economic	Improving economic climate, provision of jobs, new office space, etc.	
	Environmental	Environmental sustainability of site and surrounding area	

Note: Based on Strelitz, 2005; CABE, 2003; DEGW, 2002.

is also crucial. The morphology of place is unique and distinctive (Kostoff, 2001); the form of San Francisco, London, Beijing and Cairo have evolved due to the special circumstances of the local topography reflected in their morphological development. As a result the relationship of tall buildings to their local environments is also distinct and particular to both place and site.

Tall buildings can impact on a particular site, the surrounding urban grain and the skyline in a number of ways. Firstly, the point at which the building hits the ground contributes to a sense of the public realm; its relationship to the edge of the site and the streetscape often results in a treatment such as a podium which relates the building to its immediate setting (LSE, 2002; BCO, 2002a). Secondly, the surrounding urban grain may have a clear pattern or character which can immediately be affected by tall buildings through its distinctive height, being generally taller than the immediate area, and scale, its relative size and shape (Cohen, 1999). In terms of built heritage, buildings and areas represent the uniqueness of place in their protection through regulatory systems. Thirdly, tall buildings impact upon the uniqueness of the skyline of a city. The skyline, "the outline of buildings defined against the sky", can define the image of the city as graphic symbols and civic emblems (Lynch, 1960; Kostoff, 2001; Cohen, 1999; Attoe, 1981). Attoe (1981) indicates that skylines can also reflect that the skyline of a city can be intentionally created to project an image of the city as an urban collective with a particular brand. The skyline is particularly sensitive to change. New tall buildings can impact upon the skyline both positively and negatively; they can enhance a cluster of tall buildings on the skyline or detract from that cluster if inappropriately sited, for example.

Effect on historic environment

Tall buildings have the potential to impact upon those elements of the townscape that have been protected through regulatory systems, the built heritage. This traditionally includes elements such as protected buildings, areas, archaeology, ruins and monuments (Cohen, 1999). Furthermore, they also include elements such as protected parks, battlefields and the grounds of stately homes which are not necessarily part of the built heritage but which contribute to their character, scale and image.

Views, "the extent of vision", are integral to an understanding of the character and form of place (Lynch, 1960). They include panoramas or "an unbroken . . . wide view" of a place for example, views of townscapes, linear views which have a single defined object or a vista or "long narrow view". In common, the various views of the built heritage have at their heart the experience of place (Cohen, 1999; Heath et al., 2000 amongst others) from key points within or outside the townscape. As such, the experience of a view changes depending on the location of the viewer and the particular interest or background of the viewer (Lynch, 1960). There is potential therefore for views of built heritage or views as part of the experience of the built heritage to have multiple meanings (Attoe, 1981; Lynch, 1960). As such, built heritage includes not only particular tangible heritage in the form of buildings or groups of buildings but intangible elements which contribute to the character and experience of place (Larkham, 1992). Many of these elements could also be part of the broader category of context in that they relate to elements of the urban fabric.

Effect on local environment

The effect of tall buildings on the immediate microclimate of a site can be a crucial impact in the determination of the appropriateness of a particular development (Strelitz, 2005). There is potential for a tall building to create difficult conditions for pedestrians both on site and in the immediate surrounding area and therefore the assessment of microclimatic impacts is crucial (DEGW, 2002). Firstly, tall buildings can significantly change wind patterns in the surrounding streets, affecting air quality in terms of the dispersion of emissions from buildings or vehicles for example. Furthermore, the acceptability of wind to pedestrians at street level depends upon the uses undertaken; a major pedestrian thoroughfare may have different requirements for the control of wind than a street with outdoor cafes or a neighbourhood green space (Strelitz, 2005).

The quantity and quality of daylight inside a building can be impaired by new tall buildings depending on distance away through shadowing, the amount of glare created by the refraction of light from a large surface area of glass and the time of day (Höweler, 2003; Strelitz, 2005). Furthermore, tall buildings can cast quite considerable shadows across significant distances, meaning that again different impacts can be felt in different places at different times of the day. At night, the visual impact of a tall building can alter with the number and level of internal illuminations having the potential to create light pollution and environmental problems, but also the potential to improve area legibility and safety.

Relationship to transport

Due to their size and potential to attract large numbers of users, tall buildings can have a major impact upon existing transport infrastructure through the creation and encouragement of increased use of private vehicular movements, buses, trams, underground metro systems and rail networks (Höweler, 2003). The capacity of each of these elements is designed with particular usage figures, thereby requiring assessment of proposals to ascertain how that capacity will be affected and potentially suggesting where improvements could take place. In terms of built heritage, increase in traffic has been a crucial issue in area management for a number of decades (Ashworth and Larkham, 1994). Furthermore, as buildings are becoming taller, the effects on patterns of aviation are becoming apparent. The encroachment of tall buildings onto flight paths is a consideration that must be taken into account. (Strelitz, 2005). In some instances airport authorities can seek to limit the height of proposed towers due to these possible impacts.

Permeability

The way in which the building hits the ground can contribute to the permeability of the site in both physical and visual terms. In poorly designed tall buildings the ground floors of the building can create a barrier to the legibility of the site and wider area, meaning "the ease with which its parts can be recognised and can be organised into a coherent pattern" (Lynch, 1960: 2), by disorientating the pedestrian through monolithic treatments and a lack of understanding of the importance of the public realm (Lynch, 1960). Better examples improve legibility through good quality public realm works and a contextual understanding of the role of the building in the townscape (Cohen, 1999; Lynch, 1960; Attoe, 1981). Furthermore, tall buildings offer the opportunity to improve the linkage of sites and the wider area in terms of navigability through appropriate sign posting, site layout and form. Tall buildings can act as clear landmarks at the city or local level thereby creating reference points for legibility and distinctiveness (Lynch, 1960). In order to perform the function as a landmark, a tall building must be defined by its differentiation from the surrounding cityscape taking into account topographical differences.

Architectural quality

The structure of the tall building is also characterised by its architectural quality. It is with the external treatments that a building is projected onto the city in the ways outlined previously. The form of the tall buildings relates to the design of the building, its shape and treatment, whilst the massing, or physical volume of a tall building, relates to the capacity for floorspace and how this is realised in the building design; the results can produce a slender structure with a small building footprint or one with a much larger footprint leading to a bulkier and larger building. Its proportion refers to how the various elements of the building interrelate; any element of the building can dominate the structure and this varies by design. The silhouette of the building is the image of the building one sees against the skyline; it can add simplicity to a city image or indeed make it inherently more complex depending on the number and form of tall buildings (Heath et al., 2000). The image of the silhouette can change from different angles, thereby requiring an understanding of the ways in which new tall buildings appear on the skyline; its visual role in the skyline can change when viewed within a city or from outside, for example. Tall buildings can also be characterised by the materials used to dress the frame; this has changed over time from a combination of materials including glass and marble or stone composite to create a curtain wall in the pre-Second World War era, to the current style which is to use ever increasing amounts of glass in order to cut down on costs and to create a sleeker image (BCO, 2002b; LSE, 2002; Strelitz, 2005). Finally, the relationship of a proposed tall building to the immediate vicinity and to the wider city is crucial in its design and how it is assessed; should it reflect existing patterns of development, suggest something entirely new, or a mixture of both?

Contributions

Tall building proposals offer a number of opportunities for the developer to make contributions in order to mitigate some of the impacts of the development (Cullingworth and Nadin, 2002; Cullingworth and Caves, 2003). These could relate to the provision of public external or internal spaces, new facilities for the local area or population, a particular mixture of uses or social housing provision, for example. How this is negotiated and implemented varies but usually involves a legal agreement between the various parties. It is possible for such contributions and agreements to relate to the built heritage; perhaps the development of a tall building could provide an opportunity for the restoration of a protected building or the recording of a hitherto unknown archaeological site.

Sustainability

Tall buildings have the capacity to impact upon physical, social, economic and environmental sustainability in a number of ways (Strelitz, 2005; Jones and Slinn, 2006). Firstly, in the re-use of underused or derelict land they can contribute to the physical regeneration of a city. Likewise, they can impact upon social issues through the provision of new or improved facilities, opportunities for work or housing, for example, and through economic opportunities of job creation, new office space or tourism development (House of Commons (HoC), 2002). Finally, tall buildings can impact upon environmental sustainability in a number ways; they could attract staff or occupants who all commute by private car, could implement sustainable air conditioning or heating systems, undertake a carbon dioxide neutral development or offer incentives for users of the building to use public transport (Strelitz, 2005). Assessment techniques and the negotiation of planning approval will involve discussions about each of these elements.

Conclusions

During the determination of proposals for tall buildings in the planning process, the impacts outlined in Table 2.1 have the potential to occur. Depending on the site, place and proposed tall building characteristics, varying combinations of these impacts will need to be addressed using regulatory frameworks and assessment techniques that are particular to a city. It is through the implementation of these processes that the significance of the potential impacts are determined and mitigated. Furthermore, the process of assessment is not just undertaken to decide whether a tall building should be approved or rejected based on a judgement regarding the significance of those impacts, rather the management of impacts, their mitigation and the influencing of the decision-making process by interest groups play a large part in the determination of proposals. A number of regulatory methods and assessment techniques for managing tall buildings have therefore evolved to address these issues and are outlined in detail in the following chapter.

3

THE EMERGENCE OF PLANNING FRAMEWORKS FOR TALL BUILDINGS

In most planning systems across the globe, mechanisms have evolved to assist decision-making during the assessment of the impacts of tall buildings. In this chapter the focus of interest in these tools centres specifically on assessing the impact of tall buildings on surrounding townscapes as outlined in the previous chapter. These mechanisms are drawn from a range of international experience. It is not the case that all tools are currently being used, and one aim of the chapter is to explore the potential of mechanisms that might be used. The chapter attempts to review those tools that have evolved to assist in managing tall building proposals, recognising that they can guide appropriate development as well as restrict inappropriate development. The chapter will therefore outline existing decision support tools that may assist tall building management, given that there is a phase of regulatory searching taking place across the globe for appropriate methods.

As previously outlined, assessment tools are many and varied and are designed as supporting mechanisms for decision-making. The use of decision support tools rests on the rational assumption that they help improve decision-making through the collection, analysis and presentation of value-neutral and objective information on the basis of which the decision-maker makes a decision (Kørnøv and Thissen, 2000; March, 1994). Having said that, much of the literature points to other characteristics of the decision-making processes in practice: cognitive limitations; behavioural biases; the ambiguity and variability of preferences and norms; distribution of decision-making amongst actors and across time; the notion of decision-making as a process of learning and negotiation between multiple actors; and finally, the role and effect of information in planning decisions (Healey, 1992; Kørnøv and Thissen, 2000; Kumar, 2003; Forrester, 1989).

Firstly, the cognitive limitations of decision-making reflect that a decision-maker is bounded by the limits of his or her experiences with the result that there is no way that all consequences and preferences of a possible decision can be included with the decision-making process. In terms of decision support therefore, this means that the amount and type of information is limited, becomes laden with particular meaning and value, thereby bounding the rationality of the decision-maker (Forrester, 1989; Kørnøv and Thissen, 2000; March, 1994).

Secondly, decision-making does not necessarily follow rational patterns, rather it follows habits, traditions and can imitate practice accrued over time. As a result the use of decision support tools might be subject to a series of informal or subconscious rules that limit the decision-maker. The ambiguity and variability of personal preferences and norms likewise, informally and subconsciously limits the perspective of the decision-maker. Personal preferences can change over time giving an added level of complexity to decision-making. Kørnøv and Thissen (2000) suggest that the notion of decision-making as a process of learning and negotiation between multiple actors reflects the mutual dependencies and distribution of power and authority between participants in the decision-making process. In multi-stakeholder situations it is possible that high levels of confusion can occur due to competing preferences and variables and the distribution of power (March, 1994). In this sense, perceptions and understandings of a given problem can vary widely amongst actors and be reflected in the decision-making process.

Finally, literature on planning as a communicative action is useful in analysing the role of information in decision-making. It suggests that information in planning decisions must be identified in the communicative actions of participants in the decision-making process, through actions such as meetings, review procedures, conversations, reports and memos (Kumar, 2003; Lauria and Soll, 1996).

It is within this context that decision support tools in the assessment of proposals for tall buildings might be viewed. The remainder of this chapter analyses various decision support tools that have been utilised in different places at different times, focusing on their purpose, format, use, strengths and weaknesses. It is divided between those mechanisms which are designed to shape development at the outset of the development process (such as through development plan policy or zoning ordinance), and those that are designed as decision support during the process for applying for consent to develop in accordance with a plan or zoning ordinance (such as design review, environmental impact assessment (EIA), etc.). The chapter also outlines which of these decision support tools are used, or could be used, in the management of proposals for tall buildings and how these relate to the impacts outlined in the previous chapter. The following section relates these methods to the regulatory context in England.

The regulation of development and decision support

A number of decision support mechanisms exist which provide a framework for the regulation of proposals for development. These mechanisms provide a baseline against which proposals are assessed in the first instance. For example, does the proposal comply with national planning policy, or is it proposed in an area that is zoned for another use? How might a planning document or zoning ordinance seek to regulate tall buildings? The following section outlines the use of the following mechanisms: development planning; zoning and its control mechanisms; and design guidance and associated mechanisms.

Development planning

Development planning is a framework for discretionary decision-making that is prevalent across the UK, Ireland, Australia and many of the Commonwealth countries. Plans are indicative only and do not imply that planning permission will be granted if the proposals are in conformity with that plan. In other words the system of development planning offers flexibility and commitment (Cullingworth and Nadin, 2002). Generally permissible uses and types of building are outlined in such plans, which form the basis for detailed proposals to be submitted to the administering authority for approval, as a framing device (Healey et al., 1995).

The form of development plan varies greatly but they usually consist of a clear statement of purpose, general planning policies, specific policies and proposals that relate to sites and buildings, and accompanying maps. We can say that development plans are vehicles for "promoting specific policy and development scenarios" as well as for "negotiating and articulating shared visions with a broad range of stakeholders" (Carmona et al., 2003: 18).

The role of both the professional planner and elected councillor in local government is primary in that the discretionary nature of the development plan requires professional competencies on behalf of the planner, and democratic accountability on behalf of the elected councillor. Plans are required to provide a context for decision-making that guides regulatory and investment decisions (Faludi, 1987).

Zoning and its control mechanisms

Zoning is used to control the use of specific buildings and areas and is distinct from the concept of the discretionary development plan in that a zoning ordinance is a more rigid form of control. The ordinance is prescriptive and detailed meaning that development in accordance with the zoning ordinance can proceed. The requirement for assessment of proposals therefore takes place within a clear and mandatory framework of regulation; it provides a level of certainty which stimulates confidence in building and investment and provides a context for tall building regulation which recognises that the city is both dynamic and evolutionary (Babcock et al., 1985). Zoning ordinances often include detail of buildings and areas protected by the state and may well include social elements to the character of neighbourhoods and street, in contrast to development plans which would ordinarily not cover such detail (Cullingworth and Nadin, 2002).

Zoning began in the United States as a passive instrument that sought to set limits on the size and use of buildings and plots, indicating to developers what can be built; so called "as-of-right" development control and is prevalent across Europe and North America. It has been used in the UK in the 1980s as Simplified Planning Zones and Enterprise Zones. In its original form zoning has been seen as a negative and exclusionary system of control. Kwartler (1989) and Punter (2000) suggest that in effect, zoning is a method of maintaining and protecting property values and improving environmental quality by directing bad-neighbour uses to appropriate locations. Zoning ordinances vary widely but as a minimum impose legal restrictions on the right to build which may include specified maximum height or floor space ratios, for example. As a result, zoning has had a major impact upon the way in which cities develop, often creating uniform townscapes (Punter, 2000). As a result of the prescriptive nature of zoning, development that conforms to the detailed zoning requirements for a site or area is automatically granted consent, thereby creating a level of confidence in the market.

One zoning support mechanism of interest is height and set-back regulation. Height and set-back regulations are used to provide a control over the height and dominance of buildings on the streetscape and evolved in early twentieth century America to control the bulk of buildings. Street width is the basis of this form of regulation and stipulates that the height of building should relate to the width of the street; for example, the zoning regulation, development plan or building regulation would show a height control district where the height of buildings should not exceed twice the width of the street (Weiss, 1992). Furthermore, if the building were to be set-back, then greater heights would be allowed (Sussna, 1989) (see Figure 3.1). In most medium and higher density districts, the height of a building's front wall at the street line is generally limited to a specified height or number of stories. Above that height, a building is required to set-back behind a theoretical inclined plane – the sky exposure plane – which cannot be penetrated by the building wall. However, a tower rising without set-back which covers only 40% of its plot, for example, is permitted to penetrate the sky exposure plane. This is due to the consequent compensating slender profile which provides more open space at the street level. In most low density areas, there are specific maximum perimeter wall heights above which the building usually must have a pitched roof or be set-back before rising to the permitted building height. Building height is therefore determined by the interplay of zoning regulations with a developer's design and economic concerns (Weiss, 1992; Sussna, 1967).

A second support mechanism and form of volumetric control, plot ratio, can be described as the "ratio of floor area permitted on a zoning lot to the size of the lot" (Smith, 1983) and is normally a support to zoning regulation in North America but is also used in discretionary planning systems such as the one in England. It is expressed as a ratio: a ratio of 6.0 on a plot of 10,000 square feet would allow a building of 60,000 square feet for example. As a result, plot ratios can give developers flexibility in deciding what type of building is appropriate for the plot and their requirements; a developer can choose, for example, to erect a low-rise building covering most or all of the plot, or a higher building covering much less of the ground area (Wakeford, 1990). Interest groups and lobbyists are often able to force through amendments to the plot ratio of a particular neighbourhood with political support. As a result, more sophisticated methods of plot ratio in combination with other zoning instruments have developed.

ALTERNATE REQUIRED FRONT SET-BACKS

Depth of Optical Front Open Area (in feet)		Height above "Street Line" (in feet)	Alternate "Sky Exposure Plane"			
			Slope over "Zoning Lot" (expressed as a ratio of vertical distance to horizontal distance)			
			On "Narrow Street"		On "Wide Street"	
On "Narrow Street"	On "Wide Street"		Vertical Distance	Horizontal Distance	Vertical Distance	Horizontal Distance
R6 or R7 Districts						
15	10	60	3.7 to 1		7.6 to 1	
R8 R9 R10 Districts						
15	10	85	3.7 to 1		7.6 to 1	

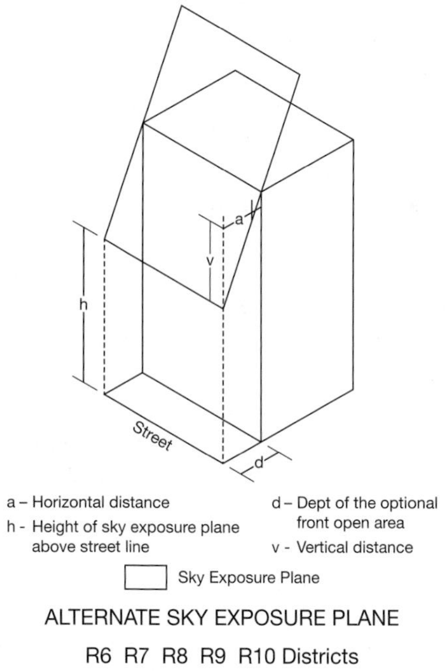

a – Horizontal distance
h - Height of sky exposure plane above street line

d – Dept of the optional front open area
v - Vertical distance

☐ Sky Exposure Plane

ALTERNATE SKY EXPOSURE PLANE

R6 R7 R8 R9 R10 Districts

FIGURE 3.1 Example of a height and set-back regulation, New York City Zoning Ordinance

Historically, plot ratios replaced height limits and were intended to allow architects to build taller without placing undue stress on transport infrastructure (Kitt-Chappell, 1990). Plot ratios are a useful method of height control in that the lower the ratio, the lower the potential height of buildings. Thus, in an area of sensitivity such as in areas of heritage value, the predominant building height can be enforced through an appropriate ratio. In areas of high land values, there is intense pressure to increase the height of buildings to maximise the potential return on investment.

A third support mechanism, transferable development rights (TDRs) or transferable air rights, are a crucial part of contemporary zoning practice in North America (see Figure 3.2). They are a mechanism permitting the transfer of development rights from designated landmarks (that is protected buildings and monuments) to nearby plots and can have major impacts upon building height at the plot, street and skylines levels. Without special designation and protection, landmarks are often vulnerable in zones that permit high density development. Each zoning plot contains an envelope of air space that can be filled by a building. Since most landmark buildings in central areas of the city do not use the full envelope, their unused development rights may be sold to developers of adjacent plots. This allows, in theory, the retention and preservation (in the US sense of the word) of landmarks while at the same time allowing owners reasonable economic use of their properties. Some or all of the unused development potential of the landmark can be transferred to an adjacent lot. The transferred development rights allow the adjacent building to be larger than usually permitted, with the extra bulk in the new building offset by the smaller landmark structure. As part of the transfer, the developer must prepare an acceptable proposal to preserve and maintain the landmark.

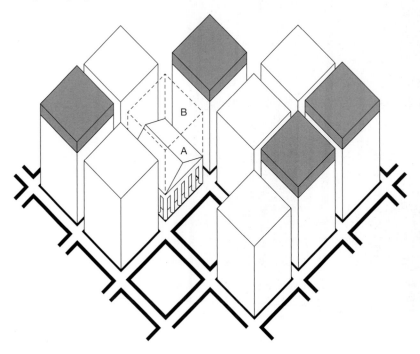

The air rights (B) of the protected building (A) are transferred to the adjacent buildings by agreement, resulting in their increased height, shown in black.

FIGURE 3.2 Transferable development rights, New York City Zoning

Finally, incentive zoning has been described as a reaction to the inflexibility of as-of-right development control through zoning regulation (Smith, 1983; Wakeford, 1990) (see Figure 3.3). It is a system through which developers are given bonuses in exchange for providing a range of amenities that are required or desirable by the "community". Such incentives usually grant higher densities or floor areas to a particular development. Consequent amenities can include public plazas, open space, desired site designs, public transport provision, and under-writing of social housing amongst other things. In other words, the premise of this type of regulation is that the integrity of the zoning ordinance can be weighed against clearly defined public benefit (Wakeford, 1990).

FIGURE 3.3 The Seagram building, New York City, showing privately owned plaza with public access

Incentive zoning is administered as part of zoning and can have radical implications for the setting of new buildings. This form of supporting regulation remains as contentious today as it did when first trialled in Chicago in the late 1950s. The creation of plazas, for example, has been particularly contentious. In effect, the creation of "public" plazas has often been used by developers to win approval for buildings at great density whilst in reality, the public access to these spaces became restricted over time under the banner of safety. In effect, this has resulted in the privatisation of the public realm in many instances. In a study undertaken by Professor Kayden, of 320 building projects analysed in New York City, nearly half did not follow the requirements of the building permits issued by the City in restricting public access to plazas (Dankwa, 1996). As a result of incentive zoning, the plot, streetscape and cityscape can be radically changed, with many established buildings and neighbourhoods crowded out by new glass boxes which have taken on board the incentive zoning potential (Wakeford, 1990). As such, the use of incentive zoning can have a major impact upon the built heritage in terms of altering the character of neighbourhoods and destroying the context of protected buildings and sites.

Design guidance and associated mechanisms

Design guidance has developed to provide advice to developers and architects on how proposed buildings and spaces should be designed (Adams et al., 2011). They can take the form of a variety of planning and other tools: supplementary planning guidance; nationally adopted guidance; design codes; design statements and site briefs, for example. Such policies can operate at various levels of government from the national to the municipal, but at their core, seek to address how specific issues can be overcome; location, townscape analysis, plot attributes, urban design issues, impact minimisation, materials, height, skyline, streetscape and plot implications of development, setting, and whether the proposal would improve the use of the plot, for example, as such guidance identifies criteria against which development proposals can be evaluated. These policy guidance documents take a number of forms but can be characterised by the involvement of interest groups in their adoption (Punter, 1999; Wakeford, 1990; Carmona et al., 2006).

As a proactive rather than reactive regulation, design guidance allows informed decision-making by indicating that the developer should meet a detailed set of criteria in a planning submission, thereby providing an adequate level of detail for the proper evaluation of a proposal. Guidance can therefore be a useful tool in maintaining, protecting and enhancing the character of a given place by indicating what form of development would be acceptable in a given location. The status of the policy is crucial: what is the weight given to it in the decision-making process; what level of information is required to be provided to meet the guidance; who assesses proposals against it? Is it binding on developers or are there measures that can be undertaken which circumvent some of the requirements of the guidance? As such, the use of guidance in the control of building height depends upon both political will and the type of planning which is undertaken. Indeed, the success of such guidance is determined by the way in which conflicts are resolved between actors through the design review process.

One element of design guidance, for example, can be the designation of specific areas for tall building clusters (see Figure 3.4). LPAs (Local Planning Authorities) can manage economic growth effectively by diverting pressure for development away from areas of heritage value. Furthermore, clustering can contribute to the character of a city by creating an identifiable contemporary skyline alongside the historic skyline. A number of cities have developed ways in which clustering of tall buildings assist in the conservation of important heritage landscapes. The use of clustering requires a mature approach to managing urban change in that it recognises that tall buildings can contribute to the cityscape and that this does not necessarily result in the destruction of the character of the city. Furthermore, clustering attempts to discourage tall buildings from being developed at random locations across the city that would create a dispersed skyline of little or no quality which also negatively impacts upon the existing heritage and value of the skyline.

Clustering involves a number of elements including the plotting of sightlines and views of protected monuments, buildings or areas, an understanding of the topography of the city or area, and a townscape analysis including an understanding of townscape character and value. Thus, a detailed knowledge of environmental, social and economic issues is gathered. The regulation of clustering manifests itself in recommendations through adopting policy guidance as indicative frameworks, or in mandatory rules explicitly forbidding tall building within certain areas.

A number of cities have developed ways in which the management of key views, often as part of design guidance, of important heritage landscapes can be protected from overly tall building proposals (see Figure 3.5); in Washington DC for example, the zoning ordinance of 1973 restricts height and views of key federal buildings such as the Capitol and Washington Monument; in Paris the city's *plan d'occupation des sols* encapsulates protected views along key axes such as the Champs Élysées; and, height restrictions in the historic centre of Beijing are designed to protect views of the Forbidden City. The protection of views of important buildings, sites, areas and landmarks can be a key element in tall building management. View protection can utilise a number of methods including: protected views into and out of the city; viewing cones where development is not allowed; city panoramas which encapsulate views of metropolitan areas from a distance; townscape views of particular character areas; and local views which are important in defining streets or corridors. Characterisation studies are a method of examining and understanding the fabric, form, topography and design within a particular geographic area, thereby establishing its character and what makes the place special and unique (Thomas, 2004). It can underpin the development of specific design guidance in providing baseline information about the character of the area or city in question (Thomas, 2004). It can often include elements of social and economic analysis that assist in understanding that character. In establishing the essential character of a place, its significance and value can be defined. This perspective on historic change enables

FIGURE 3.4 Cluster of tall buildings, Sydney harbour

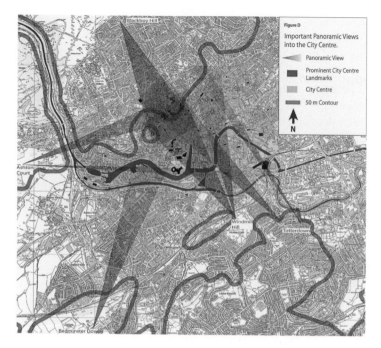

FIGURE 3.5 Protected views in Bristol

future change to be managed in ways that are sensitive to this character. It can be used as a tool in conservation planning to either directly influence planning policy or to influence decisions on specific development proposals.

The form of characterisation varies greatly but it usually includes a broad statement of intent, a detailed analysis of the character of the place in question, and recommendations about how existing character can be protected, maintained and enhanced, including guidance on how certain issues should be dealt with. In particular, they can be useful devices to encourage the containment of building height to a prescribed level (Thomas, 2004). As characterisation studies can contribute to a detailed understanding of place, they are an invaluable method for conservation of the city; only with a detailed understanding of the character of such a city can its protection and evolution be effectively planned.

The particular approach to characterisation studies indicates a democratic and sophisticated process which seeks to map the historic landscape of the city and examine how the city is used and the relationship between place and people (EH and CABE, 2002). As a piece of work however, this type of study is not only comprehensive, it requires highly skilled characterisation and translation of results of the survey into meaningful and useful information. As with other regulation, the bureaucracy and decision-makers work within a politicised and inherently complex environment where trade-offs occur and decisions are made according to a number of factors being taken into account. The use of characterisation studies is intended to facilitate informed decision-making through a detailed understanding of the landscape. They are used, in different guises, across Europe, the Middle East, the Americas and Oceania.

Decision support and the design review of proposals

The use of decision support to assist decision-makers on the submission of an application for new development or as part of preparations for a planning submission (pre-application discussions, for example) is varied. Some tools have evolved in specific situations to assist decision-makers in understanding the form of development and how it relates to the existing city fabric. An attempt is made to outline the main decision support tools below and examine how they are used in the development process. The main assessment tools reviewed are impact assessments, design review and visualisation.

Impact assessments

Impact assessments such as environmental impact assessment (EIA) are a systematic and integrative process designed to consider possible impacts of development prior to approval being granted by the planning authority and can be a key element in the design review of proposals picking up the non-visual as well as visual elements of a proposal (Wood, 2003). Various methodologies have been developed with EIA that have in common a requirement to supply decision-makers with information which provides an indication of the likely consequences should a development proposal proceed (Bartlett and Kurian, 2003; Wood, 2003). The political nature of impact assessments is unavoidable. Indeed, impact assessment is considered "within a political decision-making arena, and is therefore influenced by its norms and values, as well as by its procedures" (Wood, 2003: 3) and is therefore a fallible process. The information provided in EIA is produced by professionals who, as has been outlined earlier, have their own experiences and norms and who therefore produce information with an implicit bias. In other words, the information is value-loaded. Bartlett and Kurian (2003) recognise that there is an implicit assumption therefore, that impact assessments change outcomes by influencing political decision-making.

Wood (2003) recognises that impact assessments are not designed to stop developments from proceeding, rather the key is to become aware of the consequences of that development in advance, and make mitigatory requirements of the developers. Impact assessments function within the development process in four clear ways:

1   as an environmental protection, serving both as tool and as a forum for dialogue;
2   as an analytic tool, supporting rationality in the face of uncertainty, conflict, and shortage of problem-solving resources;
3   as a vehicle for public involvement, encouraging dialogue between actors and the general public; and
4   as an aid to the decision-making process (Sager, 2001).

There has been much experience with EIA as a project level assessment. EIA systems are widespread; the countries of the European Union (EU), USA, Canada, Australia, New Zealand and Hong Kong have all highly developed systems. In terms of tall buildings, a screening decision as to whether an EIA is required needs to be made at the outset by the competent authority. If so, a clear statement from the competent authority needs to be made about the scope of the information provided and what tools it is likely to use (Wood, 2003).

Design review

Design review is an administrative mechanism to control the visual quality of proposed additions and alterations to the built environment (Kumar, 2003). Typically, design review takes place within a development control process by professional planners and is prevalent across the globe in various formats. In southern Europe, the aesthetic review of new building proposals has a long history of assessment by learned architects, historians and artists for example, whilst in North America most large cities have formal design review processes that legally involve key actors such as planners, conservationists, public agencies and the public itself (Kumar, 2003).

The increasing use of advisory panels in various guises (architecture panels, heritage appraisal panels, community panels) including a range of individuals representing different actors in the development process (such as amenity, environmental and interest groups, architects, historians) points to the acceptance of an advisory role to appointed professionals and community representatives in the development control process (Punter, 2000). The input of these panels into the development control process is usually welcomed and taken seriously; they usually relate directly to design guidance which is adopted by planning authorities.

Membership of such panels can be based upon democratic election of community representatives, for example, and the co-opting of learned and experienced professionals who can provide impartial advice. At the core of such panels is the need for members to declare interests so that the design review process is transparent and engenders confidence (Wakeford, 1990). Kumar (2003) suggests that design review is a highly controversial aspect to the development control process due to the subjective nature of views expressed by the panel. The decisions reached by such panels can be the result of bargaining and compromise and reflect the views of an elite group of professionals that also incorporates community representatives who may or may not have a design or planning background.

Design review as a process usually involves the circulation of development proposals amongst panel members, the individual assessment of proposals and then convening of a meeting where the various views and opinions on these proposals are discussed (Kumar, 2003). The outcome of such meetings can range from outright rejection to outright acceptance. Both of these extreme positions are rarely expressed, rather the panel normally would make a number of suggestions for making the development proposals acceptable in design terms. Unless the panel has a formal role in the development control process recognised by statute or practice, the design review panel will report to the planning authority directly. This authority has a right of discretion over whether to incorporate the recommendations of the panel and therefore can ignore or accept, in total or in part, those recommendations.

The result of design review by advisory panels is a negotiation which reflects the dominant interests of the involved actors at the time of assessment. Depending on the mandate of the panel, such design review can assist in the protection and enhancement of the existing skyline, street and plot through the application of rigorous and professional assessment of the aesthetic merits of a development proposal. The approval of development does however rest with politicians who are at liberty to pursue an agenda which may or may not confirm the decision of the advisory panel in a development control decision (Cullingworth and Nadin, 2002). Kumar (2003) suggests that design review is a contentious and unsatisfactory process due to the amount of discretion, vagueness and lack of predictability, and the potential abuse of the process by actors intent on specific outcomes.

Visualisation

Visualisation tools might be used during the planning process to assist decision-makers, and indeed, all people concerned with the development process form an image of what the proposed development will look like *in situ* through the provision of information (see Figure 3.6). Typically, this will involve a rendering of the building itself as well as a montage of the building in its context (Barden, 1999). There are a number of forms of visualisation that are often used in conjunction with one another; models, photo montage and geographical information systems (GIS) are the main categories of visualisation.

The use of models in architecture has a rich history; representations of a proposed building have assisted non-architects in understanding the form of new development and how it sits within its context for millennia (Watkins, 2000). They can be made from a number of materials and aim to assist the lay person in understanding the built form which is being proposed. Photo montage likewise seeks to show how existing townscapes will be affected by new development by showing a mock-up of that new development in context by way of photographic image. In GIS and computer-aided design (CAD) the same is true but using sophisticated software to model images of the proposed buildings, what it could look like in context and even what the wind effects of that building may be, for example. Malczewski (2004) suggests that each of these methods involve both the representation and visualisation of data and information (functional) and the manipulation of that data and information to assist decision-making (communicative). As such, in the regulation of building height the GIS system can both represent the existing height and pattern of buildings within a particular locality whilst over-laying the policy-based framework on a map. Furthermore, the use of GIS offers the potential of modelling images of proposed development onto the built environment through the production of scenarios which can assist in decision-making.

FIGURE 3.6 Model of new and proposed tall buildings, City of London

Advances in GIS technology and the use of CAD alongside GIS mean that three-dimensional images can be produced which assist in annotating building proposals so that they can be analysed and assessed (Barden, 1999). The impact of a building proposal on the skyline, street and plot can theoretically be modelled which would also assist in summarising the key policy and planning issues to be resolved in the assessment of a project. Furthermore, modelling can assist in the understanding of cumulative impacts of a number of developments in a given area. In relation to the built heritage, modelling tools are therefore able to represent visually the impact of proposals on a Conservation Area, for example, thereby adding to the repertoire of planning authorities in the understanding of development proposals.

Conclusions

This chapter has examined the decision support tools which have evolved to assist in managing tall building proposals. It is evident that these methods are highly politicised and complex, and characterised by a wide range of interests. It is through the political and policy exchanges amongst these interests that decisions about tall building proposals take place. These methods have a key role in the assessment process; indeed, it is through the use of such methods that the issues, problems and debates about appropriate locations for tall buildings and their design are analysed, debated and resolved. At the core of the assessment process is the role of particular decision support tools; what is their remit, who produces the information used, who uses the information, what is and is not included, how rigorous the analysis is of the information, and how is the information included reflected in the decision-making process. In this context significant questions are raised. Does the basis for decision-making vary between places, and if so, how and why? What is good practice in tall building management and assessment, and where can it be found? What can we learn from experience elsewhere? Furthermore, how are the value judgements in the evaluation of proposals for new tall buildings made? Who makes them and how? The following chapters will explore how some of these issues are brought to ground in a number of locations across the globe.

4

THE CONSERVATION CHALLENGE OF TALL BUILDINGS

A particular contribution to debates and discussions about the role of conservation planning is made in this chapter in a number of ways. Firstly, it identifies the inherent conflicts that exist in conservation planning between the will to protect and to manage change effectively. Secondly, it offers some reflections on the conservation challenge that tall buildings pose. Thirdly, and building on chapter three, it reflects upon the relevance of decision-making tools which relate to conservation planning. Finally, it examines the system of built heritage protection in England thereby framing the first case studies in the second part of the book.

As previously stated, this book focuses on the problems of managing proposals for tall buildings in cities where the built form reflects a palimpsest of development over time, what can be termed hybrid heritage (While and Short, 2006). Phelps et al. (2002) suggest that the built heritage is a cultural and social construction, one that is dependent upon a "complex process of selection, protection and intervention" (p.3). The built heritage is normally protected through selective regulatory mechanisms that seek its conservation from inappropriate development or demolition, effectively prioritising public over private interests in seeking to protect elements of the townscape for the common good (Phelps et al., 2002). Ashworth (2002) also indicates that the survival of built heritage "relates to intentional choices to create, maintain and preserve selected senses of place" (p.247) hinting that different interpretations and understandings of the meaning of place can and do co-exist. Graham et al. (2000) acknowledge that built heritage is "a cultural product and a political resource" (p.18) which reflects that particular heritages and heritage interpretations are promoted through regulatory systems and popular debates. They propose a "circuit of heritage" model which recognises that heritage is one mechanism through which meaning is produced and reproduced; it is defined by identity and is produced and reproduced in social interactions through various media and through consumption. This meaning organises our practices in terms of setting rules, norms and conventions.

Mason (2002) argues that the underlying value attached to the built heritage by interest groups is diverse covering cultural, economic, political and aesthetic values which often overlap and compete. The production of built heritage value thereby reflects dominant narratives about the development of the city (Mason, 2002; Mourato and Mazzanti, 2002). As such, it is to be expected that the dominance of any of these values that shapes the way in which tall building proposals, and their impact on the built heritage, are analysed and determined. As a result, when tall building applications are assessed by planning authorities, they are confronted not only with decisions over what the built heritage is and what value is attached to it (Mason, 2002), but the dominant logic of the local conservation regime; what is unique about the particular place, how the significance of built heritage is determined and how this is reflected in decision-making about new development proposals.

A number of commentators suggest that the built heritage can become merely the past parcelled up in a palatable form for commercial consumption, or history selectively commodified for political ends through conservation planning systems (Shaw and Jones, 1997; Hewison, 1987). Ashworth and Larkham (1994) indicate that the increasing commodification of the built heritage, or evolution of a "heritage product", has seen the justification for heritage protection shift to a consumerist orientation where the relics of history become a product in the market to satisfy consumption. Tunbridge and Ashworth (1996) characterise these often competing meanings of heritage as dissonant. This refers to the underlying contestation about heritage which Graham et al. (2000) indicates has two elements: that there is a paradox between heritage as product and as people's sacred places; and that heritage belongs to "someone and therefore does not belong to someone else" (p.4).

Conflicts in conservation planning

Conservation planning in general and local conservation regimes in particular, reflect a number of common elements. Firstly, conservation planning is an inherently political and multi-scaled activity; it must gain political legitimacy for its decisions at local as well as national level (Tewdwr-Jones, 1995). At the local level, heritage governance is complex, "characterised by the interconnection of a variety of organisations and interests" (Strange and Whitney, 2003). It is within this context that conservation planning involves a complex set of groups who compete for their own vision of the future of the city and of the urban development process (Strange and Whitney, 2003; Larkham, 1996; Ashworth, 1997; Hobson, 2004; Madanipour, 2006; While, 2006). It is in the political and policy exchanges between these groups that decisions about development are reached; power relations define how issues are resolved or at least determined in such exchanges (see, for example, Forrester, 1993; Healey, 1997; Healey, 1988). Organisations reflect differences in status, power, authority, information, expertise and interests thereby leading to trade-offs which become obvious during the determination of planning problems (Forrester, 1993).

Secondly, conservation planning is a technical activity which uses a wide range of tools during the assessment of proposals to "ensure that decisions are taken in line with . . . prevailing rationalities" (Murdoch, 2000: 4). These tools are also politicised in that they reflect the interconnectedness of organisations and interests in their content and are therefore rarely objective or value-neutral.

Thirdly, it attempts to manage space through the selective protection of elements of the townscape. According to Hobson (2004), it can only do this through harnessing other development processes which lie outside its core competencies. In this sense, conservation planning is dependent on a number of externalities which it has little direct control over. Conservation planning practices are therefore dependent upon wider planning practices which are:

> "an ensemble of social relations, networks and nodes of dynamic and often inventive social interaction, patterned by . . . legal, governmental and professional systems, and by customs and habits built up over the years. They embody ways of thinking and ways of acting, which interact in complex and often ambiguous ways."
>
> *(Healey, 1997: 56).*

Finally, one other crucial characteristic of local conservation regimes is its criticism by pro-development interests. It has been suggested (While, 2006; Tait and While, 2009 amongst others) that whilst the principles of conservation planning are supported in general terms, conservation planning is periodically criticised by pro- . development interests due to the direct costs it imposes; repair and maintenance of protected structures, opportunity costs of alternative development, and the wider issue of conservation and change in the built environment.

The inherent tensions between the often conflicting elements of conservation planning are played out in a number of ways. Firstly, the potential conflict between conservation planning as the management of change versus conservation planning as an essentially preservationist process is at the heart of the debate about the future of cities and the status and role of built heritage. Larkham outlines this tension in the key question "how much originality, how much change?" (1996: 38). The outcome of either approach relates to the ideas of unity and diversity in the cityscape; in instances where there is a unity and coherence of cityscape such as in a Georgian square, Larkham suggests that the focus for conservation planning should be preservationist. In cityscapes that exhibit diversity, where no one style predominates and which could be defined as hybrid, the focus for conservation planning should be to manage change in an appropriate manner (1996). In terms of development within either context, Ashworth (1997) indicates that in environments where the imperative is preservation (cityscapes exhibiting unity), then conservation planning should aim to slow the pace of change. Conversely, in situations where conservation planning is designed to manage change, Ashworth outlines this as essentially an option for development.

Secondly, the role of new buildings in built heritage environments are a particular challenge in this regard. In instances where there is clear unity in the cityscape it is simple to both protect and enhance what is important, whereas in hybrid townscapes, it is more difficult to protect the built heritage from inappropriate development (Cohen, 1999; Larkham, 1996; Tait and While, 2009). With new buildings, both notions are challenged; how can unified cityscapes be preserved if new buildings encroach on short or long views, and dominate the settings of important buildings or areas? Likewise in managing change in the built environment, how do new buildings fit into a diverse cityscape? Should new buildings be discouraged in instances where they affect unified cityscapes and encouraged in diverse cityscapes? The question of new buildings within built heritage environments therefore relates primarily to the idea of approaches to the management of urban change, namely for cities with built heritage to evolve in a managed way and to not only retain their distinctiveness but to improve on it through proper planning and contributing to a twenty-first century city (Hobson, 2004). In proposals for development this can relate to discussions about the form of development at the site, neighbourhood or metropolitan level; are mimetic or pastiche approaches to the challenges of context appropriate, or are radical architectural solutions the order of the day? Both approaches can lead to concern; the former can lead to development which shows no regard for context, the latter to development which leads to an inauthentic rendering of a different style.

Thirdly, Hobson (2004) indicates that changing economic forces have resulted in a shift in the focus of conservation planning from the protection and enhancement of built heritage to the idea that the built heritage contributes to place distinctiveness and as a tradable resource which cities employ in the market to attract investment, development and jobs. The idea that the built heritage of a particular place contributes to local distinctiveness permeates much of the literature on conservation planning. For example, Strange (1999) suggests that the increasing importance of local distinctiveness in discourses around place marketing is a reflection of the local impacts of globalisation which, seeking to eliminate temporal and spatial barriers between places, results in the physical identity of place assuming greater importance. The extent to which conservation planning is able to positively undertake this task is a current area of debate in conservation planning practice; how can conservation planning contribute to a sense of place through the protection of built heritage assets and how can this be translated through the development process?

Finally, Strange argues that as a result of attempts at integrating sustainable development into the practices of conservation planning, we are witnessing a new discourse around conservation, termed post-conservation. It reflects that the rhetoric of sustainability is employed as a method whereby concerns about accommodating development – accompanied by a much diluted form of conservation – can be expressed within a context of physical and economic growth which is both desired and necessary, and that its impacts can be managed (Strange, 1999). Thus, development is the prime concern with conservation planning relegated to a supporting role where it agrees with the prevailing rationalities and norms of that discourse. The current tall building phenomenon is one element of this; proposals for tall buildings are being submitted across the globe and the same core issue of heritage governance and management within a context of a need for economic development is the basis for assessment.

Tall buildings: the conservation challenge

Tall buildings, like any other new development, are proposed within cities that are in a continual state of flux reflecting the physical legacy of preceding and current generations' aspirations, uses and limitations (Hobson, 2004). Proposals for tall buildings may present particular challenges in hybrid heritage cityscapes. In instances where there is clear unity in the cityscape it is possible to protect what is important using tools and processes which attract consensus amongst interest groups in regulating out (or in, for that matter) tall buildings. In other cities which display greater diversity in the cityscape, even where elements are or can be protected, it is more difficult to protect that built heritage from inappropriate development particularly as there may be conflict over what built heritage should be protected and how (Cohen, 1999).

Much of the media attention in England around new tall buildings has focused on London and the impacts of numerous towers on the fabric of this world city, mainly due to the height of proposals coming forward and the number of proposals in the 1990s and 2000s. These debates are increasingly reflected across provincial cities, albeit attracting less national media attention but a considerable amount of interest from English Heritage (EH) and the local media. In these cities, incremental approaches to managing tall buildings are evolving partly as a result of the status and breadth of existing national guidance and that unique approaches are required to address the challenges of different places and sites. Birmingham has developed a planning policy framework for the positive encouragement of tall buildings in particular locations whilst Newcastle's approach to place characterisation is leading to an evolving restrictive policy. In London, innovative ways of protecting particular elements of the built heritage are emerging through the Greater London Assembly and London Boroughs, whilst Manchester is resisting calls for any form of tall building policy. Some of these cities are reacting to such development proposals in a vacuum of knowledge about the cumulative impact of tall buildings being proposed, their impact upon the built heritage of the city and the wider social and economic fabric, and the utility of assessment and decision support tools. Furthermore, interest groups involved in decisions about tall building proposals have little idea about the impacts of regulatory and assessment procedures on decision-making, about what decisions are being made and how, and what the impacts of such decisions on the fabric of cities are. Understanding of these issues often remains patchy with little or no discussion of the issues at a strategic level. It is in this context that this research seeks to uncover the variety of approaches to managing tall building proposals in the major regional cities of England and examine the implications of these approaches within a wider national context.

Decision support in conservation planning

A key theme of the book is to investigate the role and function of emerging assessment tools in dealing with the built heritage challenges of tall buildings in particular places. Assessment tools are designed as supporting mechanisms for decision-making. In terms of conservation planning, there is little literature about the use of support mechanisms in decision-making yet there is a broad literature in planning more generally which is potentially useful. Various methods have been developed and are emerging for the assessment of tall building proposals yet have in common a requirement to supply decision-makers with information which provides an indication of the likely impacts should a development proposal proceed (Bartlett and Kurian, 2003; Wood, 2003).

Assessment of proposals is considered "within a political decision-making arena, and is . . . influenced by its norms and values, as well as by its procedures" (Wood, 2003: 3). The political nature of assessment tools is thereby unavoidable. Indeed, Bartlett and Kurian recognise that there is an implicit assumption that assessments change outcomes by influencing political decision-making (2003). There is a minimum intention that they assist the decision-maker yet also an explicit recognition that assessment in practice is rarely as objective or value-neutral as they might be expected to be (Formby, 1989). Those involved in the development process – developers submitting information into the planning process, planners determining compliance with policy, elected officials who decide whether planning permission should be granted, for example – reflect on a large number of trade-offs including between built heritage issues and socio-economic issues, the acceptability of possible impacts on the built heritage when balanced against investment and regeneration, and that decisions themselves reflect power relationships and dominant narratives about the direction and rate of urban change. As such, assessment tools can be used and abused by groups to justify their position. Indeed, it must be remembered that documents submitted as part of development proposals are normally drafted and published by experts employed by the applicant for planning permission. There is therefore a suggestion that the information contained within the documentation could be biased in favour of the development (Wood, 2003). The ability of decision makers to challenge information contained within such documents is limited given the limited resources available for such tasks and the lack of specific expertise in such diverse areas as computer modelling or detailed photo montages (Bartlett and Kurian, 2003). It is within this context that one of the main objectives of this research will examine and analyse the methods used in assessing tall building proposals within conservation planning.

Built heritage protection in England

The protection of built heritage in England is the primary responsibility of the Department for Culture, Media and Sport (DCMS) with some powers exercised under planning legislation that are the responsibility of the Department for Communities and Local Government (DCLG). The Planning (Listed Buildings and

Conservation Areas) Act 1990 (the 1990 Act) lays the foundation for the contemporary system of heritage protection in England. It is supplemented by *Planning Policy Statement 5: Planning for the Historic Environment* (PPS5) (DCLG, 2010) which seeks to provide full statements of central government policies for the identification and protection of the historic environment.

The system of protection in England (as in France and The Netherlands, for example) has a long history starting in the late nineteenth century with attempts at protecting ancient monuments through the Ancient Monuments Act 1882, the first time that the state had acknowledged an interest in the preservation of buildings or monuments (Cullingworth and Nadin, 2002). The Royal Commission on the Historical Monuments of England was instructed, from 1908, to record such buildings and monuments although the emphasis remained on recording rather than their conservation (Cullingworth and Nadin, 2002; Hobson, 2004). Not until the 1960s however, was a comprehensive survey of historic buildings undertaken. This survey which was undertaken county by county was the first attempt at identifying historic buildings; by 1969 120,000 such buildings had been identified for protection (Cullingworth and Nadin, 2002). The current system of protection has its routes in the 1960s particularly for historic buildings and areas. Listed Buildings, most recently expressed through the Planning (Listed Buildings and Conservation Areas) Act 1990, require a national list of buildings of "special architectural or historic interest"[1] to be compiled by the Secretary of State for Culture, Media and Sport with advice from EH. The national list is managed by DCMS at present although responsibility for implementing development control as it relates to Listed Buildings rests with LPAs with advice from EH (Cullingworth and Nadin, 2002). The system of listing rests on three separate designations: Grade I, Grade II* and Grade II. The grading in the statutory list is a material consideration in the determination of applications for development. Grades I and II* identify the outstanding architectural or historic interest of Listed Buildings and constitute about 6% of Listed Buildings. However, the statutory controls apply to all Listed Buildings irrespective of grade (DETR, 1994).

The Civic Amenities Act 1967 introduced the concept of Conservation Areas, the first attempt at protecting areas, to be designated by LPAs. They have a duty to "determine which parts of their area are areas of special architectural or historic interest, the character of which it is desirable to preserve or enhance"[2]. After designation, LPAs are required to take the special architectural or historic interest of the area into account in making planning decisions (Hobson, 2004). There is no standard set of procedures for designation or criteria against which a Conservation Area can be designated, although EH has gone some way towards plugging the gap in recent years with publications such as *Guidance on the Management of Conservation Areas* (EH, 2005c) and *Guidance on Conservation Area Appraisals* (EH, 2005b) which seek to assist LPAs in defining what it is that is important about the character of the designated areas.

Under the Ancient Monuments and Archaeological Areas Act 1979 (as amended by the National Heritage Act 1983) monuments or areas "which in the opinion of the Secretary of State are of public interest by reason of the historic, architectural, traditional, artistic or archaeological interest attaching to it"[3] can be designated. Scheduled Ancient Monuments (SAMs) are designated by the Secretary of State for Culture, Media and Sport. Archaeological remains can also be designated through the Act at local level and recorded at county level in the Sites and Monuments Record. Once designated, LPAs must seek their protection through the development plan and development control decisions (Hobson, 2004).

UNESCO administers the World Heritage Convention which seeks to designate areas of outstanding cultural and natural heritage of global importance to humankind (EH, 2005a). There are currently seventeen World Heritage Sites in England. In 1999, the UK government drew up a tentative list of potential future World Heritage Sites which it will consider for nomination to UNESCO for approval.

Locally Listed Buildings are designated by LPAs as buildings that have local historic and architectural value but that are not on the statutory list. PPS5 suggests that LPAs examine where buildings of local significance can contribute to the ideals of conservation planning and character of place, and adopt appropriate mechanisms for protection such as through a development plan or supplementary planning document (DCLG, 2010).

Development control and the use of decision support

In addition to the publication of PPSs at national level, regional and local frameworks exist with which to guide development and seek to protect the built heritage. At the regional level, Regional Spatial Strategies (RSS – although the status of these is currently under review) outline a spatial framework to inform the preparation of Local Development Frameworks (LDFs), Local Transport Plans (LTPs) and regional and sub-regional strategies and programmes that have a bearing on land use activities including the built heritage (ODPM, 2004).

Section 38 of the Planning and Compulsory Purchase Act 2004 requires that the statutory development plan will be the starting point in the consideration of planning applications for the development or use of land. The statutory development plan will include the RSS, any adopted development plan (unitary, local, minerals or waste) as well as emerging LDFs required under the new Act. LDFs are intended to streamline the planning system by promoting a proactive, positive approach to managing development through a core strategy, site specific allocations of land and area action plans (ODPM, 2004). At the heart of LDFs is a broad core strategy and area action plans which will provide a detailed planning framework for the management of the area (McPherson, 2006). Each element of the LDF should reflect the conservation planning imperative of the LPA; the core strategy will need to contain broad conservation aims whilst area action plans will operationalise these at the local level. The local community and other key actors will be required to be involved in both of these stages (McPherson, 2006; Brown, 2006).

In England, local planning authorities (LPAs) administer the system of granting planning permissions for new developments. This system can be characterised by a number of key elements: the role of pre-application discussions between key actors; the formal submission of a planning application and acceptance by the LPA; consultation with statutory and non-statutory bodies; a planning officer report weighing up the consultation responses and assessing whether a proposal complies with national, regional and local planning policy, precedent and site visit given to the decision-making body; and the decision by elected members (Cullingworth and Nadin, 2002). Decision support mechanisms can take place either informally or formally at any or all of these stages. For example, during pre-application discussions, the LPA may assess a proposal broadly against a tall building policy, as well as assessing it more robustly in the report to members in the later stages of the planning process.

These built heritage assets are protected from inappropriate development or demolition in a number of ways. Firstly, during the planning application process, as outlined above, built heritage issues are material to the determination of that application. As such therefore, there is a duty under both PPS5 to consider the impacts of development upon Listed Buildings, Conservation Areas, Scheduled Ancient Monuments (SAMs) and archaeological remains during the planning process. Furthermore, should World Heritage Sites and Locally Listed Buildings be involved, the LPA has a duty to consider the impact of development on those assets even though they are not protected through statute. In addition there are a number of distinct processes that seek to protect those assets. Listed Building Consent is required for works to Listed Buildings which affect its character as a building of special architectural or historic interest (DCLG, 2010). The process is administered by LPAs but is subject to the involvement of both EH and DCLG if demolition is proposed or if the building is either Grade I or II*. It is customary to submit Listed Building Consent applications and applications for planning permission at the same time if both are required; the issues and solutions are often intertwined in such instances and consent for one is usually only granted where it is acceptable for both (Cullingworth and Nadin, 2002).

The second process is Conservation Area Consent which extends demolition control to unlisted buildings within the area and protects trees, and is administered locally; consent is required through this process for these works to take place. The level of control in Conservation Areas reflects the need to prevent "piecemeal erosion of the character of an area through the cumulative effects of . . . changes" (Cullingworth and Nadin, 2002: 243) although the lack of appraisal of the character of many English Conservation Areas (EH, 2005b), required by the Act but largely unimplemented by LPAs, means that this is difficult to gauge (Hobson, 2004). For works to a SAM, application needs to be made to the Secretary of State for Culture, Media and Sport through the Ministry in the form of a Scheduled Ancient Monuments Consent. Central government therefore has control of these assets and usually takes the direct advice of EH in their determination (Cullingworth and Nadin, 2002).

The designation of World Heritage Sites by UNESCO provides no additional statutory controls through the development control system. Inclusion on the list does, however, assert the outstanding international importance of the site as a key material consideration to be taken into account by LPAs in writing development planning documents and carrying out development control functions. Planning policy is required therefore to reflect the value of the sites and seek appropriate protection mechanisms which will be weighed against the merits of particular development proposals (DCLG, 2010). Furthermore, UNESCO advises that management plans are adopted for sites in order to create a framework for decision-making which attracts consensus amongst key actors (ICOMOS, 2005). This is reflected through PPS5 which encourages management plans as a planning framework within which pertinent development plan policies and other guidance can be reflected in a coordinated way. The designation of Locally Listed Buildings likewise confers no statutory control from the national level, although with the designation of such buildings through such mechanisms as the development plan, a certain amount of protection should be expected.

Design guidance and associated mechanisms in England

Design guidance, which can be expressed as tall building guidance documents and policies, have been developing in England in recent times in response to the current wave of tall buildings. They are most noticeable in the urban areas of England and exhibit a number of approaches. Each is framed, however, by the jointly produced EH and Commission for Architecture and the Built Environment (CABE) Guidance on Tall Buildings (CABE and EH, 2003, amended in 2007). This was drafted in response to a survey of public attitudes to tall buildings undertaken by EH in 2001. This research indicated that there was broad public support for tall buildings only where they are located appropriately taking into account the surrounding context, and that they should be restricted in inappropriate locations. Furthermore, the research found that key buildings and views should be protected from inappropriate tall buildings (EH, 2001). The joint CABE–EH guidance document seeks to provide "advice and guidance on good practice in relation to tall buildings in the planning process and to highlight other related issues which need to be taken into account" (CABE and EH, 2003: 1.4). This guidance advocates a robust approach that requires both a strong development plan framework for decision-making supported by detailed decision support mechanisms (HoC, 2002). In reality however, the guidance has suffered from its attempt to relate to all potential tall buildings in all potential places[4]. The variation between places and the distinctiveness of local planning and conservation planning regimes suggests that a national guidance document should remain strategic and reinforce the need to have locally-based solutions which respond to local circumstances[5].

The status of the CABE–EH guidance document is unclear. In its report to the House of Commons Transport, Local Government and Regional Affairs Select Committee, the government endorsed the guidance yet acknowledged that the provisions of the guidance are insufficiently strong given the number of tall buildings coming forward (HoC, 2002). It suggested a national framework for tall buildings outlining in detail the need for locally-based development plan solutions for tall buildings and detailed criteria for proposals to meet. Furthermore however, the House of Commons report suggests that revised guidance should be flexible enough for LPAs to reflect their unique characteristics in decision-making about tall buildings. The report also alludes to the ambiguity in function of the organisations which produced the guidance: EH is responsible for protecting heritage in the face of new tall building proposals and at the same time listing post-war architecture including tall buildings, where it is argued that CABE is aligned too closely with the modernist architectural establishment (HoC, 2002). As such, the context for tall building guidance in England is somewhat flexible and contested by actors.

As will be seen, individual English cities have responded to both the increasing pressure to build tall and the framework set by the CABE–EH guidance with their own tall building policies and guidance documents. A review of approaches reveals that there are a wide variety of frameworks ranging from relatively discrete and short policy statements in development plans, to complex and broad urban design guidance documents specifically written for tall building issues. Responses to tall buildings can be characterised as being a relatively recent phenomenon although in some instances new tall buildings policies are based upon previous studies which referred to tall buildings but which were broader in nature. Birmingham Urban Design Study, for example, sought to characterise the townscape of the city in the early 1990s as a basis for planning decisions.

The use of characterisation studies in England is in its infancy although the idea of "character" in conservation planning was established under the Civic Amenities Act 1967 which brought in the concept of the Conservation Area (Thomas, 2004). The current trend to characterise place as a basis for conservation planning strategy is based on a series of archaeological programmes undertaken by EH in the early 1990s. The subsequent evolution of EH's Historic Landscape Characterisation programme led to a deep understanding of the importance of all of the elements of townscape in management and decision-making processes[6]. These archaeological programmes sought to produce databases of built heritage assets, assessments and strategies for historic towns throughout England (Thomas, 2004). In this first wave of characterisations the programme covered local market towns.

Following publication of the *Urban White Paper* (ODPM, 2000) EH conducted a review of all policies relating to the built heritage, including wide ranging consultation with actors and the public, culminating in a report entitled *Power of Place* (EH, 2000). Amongst other elements, this document called for measures which would ensure the future of the built heritage primarily as a driver of regeneration (Hobson, 2004; EH, 2000). This report has led to the extension of the characterisation programme to urban areas with studies, to date, covering Bristol and Newcastle–Gateshead. The use of characterisation is intended to assist decision-making not only in conservation planning processes (Conservation Area Consent, Listed Building Consent and Ancient Monuments Consent) but to assist planning decisions more generally by providing detailed, robust information about the character and particularity of place so that planning decisions can result in development which respects and reflects that existing character (Thomas, 2004).

Decision support and the design review of tall building proposals in England

On submission of planning applications for tall buildings, once the initial assessment against planning policy is undertaken, a number of decision support tools are utilised by LPAs in the assessment of the proposals. The application must go through a process of design review. This is required by Planning Policy Statements (PPS) with the over-arching principle being to achieve high quality architecture and urban design (DCLG, 2010). Assessment is undertaken in a number of ways and by a number of actors with the intention of commenting on the quality of proposals against specified criteria in an objective manner whilst recognising that design is an intrinsically creative process that reflects tastes and preferences and is therefore to some degree subjective (CABE, 2003).

The process of design review is not prescribed specifically through legislation or guidance but is usually bounded by development plan policy at the local level and the input of both CABE and EH from the national level. Furthermore, CABE offers more detailed advice to applicants for planning permission giving developers a sense of the quality and breadth that proposals should embody (CABE, 2003). The responses to design review are incorporated by LPAs into their decisions about the appropriateness of development. The status of these responses is interesting in that the weight of those from EH and CABE assume primacy in the development process; without the support of these organisations it is unlikely that planning permission be granted. Conversely with the support of these organisations, planning permission is more likely (HoC, 2005). A recent House of Commons report on the effectiveness of CABE's design review processes highlighted a problem that the response of this organisation to specific (tall building) proposals may limit the impact of other design review processes in the planning application (such as in the LPA and amongst other consultees). The House of Commons committee therefore suggests that the responses of CABE reflect how the design review decision is undertaken and reached, and who was involved in that decision (HoC, 2005). This should mean that the process of design review becomes more transparent and open to question specifically about how decisions are reached and who makes them[7].

The use of visualisations in the design review of schemes is strongly encouraged by both CABE and EH as well as the LPA. CABE suggests that these should consist of clear plans, drawings, models or photographs which convey the essence of the project to the reviewers although it remains silent regarding who should undertake this work (CABE, 2003). The potential for these visualisations to be objectively assessed is limited however by the skill set of the staff within the reviewing organisations; particularly in LPAs, there is often a dearth of suitably qualified staff who could challenge the accuracy of a visualisation of building (Kumar, 2003) especially given that visualisation often draws on significant resources, is designed to impress the reviewers and is difficult to challenge without political support (Kørnøv and Thissen, 2000; Forrester, 1989; March, 1994). In CABE and EH however there is potential for greater understanding of the processes of visualisation and therefore how renderings of a building may be represented in a planning application given that both organisations contain a significant amount of expertise (CABE and EH, 2003, CABE, 2002). Conflict between the opinions of the organisations on development proposals is also possible given their different mandates and focus. Furthermore, with advancements in the types and scope of visualisations, there is an assumption by decision-makers that technology can provide accurate renderings of buildings (Barden, 1999).

The use of impact assessments, particularly EIA, is widespread for development projects in England. Proposals for tall buildings fall within Annex II of the 97/11/EU Directive which requires that member states develop criteria and thresholds for deciding whether specific projects require an EIA to be undertaken (the screening element of the process). EIAs for proposals for new tall buildings are therefore not mandatory and are based upon informed decisions taken by the competent authority as to whether one is required, drawing on legal opinion and precedent. These decisions are required to be publicly available (Wood, 2003). There is, however, widespread recognition that the built heritage aspect of EIA is not given adequate regard during the decision-making process (King, 1997; Langstaff and Bond, 2002; Wood, 2003; Jones and Slinn, 2006).

EIAs are prepared by consultants specifically employed by the developers to undertake the process. In essence therefore, the body which pays for the piece of work is that which supports the project. The competent authority checks the EIA for relevance and accuracy yet often does not have the expertise and detailed knowledge to assess the content (Langstaff and Bond, 2002). In other words, the EIA is often produced as a requirement but without offering objective, competent and easily readable and digestible information to the decision-makers.

Conclusions

This chapter has reviewed the tools that have evolved to assist in managing tall building proposals from a conservation planning perspective, and to situate these methods within the built heritage context in England. More specifically, it has outlined decision support tools that may assist tall building management in England. This understanding of the built heritage context in England is augmented in the chapters on other international cities by some indication of the systems of built heritage protection in Ireland, Norway and Canada. The second part of this book details how specific tall building proposals have been determined, how decisions were made, what tools and methods were utilised, what built heritage issues emerged, how these were (or were not) dealt with, and where good practice may be located.

5

TALL BUILDINGS IN LIVERPOOL: BALANCING CONSERVATION AND CHANGE IN THE MARITIME MERCANTILE CITY

In August 2005, a planning application for a 27-storey tower and associated Listed Building Consent and Conservation Area Consent applications were approved by Liverpool City Council (LCC). Whilst the application had the support of a broad cross section of interests within the city, other tall building applications have failed to gain such support. Consensus over the benefits of specific redevelopment schemes within Liverpool has been achieved, due in part to the strong regeneration agenda of city leaders and the pro-development activity of key agencies in the city. The potential for new development in the city to impact upon Liverpool's unique character has led to local, national and international media attention. This spotlight on Liverpool's approach to tall buildings is reflected both by vigorous debate in the letters pages of the local press and by the interest many other World Heritage Site cities have in the tall building debate in the city. Furthermore, the difference of opinion between heritage organisations about the future of Liverpool (as exemplified by the current tall building debate) has meant that this spotlight on Liverpool continues. Decisions about tall buildings are taking place within a context of an emerging tall buildings policy framework, concern about the management of the World Heritage Site status conferred on the city in 2004, and growing discussion about the character and identity of Liverpool in the twenty-first century.

Context for development in Liverpool

Liverpool is located on England's north-west coast, in the county of Merseyside. The region has a population of just over 1.3 million and is comprised of five local authorities. These local authorities centre around the city of Liverpool, which has a population of 435,000 (Office for National Statistics (ONS), 2008). Liverpool is a city of world renown. In the eighteenth and nineteenth centuries the city was central to the expansion of the British Empire, in particular to trade (in goods and slaves) and to the emigration of British, Irish and other Europeans to the new world. The port remains busy today, but was particularly so until the Second World War. Subsequently, Liverpool became synonymous with urban decay, dereliction and out-migration; its population has dropped, from 850,000 in 1930 to 435,000 in 2008, as people have left to find work in other parts of the UK and further afield (ONS, 2008).

More recently however, Liverpool has started to attract worldwide attention again. The city was European Capital of Culture in 2008 (ECOC08), and its population is expanding again, albeit slowly (Allinson, 2010). Furthermore, in 2004, UNESCO declared the city's waterfront to be a World Heritage Site, worthy of protection. Indeed, the Liverpool brand is a powerful one which projects both positive and negative images. Liverpool's built heritage has been central to its attempts at regeneration since the early 1980s, as is reflected by the Albert Docks redevelopment, the valorisation of the city's Georgian buildings and the work of English Heritage and LCC in seeking World Heritage Site designation.

Liverpool is built on the Mersey River and faces the Wirral to the south and to the west. The city centre occupies a shallow amphitheatre, formed by a steep sandstone escarpment that curves to the rear between Breeze Hill and Dingle (see Figure 5.1). This ridge frames the city centre, and provides a dramatic backdrop for the city. Key landmark buildings punctuate the ridge and give the skyline clear focal points: the Catholic Cathedral, finished in 1967; the Anglican cathedral, finished as recently as 1978, although started in 1904; the BT tower or beacon, from 1970; the Three Graces (Royal Liver Building from 1911, Cunard Building from 1918 and the Port of Liverpool Building from 1907 – see Figure 5.2); and, the commercial core to the north. All the above punctuate the skyline, accentuating the ridge as a natural formation and giving clear character to the city.

FIGURE 5.1 The Liverpool waterfront

FIGURE 5.2 The Three Graces, Liverpool

The city has developed radially, from the historic medieval and Georgian port settlement. Along the river frontage, docks stretch both north and south, with their associated nineteenth century warehouse buildings, many of which survive and have been converted to satisfy a variety of uses. The city centre occupies a position at the centre of the amphitheatre, on a sliver of slightly higher land which runs towards the point where the Pier Head has now been constructed. An inner residential area (developed between the city centre and the escarpment, mainly to provide accommodation to the dock workers) and a residential ring of Georgian, Victorian and early twentieth century houses occupy the plateau behind the escarpment, with more modern suburbs stretching beyond this point to the Lancashire plain. The city's waterfront is highly revered, and it is argued that it is one of the world's great panoramas (UNESCO, 2004). Whatever the case about these claims, it is clear that the view of the waterfront matters, and that it is particularly sensitive to change.

In 2004, UNESCO declared the central areas and docklands of the city a World Heritage Site. The bid for designation attracted a large number of organisations in support, but led by LCC (see Table 5.1 on p. 63). The city was inscribed onto the World Heritage List for three main reasons:

> "*Liverpool was a major centre generating innovative technologies and methods in dock construction and port management in the 18th and 19th centuries. It thus contributed to the building up of the international mercantile systems throughout the British Commonwealth; . . . The city and the port of Liverpool are an exceptional testimony to the development of maritime mercantile culture in the 18th and 19th centuries, contributing to the building up of the British Empire; . . . It was a centre for the slave*

trade, until its abolition in 1807, and for emigration from northern Europe to America. Liverpool is an outstanding example of a world mercantile port city, which represents the early development of global trading and cultural connections throughout the British Empire."

(UNESCO, 2004)

The boundaries of the World Heritage Site were drawn around six main areas: the pier head with the Three Graces; Albert Dock, from 1847; Stanley Dock, from 1858; the historic centre around the commercial area; William Brown Street Cultural Quarter; and Lower Duke Street. This designation has attracted the general support of the many agencies and government bodies involved in regenerating the city. Yet, there is "concern within the business community that the tightly drawn boundaries are stifling investment"[1]. Furthermore, due to the ongoing inter-urban competition between Liverpool and its near neighbour Manchester, there is ongoing concern that Manchester is taking the "lion's share of development in the north-west, leaving Liverpool as second best, as usual"[2].

The *World Heritage Site Management Plan* (LCC and DCMS, 2003) submitted to UNESCO in December 2003 was adopted by UNESCO, ICOMOS and LCC for the purposes of managing the site. Furthermore, an officer employed to draft the management plan was retained within the City Council structure as the World Heritage Site Officer, responsible for implementation of the management plan[3]. The plan sets out the management objectives for the World Heritage Site, which are aimed at guiding future management of the site. In line with the World Heritage Site approach, a buffer zone has been designated, which is more broadly drawn and includes the setting for the centre of the city. The Lime Street Gateway site considered in this chapter lies within the buffer zone, and as such it is subject to the objectives of the management plan.

TABLE 5.1. Organisations supporting the bid for
World Heritage Site status in Liverpool

City of Liverpool
English Heritage
North West Development Agency
Liverpool Vision
University of Liverpool
John Moores University
Department for Culture, Media and Sport
Environment Agency
Government Office for the North West
Mersey Partnership
European Capital of Culture Bid
National Museums and Galleries on Merseyside
Liverpool Partnership Group
Merseytravel

In approving the World Heritage Site, UNESCO requested that City Council planning policy be in conformity with the special qualities of the site (LCC, 2004). This is specifically because UNESCO and ICOMOS were concerned about proposals (such as the Fourth Grace) coming forward which had the potential to impact negatively on the character of the site at the time. Furthermore, UNESCO and ICOMOS have been more generally concerned about the impacts of tall buildings on World Heritage Sites elsewhere; therefore, they were unusually insistent that a policy framework should reflect the needs of the site here (UNESCO, 2005). More specifically, UNESCO indicated that, in applying its planning procedures, the City Council should ensure that:

> *"the height of any new construction in the World Heritage Site and its Buffer Zone does not exceed that of structures in the immediate surroundings; the character of any new construction should respect the historic and architectural qualities of the Site; and, new construction at the Pier Head should not dominate, but shall complement the Pier Head group of buildings."*
>
> (LCC, 2004: 14).

The City Council considered the management plan to be part of the city's statutory planning framework, alongside the development plan.

Liverpool has been the recipient of nearly every national regeneration initiative in the post-war period, as a result of the reduction in employment in the city and the consequent dereliction (Munck, 2003; Biddulph, 2010). Regeneration monies have not substantially changed the overall high levels of unemployment and poverty which have been evident in Liverpool (Meegan, 2003; Pemberton and Winstanley, 2010), although the kind of physical regeneration that is exemplified by the restoration of the Albert Docks by the Merseyside Development Corporation (which had a clear vision of heritage-based regeneration for Liverpool) *has* benefited the city enormously. Not until the European Union granted Merseyside Objective 1 status in 1993 were there demonstrable schemes which made a difference to both the fabric of the city and the welfare of its inhabitants (Couch, 2003). Since the mid-1990s, however, the city has been radically transformed and reinvented, culminating in the awarding of ECOC08 and World Heritage Site status in 2004. The role of regeneration in Liverpool has been a story of urban reinvention which has led to a reappraisal of the city and its image elsewhere in the UK and overseas (Jones and Wilks-Heeg, 2004, Biddulph, 2010).

City Council leaders have had a clear role in managing the regeneration monies pouring into the city. They have, historically, had an unenviable reputation (nationally) for lack of vision for the city (Ben-Tovim, 2003). During the Militant years under the leadership of Derek Hatton in particular, Liverpool reflected the conflicts between central and local government over regeneration priorities. The legacy of this period is relatively weak local government control, characterised by urban and civic mismanagement; the City Council has only recently started to cast this aside (Ben-Tovim, 2003; Pemberton and Winstanley, 2010; Cocks, 2009). The election of a minority Labour administration in the early 1990s went some way towards attracting more robust control of municipal functions, and successful regeneration projects started to appear, particularly in the city centre. The election of a majority Liberal Democrat Council in the early 2000s led to greater emphasis on firm municipal management, clear policy direction, and executive control of planning and regeneration in the city.

The positive spin on the city, generated by these developments is, however, tinged with the fear of failure. This is mainly due to the events surrounding the Fourth Grace project, and other failed projects such as National Discovery Park and Kings Dock, all of which have been controversial due to their potential impact on the waterfront panorama. The Fourth Grace, dubbed "The Cloud" by Will Alsop, was chosen in 2002 in preference to the publicly backed Norman Foster design. Liverpool Vision, the city's regeneration agency, came in for a large degree of criticism as a result. The City Council justified its decision on the basis that the Foster building contained too much office space for the city and that it would sit rather uneasily next to the adjacent buildings on the waterfront, in terms of scale and style (Davis, 2002). Readers of the two main Liverpool papers (Liverpool Echo and Liverpool Daily News) wrote in large numbers to protest this decision. Some two years later, the Alsop proposal was abandoned due to spiralling costs and disquiet over the increasing amount of office and residential development required to pay for the building (and the consequent impacts on the waterfront) (Fray, 2004). The willingness of the City Council to accept a radical design was therefore "tempered by the increase in height of the surrounding office buildings required to pay for it and the consequent damage to the waterfront composition"[4]. Repercussions from the scheme continue to be publicised by the local and national media, and the negative fallout continues, fuelling concern that LCC and Liverpool Vision are unable to deliver large, high profile projects effectively.

Since 1990, a total of eighteen tall building proposals have come forward into the public domain in Merseyside, with all but one in Liverpool itself (Short, 2008). It is also clear that there are a substantial number of proposals which are not yet formally part of the planning process, but are being dealt with by LCC in pre-application discussions. Significant numbers of buildings are therefore coming forward in Liverpool, the majority of which appear to be proposed outside the boundaries of the main conservation designations, although they are within the World Heritage Site buffer zone. Explanations for this phenomenon in Liverpool vary, although there is some agreement that it is down to increasing confidence in the future of the city. This confidence is the result of a number of factors: the attraction of money from Objective 1 status; tangible physical regeneration taking place, including the £1 billion shopping redevelopment at Liverpool One; a strengthening housing market; and, ECOC08 status[5].

In the context of the Lime Street Gateway planning application, a number of groups were involved in the planning process: LCC, English Partnerships, Liverpool Vision, CABE, English Heritage, Merseyside Civic Society, Liverpool Echo, Liverpool Daily Post, Downtown Liverpool, UNESCO and ICOMOS. Table 5.2

TABLE 5.2 Key actors involved in tall building proposals in Liverpool

Name	Tier	Focus
Liverpool City Council	Local	Planning undertaken within Regeneration portfolio administered by Executive Director under leadership of Chief *Liverpool Urban Design and Conservation Advisory Panel* (LUDCAP) made up of representatives from key agencies in city and provides specialist advice and local knowledge to City Council. Generally pro-development but concerned about heritage impacts.
Liverpool Vision	Local	Independent company established to bring together key public and private sector agencies to produce a strategic regeneration framework to guide the regeneration of Liverpool city centre. Responsible for coordinating regeneration of Lime Street Station and the improvement of public realm in front of station. Pro-development.
CABE	National–Regional	Reviewed a number of tall buildings to date; Rumford Place, Brunswick Quay and Lime Street Gateway.
English Heritage	National–Regional	Funds placement of one of its officers in LCC to assist in coordination of regeneration and planning policy as it relates to historic environment.
UNESCO	International	Seeks to encourage "identification, protection and preservation of cultural . . . heritage around the world considered to be of outstanding value to humanity" (UNESCO, 2005). In response to increasing numbers of tall building proposals in or adjacent to World Heritage Sites, it has produced new draft memorandum to address issue (UNESCO, 2005).
ICOMOS	National	Global non-governmental organisation works for conservation and protection of cultural heritage places. Advises UNESCO on World Heritage Site matters particularly on World Heritage Sites in distress. Particularly concerned at number of proposals for tall buildings adjacent to or near to World Heritage Site.
Media	Local	*Liverpool Echo* and *Liverpool Daily News* become direct forum to debate issues about the future of the city. Have been heated debates regarding the World Heritage Site bid and implications for development in city. Pro-development but sceptical of LCC's ability to deliver.
Downtown Liverpool	Local	Independent organisation dedicated to development of vibrant modern Liverpool and to restore the downtown area to its full glory through economic development.

summarises the role of these organisations. In particular, the City Council takes a practical approach to development in the city that balances regeneration needs with concern about Liverpool's built heritage.

Concern, voiced by English Heritage, about the impacts of this approach on Liverpool's built heritage, have led to an officer being placed in the City Council to assist in coordinating regeneration and planning policy as it relates to the historic environment. ICOMOS UK are heavily involved in the impacts of development projects on the World Heritage Site and, as such, comment on all large planning applications which may be relevant. The input of this international organisation appears to be heavily resented in the city, as an unwanted intrusion[6]. The local media in Liverpool is highly critical of the regeneration approach adopted by the City Council, mainly as a result of the number of failed, or failing, regeneration projects and a consequent lack of faith in the planning and decision-making processes[7]. Furthermore, organisations such as Downtown Liverpool take the view that the City Council is pandering to the built heritage lobby and should be more forthright in making decisions about development proposals that benefit the people of the city.

Table 5.3 outlines the regulatory framework for tall buildings in the city at the time of the Lime Street Gateway tower application. In summary, the framework provided an emerging context for assessment of tall building proposals through a portfolio of documents which reflect the importance of the city's character. In particular, the city's development plan, urban design guide, draft supplementary planning document on tall buildings and the World Heritage Site management plan all relate directly to the assessment of proposals. The World Heritage Site management plan was clear, in requiring a robust tall building strategy to be written, yet the draft strategy was partly written to support the designation of towers in the vicinity of Lime Street station[8].

Lime Street Gateway Tower proposal

On 28 April 2005, a planning application for a tower and associated Listed Building Consent and Conservation Area Consent applications were submitted to LCC for determination. The signature tower at the centre of the proposals was 27 storeys and 86 metres high, in an elliptical shape (see Figure 5.3) comprising a mixture of uses, including retail, office and residential uses. Table 5.4 outlines the detail of these applications. The City Council assessed the three applications as one, and they share a committee report examining the pertinent issues. The applications were submitted by English Partnerships and Liverpool Vision, and were accepted as valid on 3 May 2005 with a target committee date of 3 August 2005.

The site is located to the south of Lime Street Station in Liverpool city centre, bounded by the station (dating from 1850 and Grade II listed) to the east, the Grade II listed Lime Street Chambers (from 1871) to the north, Lime Street to the west, and Skelhorne Street to the south. New student housing of eleven storeys has been erected to the south of the site on Skelhorne Street, forming an imposing block of

TABLE 5.3 Regulatory framework for tall buildings in Liverpool

Planning policy	Level	Tall buildings mentioned?	Key planning principles in relation to tall buildings	Other comments
CABE–English Heritage Guidance 2003	National	Yes	Encourages LPAs to develop plan policies to deal with tall buildings. Directs tall buildings to specific locations through strategic policies. Engages with communities in development of policies. Discourages piecemeal/ad-hoc decision-making.	Material planning consideration. Re-issued in 2007 after determination of this application.
Regional Spatial Strategy 2003	Regional	No	Defines Liverpool as a focus for development and investment. Key gateways in the city require enhancement as befits their role as international gateways (ODPM, 2003).	Suggested policy which recognises importance of strategic views along River Mersey. 28 strategic views suggested, though not all of them were acknowledged as being of regional significance.
Liverpool Unitary Development Plan 2002	Local	No	None in relation to tall buildings	In the process of being replaced by new LDF
Liverpool Urban Design Guide 2003	Local	Yes	Tall buildings can create new landmarks and frame vistas if sited correctly.	Supplementary planning document.
Draft Supplementary Document (SPD) on Tall Buildings 2004	Local	Yes	Indicates three proposed clusters of tall buildings at Kings Dock, the commercial quarter and Lime Street Station. Reiterates the guidance set out in the joint CABE–EH document (LCC, 2004).	Prepared by LCC, EH and Liverpool Vision. Approved for consultation in December 2004. ICOMOS suggested the policy did not accord with the World Heritage Site Management Plan.
World Heritage Site Management Plan 2003	International– local	Yes	Refers for the need of the City Council to prepare a tall buildings policy as soon as possible using CABE–English Heritage guidance as a base.	

FIGURE 5.3
The proposed
Lime Street
Gateway Tower

TABLE 5.4 Planning and related applications submitted for the Lime Street Gateway site in April 2005

Application	Detail
05L/1413	Planning application to create a public space and to construct 27-storey mixed use building including retail and office units and 152 residential units following the demolition of Concourse House and adjoining retail units. Works to include closure of subway link between Lime Street and St Johns Centre and modification of subway connection to Merseyrail off Gloucester Street entrance to Lime Street Station and associated alterations to access.
05L/1416	Listed Building Consent application to carry out minor alterations to the front façade of Lime Street Station and the southern façade of Lime Street Chambers associated with the removal of Concourse Shops and the Gloucester Street steps in connection with the redevelopment of Concourse House and the adjoining retail units to provide a new public space and a 27-storey mixed use building.
05C/1426	Conservation Area Consent to demolish Concourse Shops and Gloucester Steps in association with the creation of an area of public open space in front of Lime Street Station as part of the Lime Street Gateway Scheme, including redevelopment of adjoining Concourse House.

low quality buildings to the side of the station and rear of the site. It is opposite the Grade I listed St. George's Hall (from 1855) to the west, and the Grade II listed Crown Hotel (1905) to the south, and it is partially within the William Brown Street Conservation Area and the World Heritage Site, and partly within the World Heritage Site Buffer Zone. Since the 1960s, the site had been occupied by two buildings: the Richard Seiffert-designed modernist Concourse House (from 1968), and a row of small retail units which form a south facing perimeter with the station, built at the same time (both now demolished). The immediate vicinity of the site suffered from poor pedestrian flow, brought about by the lack of legibility in the current public realm (Sharples, 2004). There have been many attempts at removal of this tower on the site to open up views of the station; the tower proposal, as part of its justification, seeks to remedy this problem.

The applications were the culmination of a year-long process of pre-application discussions involving a number of key agencies, including: LCC, English Partnerships, Liverpool Vision, CABE and EH. In consultation with the City Council, the applicants developed a comprehensive series of decision support documents to support the applications during the pre-application discussion phase; these included a heritage impact assessment, a visual assessment and a planning statement. During these discussions, solutions to the questions raised by potential impacts on the surrounding environment were agreed between the parties, as well as the methods of assessment and presentation. There are no publicly available records of this stage in the planning process[9]. Potential impacts can be summarised as follows:

1   A *Heritage Impact Assessment* was undertaken as part of the Environmental Statement. The report assessed the broad visual impacts of the proposals on Liverpool's historic fabric in four areas: the setting of heritage assets within the visual zone of influence; direct physical impacts on built heritage, which exist within the development site; direct physical impacts on the various themes of historic significance to which the area's historic fabric provides testimony; and impact upon the existing townscape character (DIA, 2005).

2   A *Visual Assessment* element of the Environmental Statement detailed the potential visual impacts of the proposed development on key monuments and views, undertaken with the assistance of the University of Salford. This assessment evolved with the direct input of the City Council, EH and CABE during pre-application discussions[10], and involved a number of clear stages: agreeing view locations; analysing the significance of view locations; assessing the sensitivity of views from different view locations; identifying the sensitive receptors; identification of impacting elements of the proposal; assessing the impacts; and mitigation.

3   A *Planning Statement* described the proposal in detail and analysed the planning policy background to the proposals. In particular, the report outlined the statutory requirements for each of the built heritage designations and then described the planning policy context for each. It then refers the reader to the Heritage Impact Assessment for further detail, to ensure that the proposal is fully

consistent with planning policy, and that there are no planning policy constraints on granting planning permission.

4   A *Character Appraisal and Tall Building Rationale* analysed the townscape in the vicinity of the site, and the capacity for change. Furthermore, it offered detail to the four options for the site outlined in the ES. It referred to the other documents for detail, particularly the Heritage Impact Assessment in relation to built heritage issues.

The City Council, following its strategy of maximum engagement with agencies and the public, consulted widely on the proposals with key organisations, residents' groups, and individuals. The Council attempted to reach everyone who could have a possible interest in the redevelopment of the station[11] (see Table 5.5). The tall building debate was such that a vigorous campaign, both for and against the tower, was waged by a number of organisations and individuals in the pages of the Liverpool Echo and Liverpool Daily Post. Both papers seemed to support the regeneration of the tower in principle, but were unsure (editorially) whether this was the right scheme or whether it could even be delivered. Furthermore, widespread concern was expressed through the letters pages, to the effect that not only did the City Council not seem to know what the cumulative impact of all the tower proposals coming forward were, but that the impact on the newly designated World Heritage Site was either unknown or was being marginalised.

A number of objections, as well as letters of support, were received by the City Council in response to the consultation. The organisations which had been closely involved with the proposals from the pre-application stage supported the application. The views can be summarised by the following quote from EH:

> "*EH recognises that the proposals are an important element in the strategic planning of Liverpool . . . and also appreciates that the potential regeneration benefits the city as a whole. As such, the principle of development . . . is welcomed and supported . . . [although] . . . in relation to the historic built environment . . . the site is very sensitive.*"
>
> *(EH, 2005: 1).*

Objections to the proposals recognised the stance of EH, but had greater concerns about potential impacts on the built heritage of the city. These objections relating to the built heritage can be summarised as follows: impact of the tower on the William Brown Conservation Area and the wider skyline and waterfront (Victorian Society, Railway Heritage Trust and individual objections); cumulative impact of tower proposals across the city (LUDCAP, Victorian Society and individual objections); and assessment of the proposals against a backdrop of UNESCO actions (ICOMOS, Victorian Society, residents groups, individual and LUDCAP objections). Interestingly, the main objections were made by heritage organisations and were related to heritage issues, even though EH and the City Council supported the application. This was somewhat unexpected, given that local planning regimes

TABLE 5.5 Consultations undertaken for Lime Street Gateway Tower planning application

Internal consultations	Consulted	Outcome
Conservation/Historic Environment	■	□
Environmental Health	■	□
Housing	■	□
Operational Services	■	□
Traffic and transport	■	□
Members	■	□
Individual residents	■	□ and □
Local residents (groups)	■	□ and □
Local businesses	■	□ and □
Local business individuals	■	□ and □
City centre Manager	▣	
LUDCAP	■	□ and ■
Design Review	■	

External consultations	Consulted	Outcome
Local airport/Civil Aviation Authority	■	◄
Countryside Agency	■	◄
Environment Agency	■	
English Nature	■	□
Passenger Transport (Merseytravel)	■	■
Police	■	□
CABE	▣	□
EH	□	
Georgian Society	▣	□
Victorian Society	□	
20th Century Society	■	
Local civic society	■	□
Ancient Monuments Society	■	
Railway Heritage Trust	■	
Society for the Protection of Ancient Monuments	■	□
Council for British Archaeology	▣	
Adjoining local authorities	■	
Friends of the Earth	■	
British Telecom	■	
Department for Culture, Media and Sport	■	
United Utilities	■	■
Government Office	■	
Chamber of Commerce	■	
British Gas	■	
Members of Parliament	■	
Network Rail	■	□
Fire and Rescue Service	■	◄
Liverpool Vision	■	■
Green Party	■	□

KEY

■	Consulted by local planning authority	
□	Support planning application	
▣	Support planning application with comments	
◄	No comment or response on planning application	
□	Object to planning application	
▣	Not consulted	

would normally rely on consensus to drive the built heritage agenda forward (Hobson, 2004). ICOMOS, for example, was particularly troubled by the approval of "the tower in the absence of a robust and defensible . . . [tall buildings] . . . policy and . . . [would] . . . be discussing these concerns with international . . . [ICOMOS and UNESCO] . . . colleagues"[12].

The role of the local, national and international media in discussions about this site (in particular), and others which are attracting tall buildings applications, is an interesting one. The debates were played out in the columns and letters pages of the local newspapers in a democratic manner which saw much heated debate. It is suggested that a level of sophistication had been achieved by ordinary citizens in discussing the future of their city in the local media[13]. Having been let down by the failure of the Fourth Grace proposal, local people feel that it is imperative that LCC, and other agencies in the city, makes sure that it "listens to the Liverpool public in seeking to approve such contentious proposals"[14].

Assessment of the Lime Street Gateway Tower proposal

The supporting documentation, submitted as part of the planning application, was particularly comprehensive. Moreover, the built heritage issues that related to the proposal, perhaps unsurprisingly given the newly declared World Heritage Site, took a disproportionate amount of time to resolve during the pre-application discussions, compared with the other issues, although the Committee Report does not reflect this. The application was approved on 23 August 2005, in terms of the removal of Concourse House as an obsolete and unsightly building, the delivery of a long-awaited public realm and environmental approval works in front of the Grade II listed station, the upgrading and improvement of access to facilities for rail passengers, to reveal and enhance the colonnaded façade to the station, and delivery of a landmark building with active ground floor uses that will complement and enhance the appearance and function of the new public realm and "will act as a signature building to guide, promote and attract visitors to this historic and architecturally important part of the city centre" (LCC, 2005b: 6.9).

The major concerns of UNESCO and ICOMOS, regarding the approval of inappropriate tall buildings (and other large scale development) in Liverpool, are reflected in the requirement in the World Heritage Site Management Plan that LCC "prepares, develops and implements a Tall Buildings Policy for the city, with special reference to the Site and its Buffer Zone" (UNESCO, 2004). The draft tall buildings guidance was used to assess the tower (even though it was still out to consultation), and the proposed cluster next to Lime Street Station was drawn into the document so that the proposed "tower was more likely to be granted [planning] permission"[15]. From an early stage in the LPA's deliberations over the planning application, ICOMOS suggested that the policy did not accord with the World Heritage Site Management Plan that had recently been approved by UNESCO[16]. Making decisions which would affect the character of the city in general, and the World Heritage Site in particular, without this policy in place was a high-risk strategy, given that

UNESCO and ICOMOS were already highly concerned about damage to World Heritage Sites from tall buildings, in places such as Vienna, Cologne and London (UNESCO, 2005).

The impact of the Lime Street Gateway Tower on the World Heritage Site and its Buffer Zone is an issue one would expect would be dealt with in great detail by the planning authority in the Committee Report. This, however, was not the case (LCC, 2005b). The report does mention the World Heritage Site on several occasions, but there is little or no analysis of the impact on either the Site or the Buffer Zone. The Committee Report merely states that the proposal has been "assessed against the requirement to consider . . . impact on the World Heritage Site" (LCC, 2005b: 1.14) without supporting evidence. The position of LCC looks precarious, given that officers are on record as stating that "had the inclusion of the Buffer Zone meant that schemes like Lime Street Gateway would not be able to go ahead, then LCC should never have supported the designation"[17]. Objections to the proposal on these grounds were not only expressed by heritage organisations. Several local people were equally concerned about the potential to damage the newly declared World Heritage Site.

The need to develop the tall buildings policy, the pressures of local and heritage organisation opinion about tall buildings, and the management issues associated with the new World Heritage Site designation, combined with increasing numbers of tall buildings coming forward, are issues which LCC is grappling with[18]. In tandem with Liverpool Vision, LCC held a closed event in July 2005, in order to determine how to take the draft policy forward, given the large number of consultation responses received; these varied from opinions that the policy was far too restrictive, to contributors who felt it was not restrictive enough (LCC, 2005a). It was universally thought that the draft policy was weak and lacked "a clear basis in sound planning principles that attracts support from stakeholders"[19].

More recently, the City Council has sought to allay fears about determining tall building proposals within a policy vacuum, through the adoption of the *World Heritage Site Supplementary Planning Document* in 2009, a policy document intended to provide a planning framework for development which will "enhance the city's heritage and boost investment, tourism and regeneration . . . [and] which will encourage economic regeneration with an emphasis on quality" (LCC, 2009). The result of extensive consultation over the past few years, the document seeks to deter the development of any tall buildings at the World Heritage Site itself. In terms of the buffer zone, the document seeks to encourage tall buildings as beacons of regeneration in specific parts of that zone. The document encourages the emerging cluster of tall buildings to the north of the World Heritage Site (to be enhanced through appropriate further development) and two other clusters away from the centre of the site (see Figure 5.4). This new policy framework marks a new direction for the City Council in outlining a realistic expression of spatial vision for tall buildings which attracts consensus from business, the public and the mainly heritage-based lobby organisations at local, national and international levels.

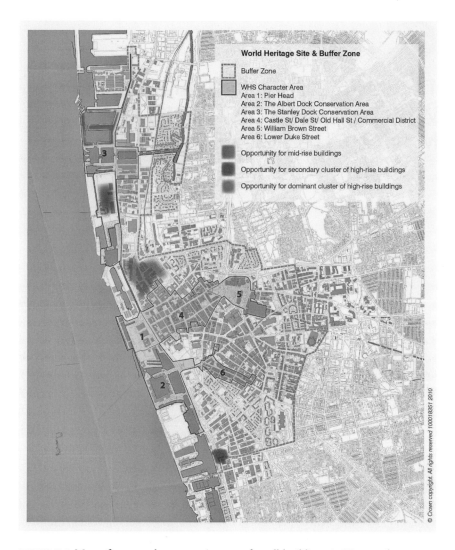

Legend within map:

World Heritage Site & Buffer Zone

☐ Buffer Zone

▨ WHS Character Area
Area 1: Pier Head
Area 2: The Albert Dock Conservation Area
Area 3: The Stanley Dock Conservation Area
Area 4: Castle St/ Dale St/ Old Hall St / Commercial District
Area 5: William Brown Street
Area 6: Lower Duke Street

■ Opportunity for mid-rise buildings

■ Opportunity for secondary cluster of high-rise buildings

■ Opportunity for dominant cluster of high-rise buildings

FIGURE 5.4 Map of proposed opportunity areas for tall buildings in Liverpool

The following chapter will examine the determination of tall building proposals in Manchester and will reflect on a number of the issues raised in the Liverpool case. What is the significance of World Heritage Site designation in decision-making for tall buildings? How are visualisations and other decision-making support mechanisms used in the planning application process? How is the need to physically regenerate reflected in decision-making about tall buildings? And finally, what is the role of local planning regimes in assessing tall buildings?

6

TALL BUILDINGS IN MANCHESTER: WHILE LIVERPOOL THINKS, MANCHESTER CONSTRUCTS[1]

In 2003, planning permission was granted for the Beetham Hilton Tower. At 47 storeys and a height of 171 metres, the building, which was completed in 2007, was the tallest residential building in the UK and one of the tallest in Europe (see Figure 6.1). It already dominates the city's skyline from a number of viewpoints and impacts significantly on its immediate surroundings. With increasing development pressure on the tightly bounded city centre, the Beetham Tower has been followed by a number of further proposals for tall buildings in the city centre, encouraged by the generally pro-development and entrepreneurial planning agendas in the City Councils of both Manchester and Salford (Ward, 2003).

Decisions about these tall buildings are being taken in the absence of a dedicated tall buildings policy, although there is design guidance for the city centre. Moreover, there have been concerns about the impact of tall buildings on the city's built heritage, both in terms of immediate impacts on adjoining Listed Buildings, Conservation Areas and scheduled ancient monuments, and more long-term impacts on the character of the city. These concerns were amplified as a result of the proposed bid for World Heritage Site status, the basis of which is the city's nineteenth century industrial heritage along the Bridgewater and Rochdale canals. This chapter places the Beetham Hilton Tower in the context of planning and design control in entrepreneurial Manchester, and investigates how the wider governance context has influenced decisions about the development of tall buildings in the city.

Context for development in Manchester

The Manchester city region is a polycentric urban system situated in England's north-west, and centred around the City of Manchester. The metropolitan region has a population of 2.56 million people and comprises ten local authorities, including the City of Manchester, with a population of 464,200 (ONS, 2008). The city has tightly

FIGURE 6.1 The Beetham Tower, Manchester

drawn boundaries that lie deep within the urban area (Hebbert, 2010). Indeed, part of the City of Salford is, for all intents and purposes, part of Manchester's city centre; this results in many planning decisions made within Salford impacting directly on Manchester, and vice versa.

Manchester lays claim to being the world's original modern city (Hall, 1998; Hartwell, 2002 amongst others), and it has a rich architectural and industrial history.

Manchester grew during the late eighteenth and nineteenth centuries to become the powerhouse of Britain's industrial revolution, as a result of the synergy of a number of key factors relating to the role of specific innovators in industrial production, an evolving system of economic organisation, and a dynamic social structure (Hall, 1998). In the second half of the twentieth century, however, Manchester also became one of the first cities to experience widespread de-industrialisation, characterised by a massive decline in manufacturing and employment (Peck and Ward, 2002). The associated population decline and physical dereliction, in both the central city and outlying suburbs, left Manchester in a parlous economic state in the 1970s. The city did, however, continue to exert influence in the cultural sphere, most notably with its sporting and music scenes.

The change of political culture in Manchester City Council (MCC) from the mid-1980s – from a model of municipal committee-based decision-making into a "working in partnership" with business and communities model – led a period of sustained physical and cultural regeneration. Since this time, the City Council has progressed an unashamedly pro-development agenda which is demonstrated in a number of ways.

Firstly, major development in the city is discussed and managed by a "coterie" of decision-makers, in advance of the formal planning application process (Peck and Ward, 2002). Encouraged by central government guidance, pre-application discussions on development proposals reflect a corporate approach to working. As such, where proposals fit into the City Council's strategies (adopted or otherwise) these are managed during the pre-application discussions, in order for the issues to be agreed "in advance of the formal planning process, and any potential problems ironed out"[2].

Secondly, the City Council firmly invests in an outcomes-based decision-making model for planning. Successful planning is consequently determined by the prestige afforded by physical development. This is particularly true of key sites in the city centre, which have an economic, social and cultural importance to the wider city and region; the development of Piccadilly, the Northern Quarter, Millennium Quarter, and Southern Gateway are paraded by the Council as tangible examples that the city is regenerating and that it is a vibrant, European and international city.

Thirdly, the city has been able to implement practical solutions to the damage caused by an IRA bomb in the central area in 1996. The widespread devastation caused by the bomb, the rallying of the development community and the quick decisions made about proposed redevelopment have all been well documented (see Williams, 2002 for example). It has been said that the particular circumstances of the rebuilding after the bomb gave a boost to the coterie-based approach to approving proposals[3]. Furthermore, the evolution of Manchester city centre as a centre of consumption and of residential use has been particularly noticeable since the early 1990s. Large parts of the regeneration of the city centre are due to residential conversion and new building projects, and they have significantly altered the form of this area. Finally, the City Council sees particular development projects, particularly tall buildings, as prestigious and dynamic, reflecting the wish of the city to project itself onto an international stage.

The entrepreneurial strategy of the City Council has delivered tangible physical regeneration, particularly in the city centre (Peck and Ward, 2002; Quilley, 2000). The city has transformed itself, visually at least. Until the recession, from late 2007 onwards, developer confidence in Manchester (as represented by the attraction of key companies such as Bank of America to the city, the redevelopment of large swathes of the city centre such as Spinningfields and the Northern Quarter, and specific tall building proposals) seemed to vindicate the approach of the City Council to a significant degree; physical development continued to be attracted to the city, transforming great swathes of the central area.

Manchester retains much of its former character as a typical British Victorian city. The individuality of the city is striking, particularly because of its strong, muscular, industrial character (Briggs in Marshall, 1994). Architecturally, the Victorian style is dominated by an interpreted Italian Palazzo vernacular style, represented in many of the city's buildings – most notably in its warehouses and commercial buildings (Marshall, 1994; Hartwell, 2002). The city centre has an almost regular grid street layout that fans out from the former Central Station, built in 1876 (now the G-Mex conference centre). The centre is permeated by clear landmark buildings, many of them from recent times, interspersed with buildings which exhibit a uniformity of mass and height (in the main). The centre exhibits a cohesive quality which belies the range of styles and types of building and space.

The city is built in a bowl at the foot of the Pennines to the east, and is characterised as mainly flat, with little difference in the height and form of the land. It is, however, framed by the Pennines which provide a dramatic backdrop for the city (Hartwell, 2002). Key buildings punctuate the skyline of the city, resulting in dispersed intervals and forming crucial points from which the form of the city can be read; as there is little topographic differentiation, the height and massing of these buildings create the skyline of the city. The varying quality of these buildings contributes to a sense that there is little character in Manchester's skyline, particularly as these are dispersed across the central area of the city. Whilst Waterhouse's Town Hall dominates the skyline in Victorian magnificence and opulence, a range of post-war tall buildings drown it out in a mass of disparate towers. Compared to Liverpool, Manchester has much less protected built heritage, yet it remains rich in terms of its industrial legacy – approximately 800 Listed Buildings, 33 Conservation Areas and six scheduled ancient monuments (including the remains of the Roman Fort in Castlefield).

A bid for the World Heritage Site status was drafted in 2005, although the World Heritage Site officer left his post during this period and the draft bid was quietly dropped by the City Council. The area presented for the initial bid in Manchester included much of the Castlefield Conservation Area and the Rochdale Canal – from Castlefield to Ancoats, including the warehousing on Dale Street and the south-west part of the Ancoats Conservation Area. The tentative inclusion of Manchester on the list of British World Heritage Sites reflected three themes: Britain's first industrial canal; its first mainline inter-city passenger railway; and the country's first industrial suburb based on steam power (MCC, 2005). These are linked by both the Rochdale and Bridgewater Canals.

Unlike Liverpool, the tentative World Heritage Site designation did not have the wholehearted support of all parts of the City Council, or of other heritage, planning and regeneration bodies. Table 6.1 summarises the bodies who lent their support to the bid at this stage; even though the list of bodies is much smaller than in Liverpool, the World Heritage Site officer indicated that this was partly due to the lack of time in preparing the bid for the tentative stage, and partly due to the need to integrate and co-opt more organisations at the next stage of nomination[4].

Like many other British cities, tall buildings in Manchester were predominantly the products of the post-war building boom. Since 1990, however, a total of 54 buildings of over fifteen storeys in height have been proposed: 30 in Manchester; 22 in adjacent Salford; and two in Trafford (Short, 2008). This is the largest concentration of tall building proposals outside of London. The characteristics of tall buildings in the conurbation vary. In Manchester, there is evidence of a mixture of uses being proposed (although the majority are residential), as well as the delivery of buildings through the planning process. In Salford, however, there is evidence that the tall buildings are predominantly residential (Short, 2008).

Two clear areas of tall buildings are evident (those built and those under construction) in Salford Quays and in the area within the Inner Relief Route in central Manchester and Salford. As there is no identifiable tall building cluster in the cities at present, beyond a disparate grouping of towers within the Inner Relief Route, the large numbers of tall buildings coming forward could be said to offer an opportunity to create an identifiable skyline which has recognisable features. The regulatory framework is such, however, that this is unlikely. This framework forms the basis against which the proposals were assessed and a recommendation by the planning officer to the Planning Committee was made. This is summarised in Table 6.2 and can be characterised by a need for Manchester to continue the physical regeneration for which it has become famous, whilst seeking to address economic and social issues. Furthermore, the lack of any specific reference to tall buildings is particularly noticeable.

With reference to the Beetham Hilton Tower, a number of actors interacted within the informal and formal planning processes: MCC, CABE, EH and the Beetham Organization. Table 6.3 summarises the role of these organisations in

TABLE 6.1 Organisations supporting the bid for World Heritage Site status in Manchester–Salford

Manchester City Council (part)
Salford City Council
EH
North West Development Agency
University of Manchester
Government Office for the NW
DCMS

TABLE 6.2 Regulatory framework for tall buildings in Manchester

Planning policy	Level	Tall buildings mentioned?	Key planning principles in relation to tall buildings	Other comments
CABE–EH Guidance 2003	National	Yes	Encourages LPAs to develop plan policies to deal with tall buildings. Directs tall buildings to specific locations through strategic policies. Engages with communities in development of policies. Discourages piecemeal/ad-hoc decision-making.	Material planning consideration.
Manchester Plan 1995	Local	No	To continue the physical, economic and social regeneration. To reinforce the city's role as a dynamic European city.	Statutory land use plan to be reviewed 2005–2006.
Guide to Development 1997	Local	No	None	Provides detailed design guidance for all development. Supplementary Planning Guidance.
Draft Guide to Development in Manchester 2004	Local	Yes	Proposals considered on their own merits. Reference to detailed issues of design. Proposals presented in context of CABE–EH guidance.	Awaiting acceptance by Council Executive at time of case study research.

TABLE 6.3 Key actors involved in tall building proposals in Manchester

Name	Tier	Focus
Manchester City Council	Local	Planning sits within Chief Executive's dept. and is characterised by corporate vision of executive control. Integration of urban design and conservation skills (headed by an architect–urban designer) within a dedicated team within the planning function means that the decision-making at executive level filters directly into the conservation–urban design decision-making process. Entrepreneurial approach to encouragement of development is led by Council reflecting relationships with other actors in city.
CABE	National	Four tall building proposals have been reviewed in Manchester to date.
EH	Regional office of national body	West Midlands office based in Birmingham. Advise local authorities in relation to Listed Building Consent applications (for Grade I and II★ buildings), Conservation Area Consent applications and planning applications which affect historic buildings and Conservation Areas situated in England.
Beetham Organization	National	Liverpool-based property construction company; proposed tall buildings in Birmingham, Brighton, London, Liverpool and Manchester. Seeks to combine landmark residential buildings with premium hotels creating mixed use schemes.
Manchester Civic Society	Local	Registered charity that has been "keeping a watch over the city" and "fostering a sense of pride in Manchester"★. Funded by members' subscriptions and donations from private and corporate sponsors. Has been sidelined in many of the decisions about new tall buildings particularly because it is seen as contradicting the views of the Council. Has little power although has a number of powerful supporters in the development and heritage communities.

★ Manchester Civic Society (2005b) *Manchester Civic Society: Its Purpose and Vision.* Manchester: MCS.

the planning application process, as well as the Manchester Civic Society who, even though not directly involved in the assessment of proposals, were concerned about the potential impacts of the tower on the built heritage of the city. Manchester's local planning regime can be characterised by "a 'can-do' approach to development and regeneration, often relegating built heritage concerns to wider concerns about attracting growth and jobs"[5]. English Heritage is the main heritage organisation involved in decision-making, and it has been criticised (in the past) for the leniency with which it treated development proposals (particularly after the bomb in 1996) that required a practical approach to rebuilding and regeneration[6].

The Beetham Tower in Manchester was one of the first tall buildings to successfully navigate the planning process outside London and progress to construction.

The following section will outline the way in which the Beetham Tower application was determined, including an analysis of assessment methods utilised during the process.

Beetham Hilton Tower proposal

The successful planning application for the Beetham Hilton Tower was the culmination of a process which included extensive pre-application discussions which involved the developer, the developer's agents, officers of the City Council, English Heritage and CABE. The application was submitted to MCC on 16 July 2003, and was for an hotel incorporating associated retailing, restaurants, bars and cafes, conferencing, and other associated facilities – including a health and fitness centre with 219 residential units (see Figures 6.2 to 6.6). The application was accompanied by a Listed Building Consent application for the demolition of the remaining part of a carriage ramp (leading up from the former Deansgate Goods Station to the Great Northern Railway Company's goods warehouse). It was agreed by the City Council that, for assessment and determination purposes, the applications should be treated as one and the same.

The site for the Beetham Tower lies at the southern corner of Deansgate and Great Bridgewater Street, in the Southern Gateway to the city centre (see Figure 6.4). The site is occupied by a remnant of the former viaduct which served the Grade II★ listed Great Northern Warehouse (from 1898) to the north. The site has unimplemented consent for the erection of an eight-storey hotel, which would include demolition of the viaduct structure. Whilst always having a central role in

FIGURE 6.2 Visualisation of the Beetham Tower from St John's Square

FIGURE 6.4 Location of the Beetham Tower in Manchester

FIGURE 6.5 The Beetham Tower from St John's Square

FIGURE 6.6 The Beetham Tower from Castle Quay

the life of Manchester, Deansgate has become the focus for much of the redevelopment of the city centre. The Beetham Tower site, at the southern end of Deansgate, provides the missing link in the recreation of the thoroughfare as the life source of the city[7]. Pre-application discussions were held in two distinct phases. The first phase involved the developer, planning consultants, and the Chief Executive and senior officers of the City Council. The second phase involved the consultants, planning officers representing the City Centre Team of the City Council, English Heritage and CABE. Thus, City Council representatives accompanied the consultants in all their presentations and dealings with both English Heritage and CABE. These discussions took place from early 2002 onwards, approximately eighteen months prior to the submission of the joint applications in July 2003, and were not publicly documented. Amongst other issues, the visual impacts of the building on the historic environment and on key agreed views were critical to the pre-application discussions.

During the pre-application discussions, the parties made a number of clear decisions about how the various issues should or should not be dealt with in the planning application[8]. This agreement was important in that it "mapped a series of issues which needed to be addressed for the planning application to be approved"[9]. It was agreed that the main issues related to the impact of the proposal on key Listed Buildings, specifically the Great Northern Warehouse (Grade II*) and G-Mex (Grade II*). Furthermore, the impact of the proposal on the adjacent Castlefield Conservation Area was deemed to be crucial, along with views from other city centre Conservation Areas. Finally, the impact on the proposed World Heritage Site was discussed at this stage, but "no particular agreement was negotiated regarding how this issue would be dealt with in the documentation accompanying the planning application"[10]. Whilst the built heritage issues were acknowledged as one element in a long list of issues in the determination of the applications, it was acknowledged that the way in which these were dealt with was crucial to the success of the applications[11].

The planning application constituted a comprehensive series of documents, presenting the proposal in the terms agreed during the pre-application discussions. Amongst other elements, the planning application comprised a PPG (Planning Policy Guidance) 15 Justification Statement, a PPG16 Archaeological Assessment, an Environmental Statement (including Visual Assessment), an Urban Design and Tall Building Statement, and a card model of the proposed tower. In summary, from the beginning of the formal planning process, significant elements in the built heritage were either ignored or only referred to in passing, all with the full knowledge and participation of the organisations and individuals represented during the pre-application discussions.

The status of the built heritage issues dominated the narrative about the impacts of the tower. Table 6.4 summarises the methods used in the submitted documentation for assessing the impact of the tower on the built heritage. The table shows that, whilst the planning application documents provide a number of useful methods to assess the impact of the tower, this is in no way comprehensive. The lack of strategic overview for the proposals – including an understanding of the attributes

TABLE 6.4 Summary of decision support mechanisms used in assessing the Beetham Hilton Tower application

Assessment or study	Submitted	Comments
Characterisation study	☐	Character of Manchester not assessed in separate study or within other.
Urban Design statement	◪	Assesses proposals against elements of CABE–EH guidance; evaluates proposal within immediate area context.
PPG15 statement	■	Full justification for proposed development in accordance with PPG15.
Tall building statement	■	Combined with urban design statement.
Traffic study	■	Addresses issue of vehicular movement/transport options.
Housing market study	■	Study of current housing supply in centre and how tower would impact.
Shadow study	■	Analyses shadow during daylight hours.
Cumulative impact study	☐	No cumulative impacts of this proposal with others provided.
EIA	■	Provides information on range of topics which require detailed investigation.
Photo montage (digital renderings)	■	Provided as part of the Environment Statement – up to 200 images provided.
Night time study	▲	Required after objection – looks at visual impact of tower at night.
GIS model of building/area	☐	None currently exists and was not deemed necessary for assessment purposes.
Card model of building	◪	Requested by Council prior to application being validated.
Card model of area	☐	None currently exists and was not deemed necessary for assessment purposes.
CAD model of building	☐	None currently exists and was not deemed necessary for assessment purposes.
CAD model of area	☐	None currently exists and was not deemed necessary for assessment purposes.
Archaeological assessment	▲	Lies within area of archaeological significance – watching brief required.
Options/Alternatives	■	Covered in Environmental Statement – alternatives for the site were discussed rather than alternatives to the site.
Bat study	▲	Required by consultee – no adverse conclusions drawn.
Acoustic study	◪	Requested by Council prior to application being validated.

KEY
- ■ Submitted as part of planning application
- ◪ Requested by planning authority
- ▲ Required as a result of consultation response/objection
- ☐ Not submitted/requested

or character of the city, the form of the city's skyline and impact upon it and analysis of the cumulative impacts of this proposal with other proposals for tall buildings – is particularly noticeable.

Two objections to the proposal were received, as opposed to near comprehensive support from all the other consultees. Table 6.5 outlines the consultations that were undertaken. Planning consultants were employed by an anonymous objector, to help inform the assessment of the proposals. The Council for British Archaeology indicated that a tower in such a crucial site would be wholly inappropriate in terms of the built heritage of the city. The submission of formal objections to the planning application proved to be an irritant to the City Council, as it was believed that all the issues which could have been addressed had been covered in the preliminary stages of discussion and the subsequent documentation produced. Interestingly, neighbouring Salford was not consulted on the proposal, even though they share a common city centre, and decisions which are made in one place can often affect the other.

The lack of consultation with resident groups in the city centre (in particular, the lack of consultation with Manchester Civic Society) adds a further dimension. Whilst publicity letters were sent to a number of individual residences in the city centre, there was certainly a feeling that the democratic decision-making process was treated lightly by the City Council, as the decision "had been made at the pre-application stage"[12]. For all the talk of democratisation in planning decision-making in Manchester City Council (Kitchen, 1997), the suspicion that the decision over the tower had been "sewn-up" by the key players in the informal pre-application discussions was widespread. The Civic Society is positive about the proposal, yet it is concerned that other proposals will be subject to an "assessment process that is as dismissive of built heritage impacts as the Beetham Tower"[13].

Assessment of the Beetham Hilton Tower proposal

The planning officer's report summarised the key issues in the determination of the applications, and made a recommendation to the Members of the Committee about whether they should be approved or not. The planning officer's report recommended that the applications should be approved, after a lengthy summary of the main issues and how these have been addressed. The planning application and accompanying Listed Building Consent application were approved, and the tower was completed in 2007. Upon reflection on the informal and formal planning process, it is therefore apparent that there are two main areas of concern: firstly, the way in which the impact of the proposals on the built heritage was assessed during the informal and formal decision-making processes; and secondly, the lack of post-decision mechanisms for assessing predicted impacts upon that built heritage.

The consultation strategy adopted by the City Council is interesting, in that it specifically excluded one of the main lobby groups in the city interested in planning issues. The ability of Manchester Civic Society to promote the conservation of the built heritage and the creation of buildings and spaces of quality in the future had

TABLE 6.5 Consultations undertaken for planning and Listed Building Consent applications for the Beetham Hilton Tower

Internal consultations	Consulted	Outcome	External consultations	Consulted	Outcome
Design and Conservation	■	□	Local airport	■	□
Environmental Health	■		Countryside Commission	■	▲
Housing	■	□	Environment Agency	■	□
Operational Services	■	□	English Nature	■	□
Traffic and transport	■	□	Passenger Transport	■	□
Members	■	□	Police	■	□
Individual residents	■	▲	CABE	■	□
Local residents (groups)	▣		EH	■	□
Local businesses	▣		Georgian Society	■	▲
Local business individuals	▣	□	Victorian Society	■	▲
			20th Century Society	▣	
			Local civic society	▣	
			Council for British Archaeology	■	□
			Adjoining local authorities	▣	

KEY

- ■ Consulted by local planning authority
- □ Support planning application with comments
- ▲ No comment or response on planning application
- □ Object to planning application
- ▣ Not consulted

been established during the late 1990s, when it assisted in the rebuilding efforts after the bomb. Particularly after "much of the dust had settled after the bombing and decisions made about the many . . . [development] . . . proposals required for rebuilding, the Trust started to question the basis for much of that rebuilding, particularly we felt . . . [that] . . . the built heritage had started to suffer"[14]. This would echo the concerns expressed about the role of English Heritage at that time, in its support for the rebuilding of the city and the leniency that it showed in assessing proposals. Since that time, there has been a palpable sense that the Society was being sidelined precisely because it "questioned the form of decision-making in the planning department and the types of development gaining consent"[15]. The Society is particularly concerned that debates about tall buildings in the city are being stifled by the City Council. The Society had not been invited to the review of the *Guide to Development in Manchester*, for example. As a result of its omission from the planning process, the Society is encouraging debate in the city by holding a number of events and by publishing articles in its journal, *Manchester Forum*, on the subject of tall buildings in Manchester. This journal is produced quarterly, is sent to all members and donators, and is provided free in libraries and public places.

The impact of the proposal on the proposed World Heritage Site is referred to in several of the documents, yet it is not analysed in any detail. The boundary (as it was agreed at that time) was not shown on any of the visualisations, nor was there any description of the aims and objectives of the designation and how new development (both within and adjacent to it) should be determined. This perhaps reflected that the City Council, whilst attaching some importance to the designation of a World Heritage Site in the city, did not see the designation as crucial to the future development of Manchester.

The likelihood of any World Heritage Site bid being successful is likely to be partly dependent upon the attitudes of the Council to proposals for tall buildings. Recognising that one of the main reasons for the designation would be to protect the importance of Manchester's commercial development during the Industrial Revolution (expressed through innovative and daring architecture at that time), the City Council sees the development of tall buildings as an extension of this innovation in the twenty-first century[16]. UNESCO, however, attaches great importance to the establishment of appropriate buffer zones around the World Heritage Site, which would restrict inappropriate tall building within this area. As has previously been explained, mounting concern within UNESCO and ICOMOS in reaction to the development of tall buildings in (or near) sites in places such as Cologne, Copenhagen and Vienna indicates that this issue is central to the way in which the Manchester bid for such status evolves. Combined with particular concern in response to tall building proposals in London and Liverpool, ICOMOS will "watch the development of the bid and events on the ground . . . [in Manchester] . . . with particular interest"[17].

The potential impact of the Beetham Hilton Tower on the SAM in Castlefield is not referred to at all, in either the planning application documentation or the Report to the Planning Committee. This omission appears anachronistic, given that the City Council claims that the character of the surrounding Castlefield Conservation Area is "unique in the world" (MCC, 2004b). Such an omission from the assessment process suggests that the impacts of the proposed tower on elements of the built heritage were not the main focus for decision-makers. It would seem that the over-riding concern related to the approval of the application and the commencement of development on the site.

In the report taken to the Planning Committee, a review of the relevant supporting documentation in relation to the built heritage issues was also a major element in the assessment of the proposals. This did not, however, critically assess the value of the documents and the information contained therein, which were accepted as providing the relevant information in an agreed format. As such, there is no contextual presentation of the information, which may suggest to the decision-makers that the visualisations or impacts of built heritage may not be entirely accurately presented or independently assessed. As a result, therefore, the information provided presents a coherent story of the benefits of the proposal, which was not questioned during the assessment process, mainly, it is suggested, because the proposal had the full support of the relevant parties.

The City Council insists that applications for tall buildings will be assessed with reference to the effect on the city's skyline (MCC, 2004a). However, there is no evidence of any characterisation of that skyline in the planning documents, either by those involved in pre-application discussions or as part of the assessment process for the tower. There is little agreement about the character of the city's present skyline: key views, for example, are not included within any of the range of available planning policy documents that guide development in the city. Moreover, the context and role of key buildings (such as the Town Hall) which punctuate the skyline, is not defined.

The lack of any clear idea of what value the built heritage of the city represents, any understanding of what the skyline represents and how it should or should not change, and the role of tall buildings within this debate are central to the future planning of the city. The lack of a metropolitan overview on issues related to tall buildings is particularly relevant in the discussion of a tall buildings policy for the city. The lack of consultation between the City Councils of both Manchester and Salford (in relation to this proposal and others, in both cities) is worrying, in that the ad-hoc approach to determination of planning applications will mean that there is no coherent vision for how the wider urban area should develop, and what the impacts of the conurbation could be on the built heritage. How, for instance, would a sixty-storey building on the boundary with Salford impact upon the built heritage of both cities, or indeed on the other Greater Manchester authorities?

Monitoring of the impacts of a proposed development after construction is required by the 1999 Environmental Impacts Assessment Regulations, in line with the mitigatory measures outlined in the Environmental Statement. MCC "undertakes no ex-post assessment activities as a matter of course, mainly as a result of staffing issues"[18]. Furthermore, the Council has responsibilities for enforcing the conditions attached to planning permissions, but again "is limited by resources for this purpose"[19]. As such, there is no way in which the impacts predicted during the planning application stage can be verified after the building has been constructed, including whether the materials outlined in the visualisations will indeed appear as they were represented. There is a suggestion that the visualisations of tall building proposals differ from the end product. For instance, it is clear that the materials utilised in the Beetham Hilton Tower are represented relatively accurately, although the slightly green hue of the glass in the visualisations is much more apparent in reality. This is particularly evident in the following photographs, where the feeling from the visualisations is that the "tower dissolves into the sky through the glazing scheme and fin at the building's summit"[20]. The visualisations were therefore relatively accurate, although there is a suggestion that some differences with the building under construction are apparent. Were the differences intentionally misleading? Did the LPAs reflect on these differences, and why is it important to have accurate renderings of proposed buildings? It is clear that MCC is resisting a dedicated tall buildings policy which would establish clear, city-wide guidance on the location, form and number of tall buildings which would or would not be acceptable and which could provide advice on the methods of presentation for proposals. The current arrangement, whereby the "coterie" of decision-makers decides whether particular proposals are to be supported by the City Council prior to developments being in the public domain, allows the objective need for a tall building policy to remain unaddressed and irrelevant to the decision-making process. The City Council does not believe that "a tall buildings policy would 'add value', as land ownership issues and the limited number of sites in the city centre mean that only small numbers of tall buildings can actually be built"[21]. Given that there is potential for a large number of tall building proposals to come forward in the near future, and that there are significant numbers of approved tall building planning applications which have yet to be implemented, this appears somewhat naïve. Furthermore, there is little evidence that the approach to approving the Beetham Hilton Tower is either unique or extraordinary. The City Council's planners are more than happy to continue their approach to proposed development, given that they have both "political support and the weight of government guidance . . . [in the shape of PPS1] . . . behind them"[22]. The effect of this approach is apparent in the changes which are discernible in the fabric of the city, not least in its skyline.

The joint CABE–English Heritage guidance on tall buildings is clear in stating that a plan-led approach should ensure that tall building proposals are considered as part of a clear long-term vision, rather than in an ad-hoc and reactive way (CABE and EH, 2003). Manchester's insistence that "each scheme is dealt with on its merits" (MCC, 2004b: 33) appears directly to contradict this. As a material consideration in the determination of applications for planning permission, CABE–EH's guidance has thus been ignored in one crucial regard. Specifically, there is no attempt in the planning application, nor is there an expectation by the local planning authority, to analyse what the impacts of the proposals would be within the context of other tall building proposals (approved and in the pipeline) in the city centre. The lack of a context for cumulative impacts, in general, and the built heritage, in particular, indicates a lack of understanding of the character of Manchester, and how development proposals enhance or detract from it. Furthermore, the guidance does not suggest that tall buildings are somehow bad for cities, rather, it suggests that a lack of rigour in assessment risks giving planning permission to buildings that do not necessarily enhance or detract from the character of the city and its protected buildings and areas. In reality, the Beetham Hilton Tower is not a bad proposal, but there is evidence that a number of elements in the assessment could have been carried out in a more transparent and inclusive way, reflecting the range of views on tall building proposals in the city, rather than simply those of the coterie.

7

TALL BUILDINGS IN BIRMINGHAM: THE NEW IMAGE OF THE CITY[1]?

In 2000, planning permission was granted for a 38-storey residential tower in Birmingham. The building followed a tortuous route to approval, which saw the original 44-storey tower reduced to 38 storeys, albeit still following the original building footprint. The developer (the Beetham Organization, as in Manchester) sought to combine landmark architectural statements with highly desirable residential and leisure accommodation. The proposals were assessed within a context of emerging CABE–English Heritage guidance on tall buildings, as well as the Birmingham Urban Design Study (1991). The issues raised by this application led to the commissioning of a new tall buildings policy by Birmingham City Council (BCC). The decision about this, and other tall buildings in the city centre, took place within a context of rapid regeneration and redevelopment – exemplified by the remodelled Bull Ring, and the re-imaging of the city, away from its much disliked post-war architectural and planning legacy and towards being a leading regional and European city (Kennedy, 2004). This chapter seeks to place decision-making about the Beetham Holloway Circus Tower within the context of the city's development politics, not least in terms of major physical regeneration efforts in and around the city centre, and the distinctive local conservation regime.

Context for development in Birmingham

In the mid-1990s, it was argued that Birmingham had an image problem (Slater and Larkham, 1996). The perceived failure of the city's post-war modernist townscapes and buildings, the associated decline in the city centre during the 1970s and 1980s, and the out-migration of capital and people from the inner city, had contributed to a picture of a city which was uneasy with itself (Holyoak, 2010). The partial regeneration of the city during the 1990s and early 2000s has gone some way towards transforming this image, in part due to the economic buoyancy which has characterised the city's recent past, and the large number of tourists now visiting the city.

Birmingham lies in the heart of the West Midlands conurbation and its local authority boundaries include the largest population of any English local authority area, with just under one million people living in the city. The Birmingham city region, the former West Midlands County Council area, comprises seven local authorities, with a combined population of 2.5 million (ONS, 2003). The city has a powerful financial services sector, and is traditionally seen as the country's second city, although it has always been somewhat in London's shadow (Holyoak, 2010).

Birmingham's townscape was recognisably and dominantly Victorian, prior to the Second World War (Jenkins, 2003). The city was built upon its role as a marketplace for the coal, iron and jewellery trades, and a vast system of canals was built here, to cope with the enormous movement of goods. The associated growth of the city during the nineteenth and early twentieth centuries led to the drawing of broad boundaries, making it the largest local authority district in the country. Indeed, Higgott (2000) suggests that the city has been shaped by this industry, rather than by tradition or topography; although the skyline and form of Birmingham is instantly recognisable, mainly as a result of key post-war buildings such as the Rotunda and Post Office Tower, punctuating the skyline, but also because the city is built on a central ridge, where most of the city centre lies (see Figure 7.1).

The huge scale of bombing during the war destroyed much of the historic core of the city, and the post-war period saw what was perhaps the largest redevelopment of any British city (Cherry, 1994; Harwood, 1999; Higgott, 2000; Kennedy, 2004). During this period, city leaders, themselves led by the city engineer Manzoni, looked

FIGURE 7.1 The Birmingham skyline

to the United States and modernism for inspiration in its redevelopment; the car became the primary arbiter of how city form should develop. The resultant separation of pedestrian traffic, and a mass of motorways, flyovers and bypasses, led to the dominance of the car and the physical isolation of the city centre to a much greater degree than in Manchester and Liverpool. Large redevelopment projects, linked to the new road network, also changed the face of the city centre. The brutalist Bull Ring development in the 1960s, for example, became the first of Britain's indoor shopping centres, and it was a national laughing stock from the 1980s onwards. Changing fashions, in terms of urban design and urban liveability, have resulted in Birmingham paying a heavy price for embracing post-war redevelopment so readily (Parker and Long, 2004).

Economically and socially, Birmingham suffered significantly during the economic downturn of the 1970s and 1980s. Industry, jobs and investment dried up, the manufacturing base of the city collapsed and the city centre suffered from falling rents and the decentralisation of shops and services to other locations in the region. The post-war architectural and planning legacy was blamed, in part, for this. In particular, the poor physical state of the city centre could hardly be conducive to a healthy economy (Higgott, 2000). The Highbury Initiative, held in 1988, was key to the rejection of this legacy. Leading built environment professionals met, as part of this initiative, to discuss a future for the city. It suggested two main ways to improve the city centre: the pedestrianisation of key routes and the improvement of architectural standards for future developments. This marked a radical departure from the immediate post-war period, in the overall focus of planning for the city. This initiative was the catalyst for a long line of regeneration initiatives which have subsequently transformed the city. In particular, Les Sparkes, as Director of Planning in the City Council, championed a number of other initiatives designed to pull the city out of the "quagmire of modernism"[2] and into the twenty-first century; the restoration and packaging of the Jewellery Quarter as an urban quarter, the remodelling of Victoria Square, and attempts at demolishing and rebuilding the hated Bull Ring were instigated by him, in an effort to project a new Birmingham (Foster, 2005).

Commentators have suggested that the planning agenda in Birmingham is dominated by a politics of urban erasure and reinvention, characterised by the development of large scale and bold solutions to planning problems, followed by equally large scale and bold solutions. Furthermore, the townscape is treated as a disputed ideological environment, where actors are able to construct a new city image, and where the rhetoric and impetus of regeneration overshadows all other concerns (Higgott, 2000; Kennedy, 2004; King, 1997; Jones, 2004). The disavowal of the recent past in the rush to regenerate suggests that the post-war townscape is of little value to the city (Kennedy, 2004). Indeed, "Birmingham's creative destruction is a compelling urban drama in which the dialectics of erasure and renewal are forever being played out" (Slater and Larkham, 1996). In comparison with the city's post-war legacy, the Victorian heritage is highly prized, much as in Manchester, with regeneration projects such as the Jewellery Quarter signifying its importance.

Whilst a large amount of the Victorian city was destroyed in the Second World War, Birmingham's historic townscapes and buildings have been used to help reinvent the city's image and attract service industries and business tourism from the late 1980s onwards (BCC, 2005). Whilst it was initially slow to designate Conservation Areas after the Civic Amenities Act 1967, the city now boasts 28 Conservation Areas, with much of the central city now covered (see Figure 7.2). Furthermore, there are nearly 2,000 Listed Buildings in the city (of which 23 are Grade I), and 13 Scheduled Ancient Monuments. The city is unique amongst the other cities examined in this book, in that it has a number of Locally Listed Buildings which are an important part of Birmingham's heritage due to their architectural, historic or archaeological significance[3]. BCC is proud of attempts at recognising the townscape value of all elements of the heritage, not just those which are statutorily protected. The local list of buildings, whilst not having any statutory status, resultant protection or interest from EH, contains large numbers of remaining post-war buildings and complete townscapes, most notably in the city centre. The site of the Beetham Tower at Holloway Circus (named the AEU building) is Locally Listed as Grade B

MAP 6.16 CONSERVATION DESIGNATIONS IN BIRMINGHAM

KEY
■ Statutorily Listed Buildings
▨ Locally Listed buildings
■ Conservation Area
✦ Site
☐ Parks and Gardens of Special Historic Interest

FIGURE 7.2
Main conservation designations in Birmingham

FIGURE 7.3
The site of the Beetham
tower prior to construction

(see Figure 7.3). The local listing is nonetheless reflected in local planning policy. The adopted policy in the Birmingham Plan recognises the local significance of particular buildings and townscapes:

> "the demolition of buildings on the Local List . . . will be resisted to the extent of the powers available. Proposals for the demolition . . . of a building on the Local List should ensure that the features of historic or architectural interest are preserved and that all new work is in keeping with the character of the original building and its setting".
>
> *(BCC, 2003)*

In common with other provincial cities, and with Birmingham's economic renaissance in the late 1980s and 1990s, there has been a marked increase in tall building proposals in the city. Since 1990, a total of 22 buildings of over 15 storeys have been proposed (Short, 2008), the largest proportion of which have remained at the pre-planning stage. Of these, eight have been built over this period, the majority being for residential purposes, although one scheme is mixed and includes leisure uses.

Decisions about tall building development in Birmingham are made by a number of key actors, who interact in both informal and formal planning processes. At the time of the decision-making process about the Beetham Holloway Circus Tower, these key actors included the City Council, government and its agencies, statutory bodies, and non-statutory pressure groups. Table 7.1 summarises the role of these organisations. The breadth of bodies, in comparison with both Liverpool and Manchester, was relatively narrow, in that BCC does not necessarily take residents' groups and businesses into account in decision-making.

The regulatory framework for assessing tall buildings forms the basis against which the proposals would have been assessed and a recommendation by the planning officer to the Planning Committee made (see Table 7.2). The framework is anchored by the Birmingham Urban Design Study. This study sought to ascertain

TABLE 7.1 Key actors involved in tall building proposals in Birmingham

Name	Tier	Focus
Birmingham City Council	Local	Development control decisions taken within Department of Planning and Architecture – reports directly to the full Council. *Conservation Area Advisory Committee*: made up of independent members of amenity societies, Councillors and key built environment professionals drawn from across the city, has a key role in making recommendations for planning permission. *Design Review Panel*: comprises personnel drawn from City Council departments which have interest in the design of landmark projects and are involved in all projects from inception.
20th Century Society	Regional group of national organisation	Aims to create understanding and appreciation of all kinds of buildings erected in Britain in the twentieth century. Involved in debates about loss of post-war townscapes and key buildings.
CABE	National	Design reviews of large projects, and those which have significant impact on surroundings. CABE has reviewed three tall buildings planning applications since 2000 in Birmingham.
EH	Regional office and national body	West Midlands office, based in Birmingham.
Beetham Organization	National	Liverpool-based property construction company. Has proposed tall buildings in Birmingham, Brighton, London, Liverpool and Manchester. Seeks to combine landmark residential buildings with premium hotels, creating mixed use schemes.

which elements of the townscape were of value, what was vulnerable to change, and what development should be directed to specific locations.

Beetham Holloway Circus Tower proposal

The proposal for the Beetham Tower was the culmination of a process which included a number of planning applications over a number of years. Table 7.3 outlines these in detail. Unless otherwise referenced, this case study refers to a resubmitted application (C/04993/00/FUL) which was submitted in April 2002. No pre-application meetings took place between BCC, the applicants, and the key actors, although the proposal did seek to address the concerns of the Planning Committee, which were outlined in the previous application (C/04991/00/FUL)

TABLE 7.2 Regulatory framework for tall building proposals in Birmingham

Planning policy	Tier	Mention of tall buildings?	Key planning principles	Other comments
RPG West Midlands/ Regional Spatial Strategy 2004	Regional	Not specifically	Urban renaissance in Birmingham. Recycling brownfield land.	Supports development which contributes to sustainability objectives.
Birmingham Urban Design Strategy (BUDS) 1990	Local	Yes	Space for new landmark tall buildings. Developing and protecting key views. Reinforcing and enhancing the city's topography.	Policy context for Beetham tower has been subsequently replaced by new policy.
Birmingham Plan 1993	Local	Yes	Importance of topography in forming city, and role in development. Tall buildings can contribute to regeneration.	Within framework of BUDS.

as relating to calls from the Civil Aviation Authority for a substantial reduction in height from 44 storeys. Figure 7.4 shows the proposed tower at 38 storeys.

The site lies on the junction of Smallbrook Queensway and Suffolk Street Queensway, on the southern side of the city centre. As described above, the site previously contained a Grade B Locally Listed Building of five storeys, used for retail and for food and drink purposes. The site lies within an area of post-war redevelopment, the character of which has been recognised by the City Council as having local merit (BCC, 2003). To the west, the site is framed by two 32-storey towers from the early 1960s, known as The Sentinels. The Queensway curves from Holloway Circus into the core of the city around the Bull Ring area. This wide boulevard is an entirely post-war composition which was originally designed to segregate vehicular and pedestrian traffic, and it has been described as "the best piece of mid-C20 urban design in the city, and the only stretch of the Inner Ring Road built as a boulevard rather than an urban motorway" (Foster, 2005: 21). The boulevard is flanked by various post-war buildings of some value (BCC, 2001), including the building that occupied the site of tower, known as the AEU building, which was protected through the local listing process as "successfully dealing with an awkward corner site by using overlapping stepped canopies" (BCC, 2001: 3). The AEU building was demolished in 2004, and the tower was constructed over twenty months from mid-2004. It officially opened in early 2006.

TABLE 7.3 Planning applications submitted for the Beetham Holloway Circus Tower

Application	Detail
Application C/04991/00/FUL	
March 2000	Erection of 44-storey mixed use tower, comprising 213 residential units, 93 sq.m. office space, 422 sq.m. of retail, plus 150 car parking spaces contained within the adjacent multi-storey car park (total height 192m), and alterations to elevations of adjacent multi-storey car park.
	Tower attracted objections, including from the Civil Aviation Authority, about the height of the proposal.
	City Council adopted objection as negotiating position, with applicants who requested it be held in abeyance pending resubmission.
Application C/00699/01/FUL	
June 2001	Demolition of existing buildings and mixed use redevelopment for office, residential units with 268 car parking spaces, Class A1, A3 and D2, 492 space multi-storey public car park, and 146 bedroom hotel; applications withdrawn on 15 October 2001.
Application C/04993/00/FUL (resubmitted application)	
April 2002	Erection of 38-storey mixed use tower, containing hotel and residential uses, at a height of 121.5 metres.
	Building was almost identical to the previous application, except for the reduction in height, and was a response to the holding in abeyance of previous application.

FIGURE 7.4
Proposed 38-storey
Beetham tower

The planning application comprised the following elements: planning application forms and relevant certificates; a local planning strategy statement; photo montages at A1 and A3 size, including visual assessments; detailed plans.

As a first stage in the determination of the planning application, BCC took an Issues Report to both the Development Control Committee and the Conservation Area Advisory Committee (CAAC) (BCC, 2000b). The original report from the application for a 44-storey tower was also taken to elected members and the CAAC by the Acting Director of Planning and Architecture. This report outlined the main issues in the determination of the application for information purposes, and it was used as the main instrument in the resolution of planning issues for the 38-storey tower, even though it directly related to the 44-storey tower application. The pertinent built heritage issues were identified as being: the impact of a building of this scale on a coherent townscape of merit; overshadowing and wind; the quality of architecture and materials; achievement of a landmark building and termination of key views; and, the potential impact on the character and appearance of Colmore Row Conservation Area (BCC, 2000b). Table 7.4 summarises the methods used to assess the impact of the tower on built heritage, in the submitted documentation. In comparison with both Liverpool and Manchester, the scope of methods utilised in the assessment process seems particularly unsophisticated. More specifically, no EIA was required by the LPA, nor was any attempt at showing (through visualisations) what the impact of the building would be, beyond immediate views of the site from the local area. The information was poorly presented, compared to both the Liverpool and Manchester cases, with bundles of maps and papers submitted without any coherence[4].

Having read and discussed the Issues Report, elected members on the Development Control Committee commented on the tower proposal. They outlined their concern about traffic generation and public transport, the cumulative impacts of all tower applications including this one, and how to deal with any masts on top of the building. Furthermore, the Chair indicated that a tall building policy should be developed to deal with each of these issues in future (BCC, 2000b). Members responded by stating that a site visit was required prior to the application being determined. The outcomes of the subsequent site visits were recorded in a memorandum from the Assistant Director of Planning to the Principal Planning Officer; this reiterated elected members concerns (BCC, 2000a).

Table 7.5 indicates which internal Council departments and bodies, as well as external bodies, were consulted as part of the planning application (the consultation responses from the previous application remained valid for the purposes of determining this application). It is evident that the consultations were comprehensive, and that they elicited a wide range of responses. Consultations were re-sent to all those who were originally consulted on the 44-storey tower proposal. Amongst other supporting comments, CABE wrote to the planning authority regarding the tower proposal, outlining its support for the proposal. CABE did, however, sound a note of caution regarding the paucity of information contained within the application. Specifically, CABE indicated that there would need to be a "full view

TABLE 7.4 Summary of decision support mechanisms used in assessing the Beetham
Holloway Circus Tower planning application

Assessment or study	Submitted	Comments
Characterisation study	☐	
Urban Design statement	☐	
PPG15 statement	☐	
Planning statement	■	Document places tower within local planning strategy framework – to be read in conjunction with photo montages.
Tall building statement	☐	
Traffic study	■	Study including car parking arrangements, traffic on adjoining main roads.
Housing Market study	☐	
Shadow study	☐	
Cumulative impact study	☐	
EIA/Environment Statement	☐	
Photo montage (digital or manual renderings)	■	Colour montages provided at A1 size for presentation purposes – A3 black and white for wider circulation.
Night time study	☐	
GIS model of building/area	☐	
Card model of building	☐	
Card model of area	☐	
CAD model of building	☐	
CAD model of area	☐	
Archaeological assessment	☐	
Options/Alternatives	☐	
Acoustic study	▲	Required after Environmental Health consultation response – covered by a condition on the planning permission.

KEY
■   Consulted by local planning authority
◻   Support planning application with comments
▲   No comment or response on planning application
☐   Object to planning application
▣   Not consulted

analysis, and a range of realistic views from different directions and distances", and
noted that it was important to ensure the quality of materials and detailing in projects
of this kind (CABE, 2002). The Twentieth Century Society likewise objected, on
the grounds that the proposal was "completely out of character with the surrounding
twentieth century townscape . . . which has retained much of its grandeur and
masculinity"[5].

   The City Council's CAAC objected to the proposal for a number of reasons.
Firstly, it was felt that the proposal failed to respect the urban design character and
uniformity of built form on Smallbrook Queensway. Secondly, the AEU building

TABLE 7.5 Consultations undertaken for planning application for the Beetham Holloway Circus Tower

Internal consultations	Consulted	Outcome	External consultations	Consulted	Outcome
Design and Conservation section	■	▲	Local airport	■	□
Environmental Health	■	▲	Countryside Commission	▣	▲
Housing	■	▲	Environment Agency	■	
Operational Services	▣		English Nature	▣	▲
Traffic and transport	■	▲	Passenger Transport	■	
Members	■	▲	Police	▣	▲
Individual residents	■	□	CABE	■	▣
Local residents (groups)	■	□	EH	■	▣
Local businesses	▣		Georgian Society	■	
Local business individuals	▣		Victorian Society	■	▲
City centre Manager	■	▲	20th Century Society	■	□
Conservation Area Advisory Committee	■	□	Local civic society	■	▲
Design Review	■	▣	Council for British Archaeology	▣	
			Adjoining local authorities	▣	
			Friends of the Earth	■	▲
			British Telecom	■	▲

KEY

■ Consulted by local planning authority
□ Support planning application with comments
▲ No comment or response on planning application
□ Object to planning application
▣ Not consulted

was recognised as elegant and protected through the local listing policies of the development plan. Finally, the CAAC described the context of the site and concluded that, whilst the Sentinels opposite occupy their own curtilage and are a distinct element in the townscape, the AEU building is surrounded by two- and three-storey buildings. In other words, a 38-storey tower would be completely out of context (BCC, 2002b).

EH had no objections to the proposal, and reiterated the details of the earlier consultation for a 44-storey tower. It felt that the main effects on the historic environment would be on views within the city centre, and into the city centre, from areas of historic and architectural value, but also felt that it was unable to object on the grounds of the impact upon the immediate historic environment, because this was outside of its remit, which relates to Locally Listed Buildings (King, 2001).

Assessment of the Holloway Circus Tower proposal

The built heritage issues in the planning application were, from the start, a relatively minor concern, set against more pressing matters for the LPA – in particular, the health and safety concerns of the Civil Aviation Authority and the transport related issues posed by the development. The planning application documentation pre-sented the proposals in a limited way and gave broad indications about what potential impacts may be, rather than being specific; indeed, the documentation could be characterised as weak, with little thought given to how the building may impact upon the historic environment. The local planning strategy was submitted at the request of EH, who could not determine from the photo montages how the proposal would work in urban design terms. The strategy was written by Ian Simpson Architects, and it attempted (assisted by photo montages) to visualise the proposal from a number of views in the immediate area of the site. Furthermore, it discussed the design of the tower within the remit of BUDS (Birmingham Urban Design Strategy). At no stage, however, was there any evidence that these views were agreed between the applicant and the LPA, and they therefore appear to be arbitrarily defined. The strategy document confirms that BUDS identifies the site in question as a preferred location for a tall (15-storeys plus) landmark building, marking a gateway into the city centre from the south.

It is clear from a number of interviews, including with those who assessed the information, that the documentation submitted as part of the planning application was "inadequate for the purposes of assessment by the planning authority"[6]. There were glaring omissions from the submitted documents, most notably a lack of any sort of EIA/Environmental Statement. The paucity of information was matched by the poor quality of submitted documents, most notably the photo montages and local planning strategy, which were criticised by the CAAC.

Perhaps reflecting the lack of documentation and poor quality of that which was submitted, the report to the Development Control Committee does not refer to any of the submitted documents directly, although it does refer to some of the views outlined in the photo montages. The report does not critically assess the way in which the tower was presented by the applicant, or indicate to members that other organisations had concerns about the paucity and quality of information provided. Furthermore, no mention of the impact of the proposal on Locally Listed Buildings was mentioned at all (BCC, 2002a). Even though members of the Development Control Committee had indicated that it was concerned about the cumulative impact of proposals for tall buildings in the city (in the Issues Report), there is no evidence of any further information being required of the applicants, and the committee report makes no mention of this issue at all.

Furthermore, the monitoring of impacts after construction, required by the 1999 EIA Regulations, has not taken place, much as in the Manchester case. As there is no Environmental Statement, the monitoring requirements rest on the proper implementation of the conditions attached to the planning consent. BCC has responsibilities for enforcing the conditions attached to planning permissions, but it is limited by its lack of resources for this purpose. It undertakes no ex-post assessment activities as a matter of course. As such, there is no way in which the impacts discussed during the planning application stage can be verified after construction, including whether the materials outlined in the visualisations will indeed look the way that they are represented. The planning permission for the Beetham Hilton Tower includes conditions which relate to the submission of materials for approval by the planning authority, a process which is undertaken by planning officers and which does not require the involvement of elected members. Figures 7.5 and 7.6 indicate the marked difference between the visualisation of the tower in the documentation submitted to the planning authority and the actual materials used in the construction of the tower. For example, the difference between the tower under construction and the adjoining, Locally Listed post-war buildings is far more pronounced than the visualisations would suggest. The way in which the tower blends in with its surroundings in the visualisation is somewhat different from reality, and the green-blue hue of the tower is in reality far more pronounced than in the visualisations. The differences appear to be far more marked than in the Manchester case.

The built heritage issues in the application were dealt with in both the "Design" and "Conservation" sections of the report to the Development Control Committee. Firstly, the character of the Locally Listed AEU was described in terms of its key features, particularly the way the building articulates the corner of the street, but the internal features were also deemed of some merit. Secondly, the CAAC objection to this building was described in terms of the proposed building being out of scale to, and character with, the surrounding area, given that the predominant height of buildings (in its view) was around six–eight storeys (BCC, 2002a). However, the report stated that the new building would provide modern accommodation and have great regeneration potential; in this respect, the benefits were thought to outweigh the disbenefits of the proposal. Thirdly, the report described how the proposed tower would be visible on the skyline from some Conservation Areas, but no adverse impact would be caused to their character. The Conservation Areas in question, the potential impact of the tower on the character of those Conservation

Areas, and the way in which the skyline could be changed by the proposal were not described or visualised. Finally, the BUDS context was described briefly in the report. The element of BUDS which required that towers should not adversely impact on any existing coherent townscape of merit, or on the environment, was likewise described. No discussions about the built heritage issues were recorded during the committee meeting to decide the application (BCC, 1993). The planning application was approved, subject to the report being sent to the Government Office for the West Midlands, which had no comment to make.

The impact of the proposed Tower on the AEU building and the adjoining Locally Listed Buildings on Smallbrook Queensway exemplifies the paucity of information that surrounded the planning application. There is no evidence that the adopted Birmingham Plan policy was utilised in the assessment of the proposals and it is not mentioned in the Committee report. The character of the immediate area surrounding the site, particularly on Smallbrook Queensway, and the impact of the tower upon it, is not discussed in any of the documents.

It could be argued that the lack of assessment of the post-war townscape of Smallbrook Queensway is, in some way, at odds with the efforts of BCC to make the area more pedestrian and business friendly. In 1998, the City Council removed the vehicular viaduct and accompanying pedestrian underpass which swept traffic down the street, and replaced it with a much lower carriageway, thereby improving pedestrian access (BCC, 2003). The effect of this was to open up the townscape, and it has resulted in an improved business and pedestrian environment, a fact which has not been addressed in any of the documents. The proposed tower is not presented within the context of an improved environment, although it will clearly have an impact upon this, at ground level. Whilst BUDS states that tall buildings should not impact on any existing coherent townscape of merit, there is no analysis of this in the committee report or local planning strategy (which purports to reflect BUDS). Furthermore, the analysis of the building did not relate directly to the existing townscape in the documentation; does the tower add something to the immediate setting, given that the AEU building is substantially lower than its immediate neighbours, for example? As has already been indicated in the report, it is outlined that the existing building assists in the articulation of the street, yet this is not analysed in a BUDS context.

Finally, whilst there is precedent for recording Listed Buildings which are substantially altered or demolished, there is no condition for recording buildings on the local list, prior to demolition. As such, no record of the building exists, beyond the Council's record of the building contained within the list itself. It would seem, therefore, that Birmingham's post-war legacy is expendable, given that there is no analysis of the impact of the tower upon it. This would fit with the earlier discussion on the status of the Victorian versus the post-war built heritage within a framework of rapid and significant regeneration. It may be that the tower proposal is preferable to the AEU buildings, but this was not discussed or visualised in any of the supporting information. Furthermore, whilst the Birmingham Plan goes some way towards acknowledging that "everyday heritage" has some importance in the way

FIGURE 7.5 (above) Completed Beetham Tower

FIGURE 7.6 (right) Completed Beetham Tower

that townscapes are experienced, the designation of a building on the local list would appear to have little impact upon decision-making. The fact that there are no sponsors of this heritage beyond the local level (that have any power), results in these buildings being subjected to more powerful forces for redevelopment and regeneration. One wonders what the situation would have been had an organisation such as EH had statutory responsibility for such buildings.

The emergence of a new tall buildings policy in Birmingham has been partly as a result of experiences of the determination of the Beetham Holloway Circus Tower applications, together with the push from CABE–EH guidance published in 2003. The new policy was developed during 2002/03, to update BUDS for the twenty-first century, combining the utility of the original policy with an increased understanding of tall buildings in the city. The tall buildings policy was widely circulated, in order to obtain the views of key actors. Consultation responses were fed into a review of the draft document. The policy is essentially an urban design statement, outlining the main principles for the determination of applications for tall buildings. The document has been adopted by the Council as supplementary planning guidance, and it is therefore material to the determination of planning applications. It provides guidance on the location, form and appearance of tall buildings. Existing tall buildings, particularly office blocks, are concentrated along the city centre ridge, and are also grouped in some local centres. The guidance document builds on this, by seeking to locate buildings in order to create clusters and points of interest, to make the city more legible. A comparative analysis of BUDS and the new policy is provided in Table 7.6. The policy is overwhelmingly welcoming of tall buildings:

TABLE 7.6 Comparison between the main principles of BUDS and the new tall buildings policy

BUDS	Tall buildings policy
Space for new landmark tall buildings.	Specific locations for tall buildings, outlined in map form. Outside these areas, tall buildings will only be allowed in exceptional circumstances.
Developing and protecting key views.	Developing and protecting key view.
Reinforcing the city's topography.	Reinforcing the city's topography, and must relate to their local context.
	Tall buildings not allowed in CAs, or adjacent to LBs, unless exceptional circumstances.
Building defined as tall over 15 storeys.	Contextual definition.
	No building shall be taller than 242 metres.
	Tall buildings should be of the highest quality.

"Birmingham welcomes and encourages well-placed, high quality tall buildings that would enhance the image of the City and the development of Birmingham's overall economy as a competitive City in the national and international context".

(Miles, 2005)

Officers at the City Council have already expressed satisfaction that the guidance is assisting in the evolution of expertise and knowledge within the relevant departments in dealing with such applications, and there is already evidence of an improvement in the quality and breadth of information submitted as part of planning applications[7]. In time, a proper review of the implementation of this policy would allow for the evolution of staff knowledge and expertise.

8

"THE BLUE, THE GREEN AND THE CITY IN BETWEEN": TENSIONS BETWEEN CONSERVATION AND TALL BUILDING DEVELOPMENT IN OSLO

In 2003, Oslo Kommune (OK) adopted a master plan for the strategically important Bjørvika area, located in the heart of the medieval centre of the city. Bjørvika is a redevelopment area of national significance, and is part of the wider Fjordcity urban expansion that seeks to utilise Oslo's strategically important fjord location to absorb development over the next decade. It represents a marked shift towards an active strategy to attract investment in Norway, and to make Oslo a city of international significance[1]. Whilst the development of the area has had the support of a broad cross section of interests within the city, the inclusion of possible tall buildings in part of the area, and the potential impact of these upon the character of the city and upon particular built heritage designations, has attracted widespread criticism and concern. Any consensus over the redevelopment of Bjørvika as a project of national importance has subsequently dissipated, with increasing concern that politicians have been favouring development interests over built heritage concerns until recently. Decisions about tall buildings in Bjørvika are taking place within a context of increasing numbers of tall building applications being received by the Kommune, reflecting a renewed economic confidence in the city, alongside concern about the management of built heritage assets, particularly the medieval old town.

This chapter will outline the context for development in Oslo including an examination of the character of the city and existing tall building development. This is followed by an analysis of the development plan context and the main actors in the development process. The move by the Kommune to promote tall buildings in Bjørvika is examined in detail, before ending with some interesting conclusions about the status of conservation planning in Norway and the emerging tension between what is perceived as local versus international cultural symbols.

Context for development in Oslo

Oslo is a city of some 590,000 people (Statistics Norway, 2010) that lies at the head of the Oslofjord in the south-east of Norway. Whilst it spans a vast area and is characterised by a dispersed population at a low residential density compared to other European cities, in Norwegian terms it is relatively concentrated. The wider city region contains more than 1.4 million people, is one of the fastest growing Scandinavian regions and is at the centre of one of the most robust economies in the world, sustained by North Sea gas (Felberg, 2005). Indeed, the population of the City of Oslo is set to grow by 11% by 2020, as a result of the improvement of the economy, increasing birth rates, and immigration from other parts of Norway and internationally (Felberg, 2005). The Kommune is particularly interested in projecting the city onto the world stage, in order to attract investment to maintain levels of employment, maintain the country's wealth over the coming century and compete with other Scandinavian capitals.

The city lies in a natural amphitheatre at the head of the fjord, and is framed by the water to the front and mountains to the rear, a context captured in the common phrase "the blue, the green and the city in between"[2] (see Figure 8.1). Central Oslo is situated around three bays at the inner reach of the Oslofjord (Pipervika, Bjørvika and Bispevika) and can be characterised by a dominant building height of between four and eight storeys in the city centre and between two and six storeys elsewhere. Bjørvika is the most historically significant (Langset, 2005), in that it was here that the city was founded in the year 1,000. The medieval town was the seat of the Norwegian king and bishop, and it flourished in the twelfth and thirteenth centuries, particularly. After the subjugation of Norway by Denmark in the fifteenth century, the medieval town dwindled and was left largely as ruins after 1624 (Langset, 2005). A triangle of medieval ruins ring the bay and characterise the form of the city: in the east, there are remains of the old settlement of Oslo (gamlebyen), including: the ruins of a number of churches, houses and palaces, and the Bishop's Palace which still stands at Ladegård; Akershus Castle and Fortress on the west side of the bay, built in the thirteenth century then remodelled; and the Cistercian monastery on the island of Hovedøya, founded in 1147 and abandoned after the Reformation.

When the railway was constructed in the mid-nineteenth century, the site of the medieval town in the east of the bay was taken over for development, causing extensive damage to many architectural and archaeological remains. Furthermore, the main city motorway to the south of Norway was constructed through the area in the 1970s. This has now partly been removed and the city's archaeological remains have been opened up to the public. Whilst the medieval remains of Oslo are ringed with roads and port related activities, they are the "most significant element of the city's heritage and . . . must be retained to keep a sense of the original character and scale of Oslo"[3].

Bjørvika lies adjacent to the country's most important transport hub, Oslo Central Station, which lies at the confluence of the three medieval elements of the city and has, according to the Kommune, the potential to reconnect Oslo to its waterfront

FIGURE 8.1 The blue, the green and the city in between

(OK, 2003). Currently, the site is used for transport related functions, such as roads, the railway and the port. There are complex problems awaiting any redevelopment: a main highway cuts off the city from the waterfront; the area is covered in fluvial deposits, polluted sediments, industrial pollution and landfills from the last 400 years; and parts of the area contain valuable archaeological remains from the medieval period. The site is owned by the national government, Oslo Kommune, the Port Authority, and a number of private landowners (see Figure 8.2).

FIGURE 8.2 View of Bjørvika from the old city

At present there are 110 buildings in the city, deemed "tall" by Oslo Kommune; buildings of over twelve storeys are defined as such. The definition of "tall" as twelve storeys appears to reflect concern about the particular sensitivity in Oslo to buildings which may affect the character and topographical frame of the city ("the blue, the green and the city in between"). The majority of these tall buildings are residential buildings, built during the 1960s and 1970s, but the two most prominent towers in the city centre are an office block and an hotel: the Post Tower (built in 1975, at 26 storeys) and the Radisson Hotel (built in 1990, at 37 storeys). Figure 8.3 shows

FIGURE 8.3 The Post Tower and Radisson Hotel

the two towers from Bjørvika. Both buildings are "universally despised", as a result of a perception that they are "foreign and alien to Norwegian culture"[4], hinting at the controversy of tall buildings in Oslo. A number of proposals for tall buildings of over twelve storeys have come forward in Oslo in the period since 2000; twenty proposals were recorded by the Agency for Planning and Building up to 2000 (OK, 2004a). Since that time, five buildings of over 25 storeys have been proposed: adjacent to the Town Hall; next to the Royal Palace; in the Grünerløkka neighbourhood; at the Central Station; and, at Bjørvika – stirring huge controversy amongst the public, local and national politicians and heritage interest groups alike. The following paragraphs outline the institutional framework for planning in Norway, as well as the characteristics of the local conservation planning regime.

The regulatory framework for planning in Oslo

Table 8.1 summarises the administrative and institutional framework for planning in Norway. This is useful in order to assist in understanding the way in which planning decisions are made in Oslo.

Development in Oslo relies on a number of key actors, who interact in planning and conservation processes. In terms of tall buildings, these are the Commissioner for Urban Development (Byråd for byutvikling), the Agency for Planning and Building Services (Plan-og bygningsetaten) and Urban Conservation Office (Byantikvaren), the State Directorate for Cultural Heritage (Riksantikvaren), Oslo Teknopol, and the Foundation for Urban Renewal (Stiftelsen Byens Fornyelse).

Planning in Norway is going through a period of change, partly as a result of the political shift away from the traditional socialist Scandinavian model. The imperatives of regeneration and development have overtaken the traditional desire to achieve consensus in planning decisions. Furthermore, there is a high degree of anxiety in the country about what is happening to the built form of the major cities, in particular (Skjeggedal, 2005). This is reflected in Oslo's planning agenda, which stresses the importance of regeneration and the creation of an internationally significant place for finance, industry and jobs. Furthermore, Norwegian planning can be characterised by the dominance of architects in shaping discourses around development and project planning. This reflects the Norwegian tradition of architects having a much higher status than planners, and therefore more power in shaping visions for the future for Norwegian towns.

The traditional consensus-building which had previously characterised Norwegian planning has given way to a system of decision-making which "favours private interests over the public good, and which judges progress by the physical transformation of the city centre"[5]. The local conservation planning regime therefore reflects this shift in focus for planning, with the result that decisions about built heritage protection are subsumed within wider concerns about regeneration. Riksantikvaren and Byantikvaren are the two bodies most involved with built heritage issues in the city. As the national body charged with the protection and enhancement of the nation's heritage, Riksantikvaren has shown particular concern

TABLE 8.1 Administrative and institutional context for planning and conservation in Norway

Area of interest	Detail
Background	Constitutional monarchy.
	4.6 million inhabitants.
Government	3 levels; central, county and local.
	National parliament Stortinget, 19 counties, 434 municipalities.
	Oslo has different system; politically responsible commissioner for one area of government.
Planning	No national spatial plan.
	Planning and Building Act (PBA) 1985 main instrument of planning – requires local and county plans.
	Municipalities must produce Municipal Comprehensive Plan (MCP) which directs land use at detailed level. Must also include long-term spatial objectives.
	System allows for third parties to forward alternative proposals for sites which are required to be debated.
Conservation	Based on Cultural Heritage Act 1978.
	Cornerstone of conservation protection in country and outlines key responsibilities in heritage protection.
	Empowers Ministry of the Environment to manage heritage protection through Riksantikvaren to the counties and municipalities.
	Counties responsible for drawing up conservation plans and dealing with heritage aspects of planning.
	Municipalities have greatest responsibility under PBA for protecting areas in MCP and for advising developers on matters of protection of buildings, monuments and areas.
	Fornminneregisteret (National Inventory of Archaeological Sites) contains about 68,000 entries of pre-1537 ruins and remains.
	Fredningsregisteret (National Register of Protected Buildings) contains all standing buildings which are automatically protected under Cultural Heritage Act (those before 1537) and contains approximately 4,000 entries.
	SEFRAK (National Register of Buildings) was set up under Act to record all standing buildings between 1537 and 1900 which remain. Approximately 500,000 entries have been made onto this inventory.
	Municipalities able to designate areas for protection under the Cultural Heritage Act.

in response to the rapid rate of change in the character of Oslo. Byantikvaren is also concerned about the character of the city, and is responsible for commenting on development proposals and how they may impact upon the built heritage of the city.

One other salient feature of Norwegian planning is that third parties are legally able to forward alternative proposals for sites and areas which must be considered by the Kommune in its deliberations over planning applications. As such, Norway has a highly developed sense of civic duty in planning, where organisations such as Stiftelsen Byens Fornyelse become involved in the detail of planning proposals and are actively suggesting improvements to development projects (Amdam, 2002).

Norway has a tripartite division of planning responsibilities (national–county–Kommune) with the Kommune required to reflect national and county (sometimes referred to as regions) planning goals in municipal development plans. In Oslo, the Kommune has county and local responsibilities, and is required to work with the adjoining county of Akershus to produce a planning strategy for the metropolitan area (OK, 2004b). The structure of local government in Oslo (and Bergen) is some-what different to the rest of the country. In Oslo, an executive City Government is elected by a majority of the City Council. The City Government advances a political programme in five areas of local government: finance, health and welfare, urban development, educational and cultural affairs, and transport and environmental affairs. Each is headed by appointees called Commissioners and is responsible to the City Council, directly. The City Government instigates and controls all work prepared by each of the divisions, and seeks approval from the City Council.

The Commissioner for Urban Development (Byråd for byutvikling) heads the Department of Urban Development, which advances the programme for planning and development defined by the Commissioner with approval from the City Council. It includes an Urban Conservation Office (Byantikvaren) and Agency for Planning and Building Services (Plan-og bygningsetaten). Table 8.2 outlines the roles and purpose of each of the above. Grete Horntvedt, Commissioner for Urban Development until late in 2006 (subsequently replaced by Merete Agerbak-Jensen, who has continued to promote development in Bjørvika), was elected to the City Government from the majority Høyre Party (conservative). Her "tenure has proved to be controversial in many respects, particularly in her approach to tall buildings"[6], partly as the result of her intention to seek physical modernisation for Oslo.

The regulatory framework for tall buildings in Oslo forms the basis against which proposals are assessed by the relevant agencies and departments of government. Table 8.3 summarises this context. The current basis for tall building regulations is in a state of flux, as "competing visions of the future . . . [of Oslo] . . . are played out"[7]. Firstly, the Oslo Municipal Comprehensive Development and Conservation Plan 2005–2020 (OK, 2006a) is the adopted plan at county–Kommune level, covering Oslo City (as a Kommune and county) and Akershus county. It is sub-divided into area-based strategies, including one for Oslo Sentrum, the central part of the city. The plan provides a framework for the Bjørvika area, which sees it as "Norway's most important development area over the next 15 years" (OK,

TABLE 8.2 Key actors involved in tall building proposals in Oslo

Name	Tier	Focus
Oslo kommune	Local and county	City Council (bystyret) and City Government (byrådet). City Council has 59 members headed by the mayor, is divided into five areas: Finance, Health and Welfare, Urban Development, Educational and Cultural Affairs, and Transport and Environmental Affairs. Government made up of Commissioners which are politicians with a political programme supported by majority of Council.
Byrådsavdeling for byutvikling (Commissioner for Urban Development)	Local and county	Heads Department of Urban Development which advances programme with approval from Council.
Plan-og bygningsetaten (Agency for Planning and Building Services)	Local and regional	Responsible for land use and transport planning through municipal plans as well as for EIAs. Grants planning permissions and responsible for policy for City Government and gives advice to both Council and Commissioner.
Byantikvaren (Urban Conservation Office)	Local and county	Supports work of Department and work of Riksantikvaren in seeking to protect city's built heritage. Advises Department on applications for development, master plans, implications of proposed redevelopment at pre-application stage on heritage and restoration practices.
Riksantikvaren (Directorate for Cultural Heritage)	National	Under direct authority of Ministry of the Environment. Responsible for formulation and execution of cultural heritage management policies. Provides cultural heritage expertise and technical advice to Ministry and counties.
Oslo Teknopol	County	Development agency established by City of Oslo and Akershus County Council. Aims to stimulate innovation and attract foreign investment to Oslo. Provides services and information to investors.
Stiftelsen Byens Fornyelse (Foundation for Urban Renewal)	Local	Community organisation designed to promote traditional architecture and urbanism. Suggested traditional urbanist solutions to redevelopment areas such as Bjørvika.

TABLE 8.3 Regulatory framework for tall buildings in Oslo

Planning policy	Tier	Tall building mentioned?	Key planning principles
Oslo Comprehensive Development Plan 2005–2020	County	No	Plans for increase in population of 11% over next 15 years. Not to encroach on green belt; contained growth. Encourages contemporary architecture.
Fjordcity Master Plan 2004	Local	No	Waterfront areas are unique with their close proximity to the city centre and to the main transport and cultural infrastructure. Bjørvika area was directed for development by the Commissioner for Urban Development through plan.
Land Use Plan for Bjørvika 2005	Local	No	Bjørvika is the most important development area in Norway at present. Zoning provisions which determine the different categories of land use and the density of development. Strategic framework.
Tall Buildings in Oslo – Principles for a Tall Building Strategy 2003	County	Yes	Tall buildings should be attracted to growth poles throughout city, particularly round transport nodes.

2006a: 3). As such, it allocates the area as a growth pole for development over the life of the plan.

Secondly, the Fjordcity Master Plan has the status of a local plan, adding detail (at the local level) to the comprehensive development plan. This plan contextualises the city's plans for its waterfront, in a series of designated areas. The strategy includes the "urban renewal of a string of waterfront properties in the heart of the city, in order to create better connections between the city centre and the fjord, providing unique physical surroundings for living and leisure" (OK, 2006b). The plan recognises the strategic importance of the waterfront area (including Bjørvika) to the development of Oslo as an internationally renowned centre for finance and industry; as such, it is the "most important development area in Norway" (OK, 2006b: 2). The plan also promotes the pro-growth agenda of the Commissioner and the wider City Council. Figure 8.4 shows the areas covered by the plan.

Thirdly, the Development Plan for Bjørvika–Bispevika–Lohavn (OK, 2003) is a local plan which was unanimously adopted by the City Council in 2003. The Plan is intended to direct development within Bjørvika, in order to fulfil the desire of the other higher tier plans to create a vibrant waterfront in this area. Figure 8.5 shows a simplified map of the area and the broad zoning categories for the Bjørvika area.

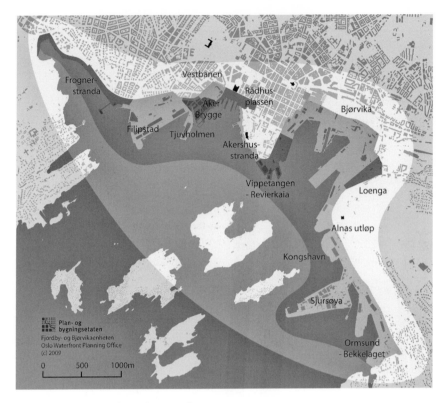

FIGURE 8.4 Fjordcity boundaries and areas

The development of Bjørvika is being financed mainly by domestic investors, including the national and city governments, the Port Authority, and many private individuals and companies (OK, 2003). The Bjørvika plan identifies approximately 900,000 sq. m. of floor space to be developed, including approximately 400,000 sq. m. for housing (or about 4,000 units), 20,000 sq. m. of office space, and 100,000 sq. m. of cultural institutions. A total of 230,000 sq. m. of space has been planned for parks and public spaces, with the balance of space relating to the associated transport infrastructure. A new national opera (by Snøhetta) has recently opened, and a National Heritage Museum, a marina and an aquarium are all planned for the future. In order to release much of the area for development, a ten-year project to tunnel the main highway under the bay is currently under approval by the Norwegian government.

The plan suggests that a number (exactly how many is not clarified) of tall buildings may be appropriate in a block between the waterfront and the Central Station, called "Barcode Row", as well as lower density housing and office development elsewhere, a medieval park, restoration of key protected buildings and ruins, a school, and a further six open spaces. Interestingly, the development will pay for the improvement of built heritage in the immediate area, particularly the medieval ruins

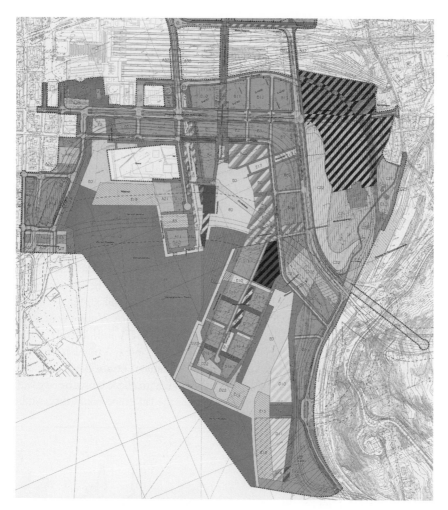

FIGURE 8.5 Land use plan for Bjørvika

in Gamlebyen and Ladegård. The detail in the plan has evolved over a number of years, and has gone through a number of iterations. The broad land uses outlined in the plan are unlikely to change, but the plan has been reissued on a number of occasions due to pressure, from the Commissioner for Urban Development and her Department, to reflect changing ideas about the height of buildings. Indeed, there was palpable tension between various interests over this issue. There is a perception that the "planning process was being manipulated by the Commissioner, as improving economic circumstances mean that more development can be accommodated in Bjørvika"[8]. The result is a development plan that is updated to reflect those changes. In addition, there is concern that the Commissioner is on record as saying that "it is at the planning application stage that the detail will be worked out in tall building proposals, and the heights of individual buildings set" (OK, 2004a: 1).

In addition to preparing the 2003 development plan, the Agency for Planning and Building produced a draft tall building strategy (*Høyhus i Oslo, vurdering av prinsipper for høyhusstrategi* – Tall Buildings in Oslo, Principles for a Tall Building Strategy) in 2002 (OK, 2002). The document was produced as a result of a number of factors: pressure from development proposals and public opinion meant that the City Government felt that it needed a coherent strategy to deal with planning proposals for tall buildings; the Commissioner for Urban Development felt that such a document would provide potential to attract appropriate development to specific growth areas in the city and that therefore, the goal of the City Government and Council to create a city of international significance would be facilitated; and the City Government came under political pressure from the City Council, as a result of community groups and individuals expressing concern about the potential loss of character due to tall building proposals. The latter was in part due to the perception that tall buildings were alien to Norway, and that they "represented a unique threat to Norwegian culture"[9].

Firstly, the strategy defined tall buildings as those of over twelve storeys. Secondly, it suggested a number of nodes around which tall buildings should be encouraged. It was felt that these nodes would provide enough space for tall buildings, whilst enhancing the city's natural form and topography (see Figure 8.6). A number of nodes were promoted through the document along Ring Road 1 immediately to the north of the city centre, at Bjørvika on the waterfront, and at a number of trans-port nodes in the wider city (Lysaker, Skøyen, Majorstuen, Ensjø, Bryn, Nydalen, Forkningsparken, Storo and Økern). The strategy sought to characterise the city with respect to tall building impacts, recognising where the landscape could successfully

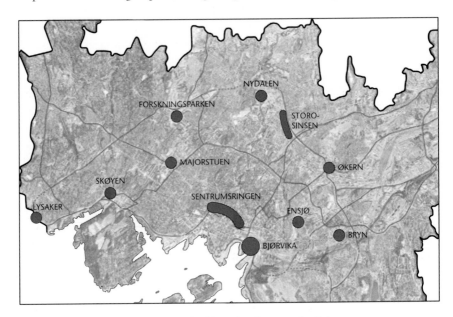

FIGURE 8.6 Proposed nodes for tall building development in Oslo

accommodate tall buildings. In 2003, the draft policy was taken by the Commissioner for Urban Development and her department to the City Council, but it was voted down on the bases that it was overly accommodating to tall buildings, the character of Oslo would be adversely affected by the strategy and the public had not had sufficient opportunity to comment on it (Herbjørnsrud, 2004).

In the original tall building strategy, buildings of 25 storeys or more were proposed in Bjørvika. The people of Riksantikvaren were so "horrified"[10] by this proposal that they visualised what the tall buildings might look like, forwarding these visualisations to the City Government (who, it must be remembered, have a duty to consider third party proposals for development) and making them available to the wider public. The City Government promptly placed a ceiling of twelve storeys on development in the area, as a result of this public concern. However, as it became clear that a certain amount of floorspace was required to pay for the clean up of the site and the proposed services, the Commissioner for Urban Development altered this ceiling to a maximum of nineteen storeys.

In response to further concern being expressed by Riksantikvaren, and the public more generally, the Commissioner of Urban Development produced a position paper in 2005 entitled *Høyhus i Oslo – strategi for videre arbeid* (Tall Buildings in Oslo – A Strategy for Further Work) (OK, 2005). The paper sought both to summarise the policy situation in relation to tall buildings and to propose a new strategy. The new strategy sought to limit the building height of buildings across the city to under 42 metres (in other words, to twelve storeys), except in Bjørvika. Within Bjørvika, buildings of over twelve storeys could be allowed, subject to specific development proposals being approved. In particular, the Commissioner and her department wanted to create a skyline of varied height in this location, to reflect the city's international importance. Bjørvika was exempt from the twelve-storey limit, precisely because of its national and international significance to Oslo and Norway. Furthermore, the Commissioner for Urban Development, City Government and Council, and Oslo Teknopol had "invested so much . . . time and money over the last 10 years into realising the potential of the area that it had to continue to attract large amounts of development"[11]. Indeed, as a major landowner and shareholder in the development of Bjørvika, it was crucial for Oslo Kommune to continue to see the area as a development site of national importance.

The evolution of a planning framework for the Bjørvika area has reflected the weakness of planning documents in Norway, which contain frameworks that are subject to influence by politicians and developers. As a result, whilst the plans for the Bjørvika site were required to recognise the impact of development on the built heritage, in effect the "architect-dominated Agency for Planning and Building, along with the Commissioner for Urban Development, was able to mould the detail of the plan away from the public eye and propose a number of tall buildings which had explicitly been rejected by the City Council in responding to the proposed tall building strategy in 2003"[12]. In this way, the Commissioner and her department were able to maintain the amount of development in Bjørvika. The planning framework for the Bjørvika plan therefore reflects that the acceptance of tall buildings in the area has evolved into a so-called gentlemen's agreement between developers and the City Government.

Tall buildings and the character of Oslo

Agreement about the key historic environment issues in the redevelopment of Bjørvika were made at an early stage (in 2002) between the Directorate of Cultural Heritage, the Urban Conservation Office, the Agency for Planning and Building, and the Commissioner for Urban Development (OK, 2003). The key issues were: the loss of historic monuments and sites; the loss of archaeological material, both on land and in the sea; the potential for development to impede legibility in the area, specifically the sight lines between the medieval elements of the city (Gamlebyen, Ladegård, Akershus Castle and Fortress and Hovedøya); the potential for the city's skyline to be dominated by new tall buildings; and creating new dominant focal points within the cityscape, which might deflect attention from the historic structure of the townscape. Whilst it was on public record that the focus of the development was the re-use of a derelict part of the city, and the reconnection of the east end with the sea and waterfront, the reintegration of Gamlebyen (the medieval town) into the fabric of the city was seen as the most important goal of development for both Rikantikvaren and Byantikvaren (Langset, 2005).

A number of views regarding conservation in the city were played out during the discussions around the development of Bjørvika. Firstly, it would appear that the Agency of Planning and Building, dominated by architects and architect–planners, adheres to an essentially consumerist view of the heritage; namely, that the built heritage is a commodity to be exploited wherever there is economic value to be realised and to be discarded if there is none. The Commissioner for Urban Development, whilst positive about the character of Oslo and the elements that constitute the historic city, was interested in her own legacy for the city – through promotion of the Bjørvika development and attracting as much physical development to Oslo as possible[13]. Furthermore, Byantikvaren, as part of the Comissioner's department, supports contemporary development solutions for sites such as Bjørvika, whilst recognising the built heritage context. Riksantikvaren, however, was particularly concerned to ensure that the maximum possible benefit accrued for the built heritage, given the opportunities that the development of Bjørvika provided for its enhancement. As such, the development of Bjørvika as a site of national importance had a number of detractors, regarding the approach to setting the planning framework and the future physical form of the area. It would seem, therefore, that the national imperative for development at Bjørvika overrode concerns about impacts of development on the built heritage elements of the city.

Discussions related to the approval of the new national opera house, the evolution of the Bjørvika plan, and the nature of the built heritage issues. The actual impact of tall buildings at Bjørvika on the city have largely been ignored by the decision-makers and civil servants in the City Government. A number of organisations have attempted to clarify, via representations to the City Council, what impacts tall buildings could have on both the broad character of Oslo and (more specifically) on Gamlebyen (Riksantikvaren, Byantikvaren and Stiftelsen Byens Forenyelse, for example). These impacts have largely been ignored, both within the Agency for Planning and Building and by the Commissioner for Urban Development; this is due to the need to maintain a minimum development footprint in order to clean the site, provide its infrastructure and pay for public realm works, as well as maximise returns on a constrained site. The visualisations produced by Riksantikvaren and Stiftelsen Byens Forenyelse were created based upon discussions that officers had had with the City Government, potential developers and site owners about how potential development might be constructed on site. In the absence of any attempt to visualise what Bjørvika might look like in the future, the Agency for Planning and Building utilised visualisations for its own purposes. Riksantikvaren provided these at public forums, so that the possibility of a cluster of tall buildings at Bjørvika could be discussed more widely. That the visualisations may represent a potential worst case scenario, in terms of the number and height of tall buildings, did not appear to concern the planners in the City Government. This was taken by third parties to mean that they are relatively accurate, at least in terms of the density, height and number of tall buildings.

   The impact of tall buildings on the character of the city does not seem to have been of over-riding concern to the city government in its discussions about possible tall buildings. Indeed, the city government's main concern relates to its desire to stop a wall of tall buildings arising, through selective use of variety in building height in the area. This is opposed to limiting building height, per se, which would add interest to Oslo's skyline. Figure 8.7 shows how the Post Tower and Radisson Hotel

FIGURE 8.7 Existing tall building blocking views between the water and hills

Tower currently block views to the north from the Bjørvika area; it does not take much of an imagination to envisage further tall buildings blocking this view entirely.

The potential for tall buildings at Bjørvika to block views of the sea and fjord from the north and east, the potential to worsen rather than improve vistas and sightlines between the medieval elements of Oslo, and the potential to destroy the historic sight lines between the Royal Palace and Gamlebyen along Karl Johans Gate, were all omitted from the planning document for Bjørvika. Interestingly, whilst the Commissioner has stated that, "the city is viewed from both the hills towards the fjord and towards the hill; development is approved with this in mind. We do not want to block the views either way"[14], it is clear that arguments about aesthetic considerations were (and still are) subsumed into wider debates about economic growth: the stated imperative of the Conservative-led City Government and City Council.

The vision for the development of the Bjørvika area will see all development completed within approximately fifteen years. As specific applications for planning permission are advanced in Bjørvika (such as the 36-storey Moderne Arkitektur og Design AS designed tower and the twelve-storey PricewaterhouseCooper building), there will be a clearer idea of whether tall building proposals are assessed in relation to heritage concerns, or whether the framework provided through the area plan sterilises such a debate. Despite general concern in Norway that there may be a lull in economic activity over the coming years, the development of Bjørvika remains of national importance to Oslo and Norway. However, the city's population views tall buildings as essentially elitist and un-Norwegian, and is generally concerned about development in Bjørvika, as expressed in the columns of the local and national papers.

Conclusions

The impact of a pro-growth agenda in Oslo on planning for tall buildings is particularly apparent. The architect-led planning regime sees physical growth as a way of promoting the city's image across the world, and of absorbing enough development to continue Oslo's economic boom. The resultant tensions within the local conservation regime is therefore significant; the impact of potential tall building proposals on the character of the city as a whole, as well as specific built heritage designations, is a particular feature. The ability of local conservation frameworks to address the issues raised by the encouragement of tall buildings is interesting. The political will exerted to promote Bjørvika was in direct opposition to the concern of a number of organisations regarding the impact of tall buildings in this location on the fabric of the city, and on the medieval remains in particular. This was despite the Bjørvika development providing much needed money to create a medieval park on the ruins of Gamlebyen. As such, the impact of the development area on the character of the city of Oslo as a whole is crucial.

Emerging regulatory frameworks to assess tall building proposals are in evidence in the city. The pro-growth agenda of the City Government is expressed through a draft tall building policy which was voted down by the City Council as being too pro-tall building. The Commissioner for Urban Development was, however, able to make an executive direction to promote tall buildings at Bjørvika, in defiance of the wishes of the Council and population at large. The Bjørvika land use plan was drafted to assist decision-makers in the assessment of particular proposals.

An essentially modernist view of development, planning and conservation is apparent in the debate about tall buildings in Bjørvika, and this is keenly felt by those working in the conservation realm. The desire for an insular Norway to embrace modernity through the adoption of internationalist symbols of development, i.e. tall buildings, is seen as representing some sort of societal progress by its politicians. As such, the built heritage is viewed as culturally recessive and part of the problem of the past, rather than part of the solution for the future development of the city, or indeed as a positive tool to manage change in the built environment.

Furthermore, the ability to present alternative proposals to the City Government is enshrined in Norwegian planning law, yet the Commissioner for Urban Development appears to over-ride any possible dissention from her view for the future of Bjørvika. This reflects wider concerns in Norway about the status of such representations in the planning process, particularly when so much power rests in the hands of Commissioners. Indeed, the perceived privatisation of the skyline through the master planning of Bjørvika appears to be at odds with the Norwegian sense of social justice and egalitarianism.

9

TALL BUILDINGS IN DUBLIN: PROPERTY-LED REGENERATION WITHIN AN EVOLVING CONSERVATION PLANNING FRAMEWORK

In June 2005, An Bord Pleanála, the Irish Planning Appeals Board, approved the Heuston Gate Tower planning application after it was appealed by a number of heritage organisations. This 32-storey tower, which would be the tallest in Ireland, was part of a building boom taking place within the country, fuelled by the "Celtic Tiger" economy, which came to an abrupt end in 2008 due to the global financial crisis. Up to 2008, the fifteen years prior to the recession had seen Ireland transform from a predominantly low wage agrarian economy into one of the richest countries in Europe. This was mainly due to huge levels of investment from the European Union under Objective 1 status, and to the adoption of the Euro in Ireland, which released massive amounts of capital into the economy (McDonald and Nix, 2005). The Heuston Gate Tower proposals galvanised heritage organisations into seeking a wider debate about the need for tall buildings in the city, both to combat sprawl across the Irish countryside and, more specifically, to lessen the impact of the tower on particular built heritage assets.

The approval of the scheme, first by Dublin City Council (DCC) and then by An Bord Pleanála, reflected attitudes to development in the city, as well as to the status of both planning and protection of built heritage in Ireland. Planning is viewed with cultural mistrust, mainly "as a result of the lack of need for planning during the decades of emigration and economic stagnation"[1]. During the late 1990s and early 2000s, the huge amount of capital flowing into the country, pressure for land (particularly for residential development), and large-scale immigration contributed to a sense of siege amongst the built heritage community. Decisions about tall buildings in Dublin therefore took place within a context of significant physical transformation in the fabric of the city. This presented a particular challenge regarding protection of the city's built heritage, whilst continuing to enable growth and change. The ongoing economic recession has allowed some reflection on changes to the character of the city from new development.

Context for development in Dublin

Dublin is the capital city of the Republic of Ireland, and lies on the eastern coast facing the Irish Sea. It has a population of 506,000, located within a wider region of over 1.6 million (approximately 38% of the Republic's population)[2]. The population has seen rapid growth, mainly as a result of migration from the smaller towns and cities of Ireland, as well as from the European Union (particularly the recent eastern European accession countries) and further afield. Indeed, the country's population passed four million for the first time since 1871, and is projected to reach five million by 2020[3]. Dublin is a vibrant city region that has been the powerhouse of the Irish economy, the so-called "Celtic Tiger", and is Ireland's gateway to the global economy[4]. It has attracted the majority of economic investment in the country, the majority of jobs created and, as a result, the lion's share of development (McDonald and Nix, 2005). As a result, the city is experiencing huge pressure to build, particularly in the re-use of brownfield land and specific built heritage elements which are at risk from demolition (McWilliams, 2005). In more recent times, the country has witnessed a GDP decline of 21% between 2007 and 2010 (Lane, 2011). The effects of this financial crisis and the contraction of the Irish economy have been particularly felt in the city, where cranes stand still, half-built properties are abandoned, and there is a palpable sense of inactivity (Waldron, 2011).

The city lies at the mouth of the River Liffey, and extends across the plains of Leinster, bounded by the Wicklow Mountains to the south and the coastline to the east. Dublin is one of the oldest capitals in Europe, outside the orbit of the Roman Empire (McDonald and Nix, 2005). It is approximately 1,000 years old, and developed as a Norse trading station during the tenth and eleventh centuries. This Norse–Viking city fused with the surrounding Gaelic culture, creating a Hiberno–Norse city until the late twelfth century. During the medieval period, Dublin grew steadily but it was not until the sixteenth century that the city physically expanded to the south and north, mainly as a result of the "invitation" of protestant merchants from England. The subsequent plantation of Ireland by the English and Scots led to the Pale of Settlement, where native Irish rights were curtailed in favour of the protestant Anglo–Irish; much of the Dublin that survives to this day dates from this period, particularly the seventeenth and eighteenth centuries, although significant buildings from earlier periods survive (such as Christchurch and St. Patrick's Cathedral, for example). The physical legacy of this period is a relatively homogenous central area, with buildings that are between four and eight storeys high. The famine of the mid-nineteenth century and the subsequent drop in population through death and emigration led to stagnation in the Irish economy for a significant period. A bitter battle for political independence, culminating in the 1916 Easter Rising, resulted in a significant portion of the city (particularly around O'Connell Street, on the northern side of the city), being destroyed by British forces. Following Irish independence, and the partitioning of the island into the Irish Free State and Northern Ireland in 1921, relations with Britain remained strained and the economy suffered as a result of a lack of investment and the emigration of its young and talented; as such, little building took place in the city until after the Second World War. Even after the war, development was often piecemeal, and lacked a planning context for decision-making (McGuirk, 2000). Central Dublin lost a staggering 52% of its population to suburbanisation and emigration, between 1961 and 1995 (McGuirk, 2000).

It has been argued that Dublin is a city of "quite exceptional character and beauty" (Bor, 1967: 2). It can be characterised mainly by its eighteenth and nineteenth century attributes, in the inner city at least; these include tightly woven streets, using consistent materials, scale and form, which are from the Georgian period in the main, but also take elements from the Victorian period. The predominant part of the fabric of the city from this period has survived mainly as a result of neglect and lack of economic activity during the twentieth century.

The city is a predominantly medium-rise city, with buildings that mainly range between four and eight storeys – this is relatively tall, compared to other cities in Ireland and Britain (see Figure 9.1). The city is built along the River Liffey which forms the main backbone of the modern city, fanning out to the north, west and east. The city gently rises from the central area to the west, providing wide panoramas of the city from the west. The skyline, particularly from the west, can be characterised by its generally medium-rise nature, although a number of key historic (and more recent) buildings punctuate it at regular intervals. To the east of the central area lies the Docklands which is experiencing a large amount of development,

FIGURE 9.1 Buildings on Henrietta Street

mainly office and residential, spurred on by a well controlled development plan framework, implemented by Dublin Docklands Development Authority and DCC. The planning of the Docklands area was DCC's first attempt at comprehensive planning on a significant scale for economic growth and, as such, had the political will from the state, business and the local population for implementation. Whilst the framework for development suggested development at between four and eight storeys (reflecting the character of the wider city centre), a number of taller buildings are coming forward in this area, with the Anglo–Irish Bank cluster the only ones built to date (see Figure 9.2). These towers, whilst not particularly tall at thirteen storeys, are significantly tall to attract concern from some heritage bodies about the development of the Docklands, although others were happy that particular tall building nodes were forming outside the historic core of the city. To the west of the city core, Phoenix Park represents the largest urban park in the world, twelve times the size of Hyde Park in London.

At present, approximately ten buildings deemed tall (over 40 metres or 11–12 storeys) by DCC have been built in the central city. These range from the Spire, a piece of art rather than a building, which was built to celebrate the millennium and is, at 120 metres, the tallest structure in Ireland, to the main churches and cathedrals in the city. George's Quay House (at 59 metres), O'Connell Bridge House (at 42 metres), and Liberty Hall (at 58 metres and built in 1965) are the only tall buildings from the post-war period in the central core of the city. A further six buildings were erected in peripheral housing estates, but three of these (in Ballymun) were being demolished in 2005.

Concern about the character of the city is currently an important topic in discourses around planning in Dublin. Up to the early 1990s, McGuirk suggests that

FIGURE 9.2 Looking east towards Docklands from the Four Courts

the local planning regime in the city was viewed as being cumbersome and ineffective by central government and developers, meaning that there was an inability to plan effectively for growth in jobs and economic opportunity, and to stem the out-flow of the population (2000). Indeed, it can be characterised by being "overly bureaucratic, with decision-making about planning applications not reflecting any adopted strategies"[5]. There is a suggestion that increasing restriction upon the role of planning within the city occurred during this period, mainly as a result of the Irish tradition of viewing planning as purely development regulation, rather than being a spatial activity (McGuirk, 2000). Furthermore, there is a traditional view of planners as advisors to government, with little power to influence decision-making. In addition, the Irish Constitution's guarantee of private property rights has contributed to a culture of mistrust around planning as being weak, ineffectual and a waste of time (McWilliams, 2005). Table 9.1 outlines the administrative and institutional framework for planning in Ireland, which is useful in understanding the dynamics of the development process in Dublin. In particular, it reflects two main

TABLE 9.1 Administrative and institutional context for planning and conservation in Ireland

Area of interest	Detail
Background	Parliamentary republic. Approximately 4.2 million.
Government	Multi-party democracy run through the Oireachtas; made up of Uachtaráin (President) and a bicameral parliament made up of Dáil Éireann and Seanad Éireann. Three levels of government; national, 29 counties and local authorities made up of five city councils, five borough councils and 49 town councils.
Planning	Department of Environment, Heritage and Local Government (DEHLG) responsible for setting national spatial strategy and development plan, protecting sites of heritage interest and value. Development plan main public statement of planning policies. Sets out land use, amenity and development objectives and policies over six years. Applicant and/or any person who has made a submission on a planning application may appeal a planning decision to An Bord Pleanála.
Conservation	National Monuments Act 1930 set up national Sites and Monuments Record (SMR). NM is building or structure which is of national importance and is recorded at the county as well as national level; approximately 800. Protected Structures (PS) introduced by Local Government (Planning and Development) Act 1999; structure of special interest from an architectural, historical, archaeological, artistic, scientific, social or technical point of view. In Dublin there are approximately 9,000 PSs. Architectural Conservation Area (ACA) which is place, area, group of structures or townscape that is of special architectural, historical or archaeological interest or one that contributes to the appreciation of a protected structure.

elements: the current planning and conservation planning framework in Ireland is in its infancy, and is an attempt to improve the role of spatial planning in managing change; and whilst the three tiers of Irish government have powers and responsibilities under the new planning system, DCC has a significant amount of power in decision-making.

McGuirk suggests that the introduction of the Urban Renewal Act in 1986 – the first attempt in Ireland at comprehensive regeneration, which sought to address derelict urban areas such as Temple Bar in social and economic terms through property incentives for regeneration – confirmed views of planners and the role of planning as "emasculated" (2000: 655). In other words, planners and planning were relegated to an advisory role, whilst the property sector led the regeneration agenda. The success of regeneration schemes such as Temple Bar have "confirmed people's views of planning as superfluous and ineffectual"[6], particularly as the regeneration of the area led to the wholescale removal of much of the built heritage of the area, leading to a re-evaluation of the importance of built heritage in the regeneration of the city (McGuirk, 2000).

Conservation planning is in its infancy in Ireland, although recent times have reflected a growing interest and awareness in its benefits to regeneration (Negussie, 2001). Whilst the protection and management of specific sites, structures or buildings does have some history in the country, positive planning for such designations by public authorities has only recently been introduced. Negussie (2001 and 2006) suggests that the conservation system in Ireland can be characterised as inefficient for a number of reasons: there is a dearth of qualified people in the field in Ireland; listing has often related to façades without any detailing of interiors, many of which have subsequently been lost; there are competing priorities for local government, with conservation coming a long way down the list – compared to economic development and tourism, for example. Above all, it is argued that there is insufficient or poor integration between conservation planning, town planning and urban design. The Planning and Development Act 2000 has sought to mimic conservation practice in the UK, by seeking to integrate conservation and planning through a development plan system which would reflect the protection of built heritage in directing development to particular sites and areas, and to set up national and local registers of buildings and areas (called Protected Structures and Architectural Conservation Areas in the Act) (McGuirk, 2000). The new act is designed to plug the perceived gap in conservation planning control, particularly as the state "has had no commitment to the protection of . . . heritage"[7].

The role of developer and development is crucial to understanding the culture of planning in Ireland. The idea that development should proceed in transforming Dublin into a world city is an attractive proposition to politicians in Ireland; after all, it is a small city in a small country, but is the centre of the Irish diaspora across the globe, and it needs to reflect this in its built form. The idea that Ireland must modernise to meet the rigours of the twenty-first century permeated much of the content of the interviews undertaken in Dublin. More specifically, there was a strong feeling that the built environment in Dublin should reflect the city's importance and that Ireland is a modern nation free from the "cultural myopia that has characterised much of the period since independence"[8]. It is argued that debates about tall buildings in the city take place within this context; one of contributing to the modernising of the state, reflecting the diminution of the role of the church and of unfettered development according to the market and the role of central government. The potential for tall buildings to meet the needs for residential, office and leisure space in the future is missing from current debates about the future of the city. The "why not?" approach to discussing tall buildings in the city dominates over the "why?" approach alternative. As such, the planning and conservation planning framework in Ireland can be characterised as weak and subordinate to development interests.

Development in Dublin relies on a number of key actors, who interact in planning and conservation planning processes to reach decisions about particular proposals. In terms of tall buildings, these are DCC, Oifig na nOibreacha Poiblí (Office of Public Works–OPW), the Irish Georgian Society, An Bord Pleanála, An Taisce ("treasury" in Irish), the National Trust, and Dublin Civic Trust. Table 9.2 outlines the roles and purpose of each of these. In addition, it refers to the Friends of Kilmainham, who had a particular interest in the planning application described in the next section.

The role of actors in development in Dublin reflects a historically strong state interest in land development, as a result of a need for the Irish state to have control over economic development from the period when little inward investment was apparent. Oifig na nOibreacha Poiblí, for example, was established in 1831, to oversee public works and the construction of public buildings and facilities. It still performs this function on behalf of the state, and works closely with DCC and developers in realising the potential of many of the sites that it owns or is responsible for. The actors involved in the development processes can also be characterised by a strong heritage interest and lobby, through organisations such as the Irish Georgian Society, Dublin Civic Trust, and An Taisce. The relative power and influence of these organisations reflects, however, the relatively weak status of conservation planning within debates about development, although this has changed as a result of the new legislation[9].

The regulatory framework for tall buildings in Dublin forms the basis against which proposals are assessed by the relevant agencies and departments of government. Table 9.3 summarises the context as at the time of the submission of the Heuston Gate planning application. At the national level, the National Spatial Strategy seeks to create a coherent strategy to integrate land use planning and transport policy over the next twenty years. Furthermore, it seeks the dispersal of government functions and economic development away from Dublin to smaller regional cities, whilst maintaining the importance and significance of Dublin to the Irish economy (Department of the Environment, Heritage and Local Government – DEHLG, 2002). This is taken forward through the Regional Planning Guidelines for the Greater Dublin Area, which interpret the national strategy at regional level. Neither of these strategies explicitly mention tall buildings. The Dublin City Development Plan 2005–2011 specifically mentions tall buildings as potential solu-

TABLE 9.2 Key actors involved in tall building proposals in Dublin

Name	Tier	Focus
Dublin City Council	Local	52 members headed by Lord Mayor. Strategic Policy Committees oversee a range of executive functions including one constituted to look at planning. Committee convenes to reach decisions on planning applications brought by Chief Planner.
Oifig na nOibreacha Poiblí	National	Established in 1831 to oversee public works; in particular, construction of public buildings, roads, bridges and harbours. Managed by executive appointed by Department of the Environment, Heritage and Local Government (DEHLG). In particular OPW is responsible for the management of all national monuments and historic properties.
Irish Georgian Society	National	Founded in 1958; seeks to encourage an interest in country's architectural heritage from all periods through education, grants, public involvement and fundraising. Society submits responses to planning applications.
An Bord Pleanála	National	Reviews planning decisions. Under jurisdiction of DEHLG. Acts as independent review body and hears appeals submitted by either developers or third parties.
Friends of Kilmainham	Local	Independent society made up of public who wish to seek to protect, preserve and proper management of historic Kilmainham Gaol and surrounding area.
An Taisce	National	Statutory consultee under Planning Act. Goal to improve physical environment of country. Comments on development projects which raise questions of national significance.
Dublin Civic Trust	Local	Non-profit making company dedicated to renewal, maintenance and enhancement of Dublin's built heritage. Trust sees itself as champion of built heritage and facilitator for open discussions about future of city.

tions to the city's land supply shortage, and the need to increase densification around public transport nodes. It also recognises the need for tall buildings to be sensitively sited, taking into account built heritage issues (DCC, 2004a). One such site identified in the plan is the site which is the subject of the case study. DCC have also undertaken some further work for particularly important development areas through the publication of area-based strategies. One strategy which is of particular relevance to this case study is the Heuston Gateway Regeneration Strategy which has been adopted by DCC for the purposes of guiding development in the area. The Strategy is a development framework that relates to the Heuston area of the inner city and includes the application site. It is a non-statutory advisory document which sets out an urban design framework for the area as a basis for assisting in decision-making about planning applications. The station is a key focal point for both Dublin and the

TABLE 9.3 Regulatory framework for tall buildings in Dublin

Planning policy	Tier	Tall building mentioned?	Key planning principles	Other comments
National Spatial Strategy (2002)	National	No	Effective integration of land use and transportation policy. Supporting the city region's capacity for innovation. Protecting landscapes.	Set goals and objectives in a spatial context for the coming 12–20 years.
Regional Planning Guidelines for Greater Dublin Area (2003)	Regional	No	Implements the national spatial strategy at regional level.	Confirms Dublin's status but encourages sustainable dispersal to smaller cities in region.
Dublin City Development Plan 2005–2011 (2004)	Local	Yes	Create positive urban design, incorporate building into urban grain and to create positive urban spaces. Outstanding architectural quality and make positive contribution to skyline. Siting should be carefully related to prominent features in vicinity and open spaces. Site must be of appropriate size and context.	Defines relational view of tall buildings. New proposals for tall buildings need to be sensitive to historic city core, specific character areas, NMs and PSs. Detailed criteria for assessment of such proposals will relate directly to DEGW 2000 study.
Heuston Gateway Regeneration Strategy (2004)	Local	Yes	Site could contain up to three tall buildings.	Development framework that relates to Heuston area of inner city. Urban design framework for area as a basis for assisting in decision-making about planning applications.
Managing Intensification and Change: A Strategy for Dublin Building Height (2000)	Local	Yes	Establishes character areas across city. Outlines areas for change which identify extent and speed of change which may or may not be permissible within tall building context.	

whole country and, as such, the development of the area should reinforce this. More specifically, the strategy seeks to create a coherent and vibrant quarter of the city, with high quality services, development, design and public spaces, all of which would consolidate and improve the existing strengths of the area.

In addition to the formal planning framework, DCC commissioned a report from DEGW on the capacity for Dublin to absorb tall buildings. It was published in 2000, and has been crucial to the ongoing debate about the appropriateness of tall buildings in Dublin. DEGW were appointed by DCC to "complement the existing development plan policies and evolve a comprehensive, dynamic policy to capitalise on the potential benefits and effects of high buildings"[10], at a time when a number of tall building proposals were coming forward. The first of any substantial height to be welcomed by DCC has been the Heuston Gate Tower, at 32 storeys.

As such, the rationale of the DEGW report (from the outset) was to find ways of absorbing tall buildings into the fabric of the city in the most appropriate way; it can thereby be characterised as pro-tall building. DEGW worked with DCC in following a methodology which sought to establish character areas across the city, defining the dominant characteristics of each sub-area, and extrapolating where tall building development could effectively be directed; thereby determining where tall buildings could be absorbed with reference to context. The DEGW report indicated areas where change could occur without damaging the character of the city. It identified potential new character areas which would benefit from substantial regeneration, although had contextual constraints and large brownfield sites without such constraints. Within the defined areas which were identified as potential sites for tall buildings, the report suggested locations for intensification and densification, linked to accessibility within the public transport network. Furthermore, the report related this approach to the regulatory framework for planning in the city, in particular suggesting the need for flexibility on behalf of the planning authority, and an increase in resources so that planning could expedite planning decisions for important projects. The report also reflected that there was potential "for real benefits for the city, in terms of planning gain from tall building projects"[11]. Table 9.4 outlines the recommendations contained within the report, which were subsequently adopted by DCC as part of the development plan. More specifically, the report identified the Heuston area as a potential location for tall buildings, subject to the "desire of

TABLE 9.4 DEGW main recommendations for tall buildings in Dublin

Policy guidance does not preclude the possibility of high-rise buildings when appropriate and where they do not compromise the inner-city skyline.

Intensify use within areas of change to reinforce character, increase vitality and provide a continuity of functions.

Allow for high rise at transport nodes.

Recognise role of high rise in signposting important locations in city.

More flexible and quick response to developers suggesting tall buildings.

policy makers and the public", (DEGW, 2000: 15) on three grounds: the proximity to a primary public transport node; a termination point of long views along the Liffey corridor; and, a converging point for road infrastructure.

The status of the DEGW report has formed a particularly important part of discussions about tall buildings in general, and is the subject of this case study in particular. At the time of the publication of the report, the City Council used the document as an informal guide to decision-making, and subsequently adopted the strategy as part of the development plan in 2005, even though no general consultation was undertaken. Detractors have postulated that the strategy "merely reflected the approach that the Council wanted to take, and the production of the report therefore allowed the Council to promote tall buildings in particular locations"[12]. Whatever the basis for the report, it is now an adopted part of the city's regulatory framework for tall buildings.

The Heuston Gate Tower proposal

In 2001, Oifig na nOibreacha Poiblí (known as OPW) commissioned a design team led by Paul Keogh Architects to prepare an application for the site owned by OPW and Eastern Health Shared Services. The site lies to the east of Military Road and south of St. John's Road West in Kilmainham, in the Heuston station area (see Figure 9.3). On 10 February 2004, an application for planning permission was submitted by OPW; Table 9.5 outlines the detail of the application. The 32-storey tower proposal can be characterised by a number of uses, including residential, offices, leisure and cultural facilities. The City Council duly registered the application on 5 October 2004.

The site for the proposed tower lies at the western edge of the city's inner city, and has a total site area of approximately 3.4 hectares. The site is roughly triangular in shape, and is bounded to the north by St. John's Road West and Heuston Station and to the east, Dr. Steevan's Hospital, St, Patrick's Hospital, and the Camac River. To the south there is a modern residential development, currently under construction, and Old Kilmainham village. To the west lies a site which has a number of structures currently undergoing demolition, and beyond that the important landmark buildings of the former Royal Hospital Kilmainham (now the Irish Museum of Modern Art) and Kilmainham Gaol. The area offers good access to Heuston

FIGURE 9.3 The proposed Heuston Gate Tower

TABLE 9.5 Detail of Heuston Gate Tower planning application

Mixed use development including works to two protected structures (Phoenix Deer Park Wall and East Gate Lodge, Royal Hospital Kilmainham) and three historic buildings which are listed in SMR (Doctor's House, Infirmary and Laundry).

Development of 14 buildings ranging from 1 to 32 storeys.

Development will have mix of uses including 197 apartments, offices, museum, health club and other cultural facilities, 19 retail units, two restaurants, public house, childcare facility, educational facility and observation deck in 32-storey building.

Proposed tower will be 124 metres to top of structure with a further 16-metre mast.

Station, the primary train node for services to the west and south of the city, and beyond. Heuston station is also connected to the inner city by the Lúas tram network, making it an important node in terms of accessibility to jobs and services in the city. Itself a Protected Structure, the station dominates the immediate area, along with other landmark buildings (such as the Museum of Modern Art and the gaol). The Heuston Gateway Tower site lies to the south of the Liffey, opposite Phoenix Park which rises to the north-west. The overall feeling is that this site marks an important transition between the densely packed inner city and the wide open spaces of the park and grounds attached to both the museum and gaol.

Contacts between the OPW, Paul Keogh Architects and the City Council were made in the pre-application stage, and mainly related to the broad principles of development on the site. The detail was not addressed, which led to gaps in the information being submitted. The main issues covered the potential impact of the building on: adjoining Architectural Conservation Areas in Kilmainham and Heuston; the Heuston station and Kilmainham Museum Protected Structures; an area of archaeological importance adjacent to the Gaol; and, a national monument (the Gaol). The key issues in the determination of the application were outlined in the Report to the Planning Committee in November 2004 as being: the visual impact of the tower on the surrounding area, and the fabric of the city as a whole; a comparison between the proposed tower and other tall buildings in the city; the conservation of buildings and structures on, or adjacent to, the site; and details of materials and external finishes proposed for the tower, and how these might influence the other three points.

Planning permission was granted for the Heuston Gateway Tower development on 29 November 2004, subject to 31 conditions. The Committee report cited the regenerative benefits of the scheme and the need to modernise Dublin through the built environment as the main issues in granting planning permission (DCC, 2004b). Furthermore, the quality of the building and the works to improve connections between the site and the surrounding area were also cited (DCC, 2004b). As is allowed through Irish planning law, the decision was appealed by the Irish Georgian Society, An Taisce, and Friends of Kilmainham, on 3 January 2005, which An Bord Pleanála duly considered. There were five grounds for appeal cited in the submission: the height of the proposed development; the potential impact of the tower on important views; potential impacts on the setting of protected structures, national monuments and historic areas; the status of the DEGW report, and its relevance to the site; and the historic evolution of Dublin and the current rate of physical change.

In reporting to the appeals board, the Inspector's report listed the issues in the appeal to be: the principle of development, having regard to the policy context; the assessment of the tall building against policy; other impacts on historic buildings on the site; the general design and amenities of the scheme; traffic and access issues; and the assessment of potential impacts contained within the EIA. In particular, the Inspector was concerned about the "status of policy and the regulatory framework used to approve the scheme" (An Bord Pleanála – ABP, 2005: 3). Each of the issues raised by the Inspector was dealt with in the report covering (in the main) the grounds of appeal from the three heritage organisations. Reporting to An Bord Pleanála in April 2005, the Inspector recommended approval of the scheme, but omitting the tall building element of the proposal due to heritage concerns. An Bord Pleanála took this report into account during the subsequent weeks, and decided to dismiss the appeals and, contrary to the advice of the Inspector, grant planning permission as per the original application (i.e. with the tall building). This was issued on 14 June 2005. It would appear that the decision of An Bord Pleanála to ignore the advice of the Inspector and appellants, in favour of the City Council, is relatively uncommon, although when one considers that the proposals were sponsored and drawn up by a body of the state on state-owned lands, and that the interests of the developer are traditionally favoured in Irish land use planning, this is perhaps unsurprising.

The documentation submitted as part of the planning application was in general deemed to be sufficient for the purposes of determination by the planning officers involved, although officers recognised that few buildings had reached the formal planning application stage at this point; therefore, there was a "huge learning curve in determining this application"[13]. The impact of the proposal on Protected Structures, National Monuments and Architectural Conservation Areas was crucial to the discussions held between the applicants, DCC planners and heritage organisations, during the assessment process. Table 9.6 summarises the decision support mechanisms involved. The Visual Assessment undertaken by Paul Keogh Architects sought to visualise the building in its proposed site, in relation to the surrounding cityscape. This visualisation took the form of a number of before and after photos, mock-ups and a model. Figure 9.4 shows a visualisation of the tower from the Liffey. Having submitted an inadequate document in the first instance, the visualisations presented in the document were agreed with the City Council. The document also relates the building to the Dublin skyline, although it does not constitute a cumulative assessment of other proposed or approved developments in the city. The EIA, whilst covering a wide range of topics, also related the proposal to the built heritage assets in the vicinity of the site. It described and commented upon the images provided in the Visual Assessment. In all instances, the building was recognised as impacting on the surrounding cityscape and built heritage assets, but the quality of the building,

FIGURE 9.4 Visualisation of the Heuston Gate Tower from the Liffey

the regenerative benefits of the scheme and the need for a tower in this location were used to justify the proposal.

The City Council consulted widely amongst key organisations, residents' groups, and individuals. However, the resultant debate about the merits of the proposals was mainly played out in the pages of the Irish Times, and amongst concerned heritage professionals. This newspaper has taken a consistently critical stance regarding development in Dublin generally, and regarding this tall building proposal in particular. The debate can, however, be characterised by the general apathy of the public, set within a context of lack of trust in, and respect for, the planning process. Indeed, it was felt by a number of individuals that there was little point in engaging with the City Council, as the applicants were a "state body, and therefore guaranteed [planning] permission"[14]. A number of objections were received by the City Council; heritage organisations, including An Taisce, Friends of Kilmainham and the Irish Georgian Society, as well as members of the public (particularly from Old Kilmainham) expressed deep concern over the impact of the tower on the area, and on the city as a whole. The comprehensiveness of the documentation was acknowledged by many of the objectors, but it was the substance of the arguments rather than the way in which the information was portrayed that became grounds for objection. Table 9.7 summarises the consultation undertaken, and the responses by consultees. As can be seen, the majority of organisations supported the application with specific comments (e.g. local businesses and City Council departments including the conservation section of the planning department), whilst local residents and heritage organisations objected to the proposal.

TABLE 9.6 Summary of decision support mechanisms in Heuston Gateway Tower application

Assessment or study	Submitted	Comments
Characterisation study	■	
Urban Design statement	■	
Planning statement	■	
Tall building Assessment	■	
Heritage Impact statement	■	
Transport study	■	
Housing Market study	■	
Shadow study	□	
Cumulative impact study	□	
EIA/Environment Statement	■	Relates proposal to built heritage assets in vicinity of the site. Describes and comments upon images provided in Visual Assessment; in all instances building is recognised as impacting on surrounding cityscape and built heritage assets but quality of building, regenerative benefits of scheme and need for a tower in this location are used to justify this (O'Sullivan, 2005).
Photo montage (digital or manual renderings)	■	Visual Assessment undertaken by Paul Keogh Architects sought to visualise building in its proposed site in relation to surrounding cityscape. Took form of number of before and after photos and mock-ups. Visualisations presented were agreed with DCC. Relates building to Dublin skyline although does not constitute cumulative assessment of other proposed or approved developments. There are no specific attempts to visualise impact of building on specific heritage assets.
Night time study	■	
GIS model of building/area	□	
Card model of building	□	
Card model of area	□	
CAD model of building	□	
CAD model of area	□	
Archaeological assessment	■	
Options/Alternatives	■	
Bat study	□	

Acoustic study ☐
Strategic Environmental
Assessment (SEA) or
Sustainability Appraisal
(SA) ■

- ■ Submitted as part of planning application
- ☐ Requested by planning authority for planning application to be validated
- ◄ Required as a result of consultation response or objection
- ☐ Not submitted or requested

TABLE 9.7 Formal consultations undertaken for Heuston Gateway Tower planning

Internal consultations	Consulted	Outcome	External consultations	Consulted	Outcome
Conservation/Historic Environment	■	☐	Local airport	■	◄
Environmental Health	■	☐	Garda Síochána	■	◄
Housing	■	☐	An Taisce	■	☐
Operational Services	■	☐	Friends of Kilmainham	■	☐
Traffic and transport	■	☐ and ☐	Irish Georgian Society	■	☐
Members	■	☐	DEHLG	■	☐
Individual residents	■	☐			
Local residents (groups)	■	☐			
Local businesses	■	☐			
Local business individuals	■	☐			

- ■ Consulted by local planning authority
- ☐ Support planning application with comments
- ◄ No comment or response on planning application
- ☐ Object to planning application
- ▣ Not consulted

Assessment of the Heuston Gate Tower proposal

Built heritage issues were a major part of the discussions about the merits of the application from the beginning, and this was reflected throughout the decision-making process. The views of An Taisce, the Irish Georgian Society, and Friends of Kilmainham appeared, however, to be ignored throughout the planning application and appeal processes, as they did not "fit into the view of the report writers or DCC that tall buildings can be absorbed into the urban fabric of the city"[15]. It is apparent that the assessment of the tower proposals reflects the context for planning in the city.

Dublin faces real problems. Prior to the recession, the increase in population and wealth and demands for land and property by an increasing population had created a situation where the fabric of the city needed to be expanded to maintain and improve standards of living and accessibility to jobs and services, in order to sustain growth. DEGW suggested that this could be achieved through an appropriate strategy that involves directing tall buildings to "activity clusters" at transport nodes with development opportunities, and recognising that high buildings have the potential to become landmarks at the local level, even in existing areas of high character. The DEGW report has been adopted as part of the city's development plan, yet there has been widespread concern that there has been little debate about the appropriateness of this strategy (O'Sullivan, 2005; Stirling et al., 2008). In particular, there is concern, from a wide range of people and organisations, about the ability of this strategy to manage proposals which may negatively impact upon the character of the city as a whole, and on individual neighbourhoods in particular.

It is clear, therefore, that planning in Ireland constitutes a complex set of processes where actors are battling over competing visions of the future (McDonald and Nix, 2005). Historically, the country does not have a tradition of effective planning, with the result that in plan-making and development control the status of policy is relatively untested in the Republic. Several commentators have taken a dim view of how regulation of the built environment has been evolving. McDonald and Nix (2005) stress that the Republic is the leader in breaking many EU Directives on the environment, whilst McWilliams (2005) points to the wholehearted embrace of a consumerist way of life that has stemmed from the economic boom. This is reflected in a laissez-faire attitude towards development, with the view that "development is good for Dublin"[16] having much resonance amongst planners.

In the case of the Heuston Tower proposal, the assessment of the proposals by both the City Council and appeal Inspector, all references to the built heritage note the concern of the authorities that the proposal "fails to comply with the requirements of the Development Plan and architectural heritage protections" (Green, 2005: 4). Even though the recommendations of the two parties were different, the decision-makers (in the City Council and An Bord Pleanála) approved the scheme without alteration. This feeds into the afore-mentioned cultural theme of the mistrust dominant in narratives about protection of the built heritage and the role of planning in Ireland. There appears to be almost universal support for tall buildings in locations such as Docklands, where clusters could provide an interesting contemporary focus for this revived part of the city, yet such buildings in the inner city do not attract equivalent support. As such, the reliance on a report commissioned by DCC for attracting and absorbing tall buildings into the fabric of the city feeds into narratives of mistrust (in conservation planning, in particular) and the practice of planning more generally, and hints at the need for consensus in plan-making, for successful futures to be planned effectively. As such, the dominance of a pro-growth agenda in Dublin, political pressure to build tall to sustain the "Celtic Tiger" economy, and the relative weakness of the planning process, suggest that issues related to the character of the city are relegated to a minimal role in decision-making.

However, it does appear that tall buildings are regulated out of the most historically sensitive sites in Dublin (in particular, the city centre), unlike in Oslo, Manchester and Liverpool, for example. The examination of the Heuston Gate Tower proposal indicates that a correct decision was made, in the sense of utilising key sites next to public transport interchanges for high density development. However, the built heritage debates were unsophisticated, and did not reflect the importance of the built heritage designations in the Heuston area. There appears, therefore, to be a need for a robust inclusive debate about the need for Dublin to utilise creative solutions for its land shortage, and for a broad consensus to emerge.

The impact of the global financial crisis upon the Irish economy and upon development projects across the state, has been severe. The Heuston Gate Tower project has been abandoned as the state's finances have contracted. The same is true of other tower proposals across the city, and indeed the country. The property crash and contraction in investment in the city has, at least, allowed pause for thought by policy makers, developers and lobbying organisations. The period since the start of the recession has seen a number of policy initiatives by planners in the city to try and reinforce the planning framework. In 2008, the City Council published a review of the DEGW tall buildings report (which had been published in 2000) which had been open to public consultation. The document reflected upon the appropriateness of the DEGW report, and in particular, its status in the planning process. As a result, the document recognises that the contested nature of the DEGW report had resulted in a lack of clarity for developers and the public, and furthermore, that resources had been taken up at the City Council dealing with ad-hoc pressure for tall building proposals (DCC, 2008). The report suggests, therefore, a revised strategy for height management that combines a criteria-based approach (over-shadowing, microclimate, residential amenity, etc.) with areas of the city where height would or would not be appropriate. This, on paper, would appear to be a more sophisticated and intelligent approach that recognises the intrinsic character of the city. The City remains "committed to the protection of the special character of the city's historic core located within the 'bowl' of the inner city" (DCC, 2008: 13).

The subsequent Dublin City Development Plan 2011–2017 (an interim document subject to consultation; (DCC, 2011) reflects this shift in its proposed policy. The plan seeks to "protect and enhance the intrinsic quality of Dublin as a predominantly low-rise city, and to provide for taller buildings in the designated limited locations" (policy SC17), "to protect and enhance the skyline of the inner city, and to ensure that all proposals for mid-rise and taller buildings make a positive contribution to the urban character of the city" (policy SC18) and "to promote a coordinated approach to the provision of taller buildings through local area plans in order to prevent visual clutter or cumulative negative visual disruption of the skyline" (policy SC19).

Of course it remains to be seen how this enhanced, and on paper stronger, planning policy regime will be implemented. The ongoing financial crisis and recession in Ireland shows no sign of abating. It is unclear, therefore, when the emerging policy regime might be tested to any significant degree. As a result, it is hoped that planning policy will act as a focus for consensus amongst politicians, developers, planners and the public around proposals for new development in the future.

10

TALL BUILDINGS IN NEWCASTLE-UPON-TYNE: RECONCILING THE PAST WITH THE PRESENT[1]?

In 2004 twin planning applications for the erection of a 32-storey tower on Newcastle's Quayside were withdrawn by the developers. The proposals were the latest in a series of tall building proposals across the Tyneside conurbation that had failed to gain planning permission. In Newcastle specifically, consensus over the type of regeneration that is appropriate in the city, together with an active historic building conservation policy, has dominated discussions about tall buildings in the city. Decisions about tall buildings are being made without a specific tall buildings policy, although there is a clear policy background, particularly in terms of a major characterisation of the Tyne Gorge, which was undertaken by a consortium of organisations in the city. This chapter places the tall building proposals rejected in 2004 within the context of rapid regeneration in Newcastle up to the recession from 2008; regeneration which has been centred on landmark iconic projects and a clear characterisation of the existing townscape of the Quayside and wider city.

Context for development in Newcastle

Newcastle lies at the centre of the Tyne and Wear conurbation in England's north-east. The region, which also includes the City of Sunderland, has a population of just less than 1.1 million (ONS, 2003), making it the smallest metropolitan region in England. The region comprises five local authorities, including the City of Newcastle-upon-Tyne which has a population of 274,000 (ONS, 2008). The city has relatively tight boundaries, drawn by the River Tyne to the south and green belt to the north, and includes the commercial centre, inner suburbs and a large expanse of open space, protected by statute, known as the Town Moor. Furthermore, Gateshead to the south is (for all intents and purposes) part of the functioning city, with strong communication and cultural links to the immediate south – although it is separated from Newcastle by the Tyne. Newcastle is increasingly being seen and projected – mainly as a result of the failed City of Culture bid which was a focus for joint working – as one unit with Gateshead to the south, and the two places are treated as one policy unit for many of the government-funded regeneration schemes being run at present. This has placed the Tyne Gorge at the centre of the region's cultural regeneration agenda. Much of the contemporary regeneration and policy literature about the city refers to Newcastle–Gateshead, the combined urban area to the north and south of the Tyne, mainly as a result of efforts by the Newcastle–Gateshead Initiative to market the joint cities for a wide range of tourists and visitors.

Newcastle has been described as "one of the most historically and morpho-logically diverse" of British cities (Buswell, 1984). Newcastle can trace its origins to the Roman occupation, and was one of the most important commercial centres in England from at least 1400 (Pendlebury, 2001). In simple terms, the urban form of the city includes a medieval walled town, overlaid with a planned Georgian new commercial centre (Soult, 2003). Perhaps the feature which most defines the form of the city and the surrounding conurbation is the River Tyne, which forms the boundary between Newcastle and Gateshead, and the gorge which fans out on a number of levels from the river (Buswell, 1984). Views of the river from both cities and from the seven bridges that link them (most of them listed structures) are central to experiencing the composition of the gorge. Furthermore, a number of key land-mark buildings define each of the levels of the gorge; many of these are protected, and some of them are from the post-war period (Figure 10.1). Buswell describes the skyline as exhibiting "melodramatic physical characteristics" (1984: 502). Many of these characteristics, particularly views of the skyline, are only obvious when viewed from outside the administrative boundary of Newcastle – mainly from Gateshead to the south and North Tyneside to the east.

The varied townscape of the city from the medieval, Georgian and Victorian periods has remained largely intact through a number of periods of comprehensive redevelopment – most notably in the 1950s and 1960s, when the leadership of T. Dan Smith and Wilfred Burns set out a vision of the city as a "Brasilia of the north" (Pendlebury, 1999), with all the attributes of a self-consciously modernist city. Key redevelopments in the city included the planning for Eldon Square, a large covered shopping centre built over the Newcastle markets, and a central inner-city motor-way which ploughed north through the city, linking the south with the northern suburbs and beyond. The city's central area did, however, remain largely intact,

FIGURE 10.1 Tyne Gorge

compared to other cities such as Liverpool, Manchester and Birmingham. De-industrialisation and economic decline in the post-war period led to massive out-migration, unemployment and under investment in the city. It also helped to preserve many of the buildings which make Newcastle unique: St Nicholas' Cathedral (dating from the thirteenth and fourteenth centuries), St Anne's Church (dating from 1768), the Vermont hotel (dating from the 1920s), and Earl Grey's Monument (dating from 1838), are all historic structures that survived this period and that retain significant functions in making the city legible. Attempts at wholesale redevelopment, and the demolition and neglect of large numbers of historic buildings in the city centre, spurred a distinctive local conservation regime, which sought to build upon public support for conservation in planning for regeneration. This distinctive regime, what Pendlebury (2001, 1999) calls Newcastle's "conservation community", can be characterised by a number of elements:

1   the evolution of a strong heritage lobby, comprised of conservation bodies, councillors, members of the public and the local media, which reflected a consensus that the built heritage of the city was under threat from neglect, demolition and inappropriate development;

2   the involvement of many local heritage groups in implementing effective conservation strategies and programmes. Organisations such as the North of England Civic Trust (formerly the North East Civic Trust), the Northumberland and Newcastle Society, and the Society for Antiquaries of Newcastle-upon-Tyne (the oldest provincial Antiquarian society), have sought to preserve and enhance the unique historic environment of the city through a range of activities. Such activities have included the restoration of particular buildings, holding seminars and lectures on issues of local importance, research, and report writing. More locally-based organisations, such as the Ouseburn Trust and Jesmond Dene Conservation Area Association, strive to improve the physical environment of their local areas through involvement in decision-making during the determination of applications to the City Council (NCC) for development and community-based activities which seek to raise awareness about the unique attributes of their areas;

3   the importance of key heritage-led regeneration initiatives (particularly in Grainger Town) in raising public consciousness about the benefits of heritage-led regeneration (Wilkinson, 1992); and,

4   the importance with which the City Council, particularly from the 1990s but earlier also, viewed heritage-led regeneration as part of a conscious effort to market the city to visitors and tourists.

Discourses around built heritage in Newcastle, unlike in, say, Manchester, reflect that approaches to conservation are both "inclusive and egalitarian"[2], which in turn reflects consensus in decision-making about particular development projects. This is despite an emphasis on the physical regeneration of the Newcastle region, characterised by a number of key actions since the 1980s:

1   Tyne and Wear Development Corporation (TWDC) was established by central government in 1987, to regenerate the riversides of both the Tyne (Newcastle–Gateshead) and Wear (Sunderland). Its main aims were to accelerate the rate of regeneration in these areas (by increasing confidence and optimism in them), and to increase the marketing of the area – to prospective businesses and visitors alike (Miles, 2005). The work of the TWDC included the refurbishment and conscious commodification of the historic buildings along the Tyne Gorge, and the promotion of new buildings in order to regenerate the city. Working with a diverse range of partners, the corporation achieved a number of tangible changes to the river front in Newcastle and Gateshead, including residential projects such as East Quayside and Royal Quays, riverside pedestrian routes along both banks of the Tyne, and leisure facilities such as the Pitcher and Piano bar development on the north bank of the Tyne.

2   Subsequently, a new phase of river front development has been based around a number of high profile flagship projects, such as the Gateshead Millennium Bridge (opened in 2001), the Sage Gateshead Music Centre (opened in 2004), the Centre for Life (opened in 2000), the Centre for Children's Books (opened in 2005), the Baltic Centre for Contemporary Arts (opened in 2002, see Figure 10.2) and the Grainger Town project (ongoing, see Figure 10.3).

3   Despite being unsuccessful, the process of bidding for the 2008 European City of Culture nomination in the early 2000s galvanised local authorities, local

FIGURE 10.2 Baltic Centre for Contemporary Arts

FIGURE 10.3 Grainger Town

community groups and a wide range of other bodies into realising that the Newcastle–Gateshead riverside was a unique resource, with international standards of attraction. The bid achieved a level of exposure that attracted increasing numbers of visitors from the UK and overseas. It also resulted in increased working between the respective Councils of Newcastle and Gateshead, which went some way towards mitigating their historically fraught relationship (NCC, 2000). The subsequent evolution of "NewcastleGateshead", even as just a label rather than as a reality, has therefore attracted a number of benefits to the city region, particularly in tourism terms.

4   Newcastle published its *Going for Growth* regeneration strategy in 2000, which sought to: create a competitive, cohesive and cosmopolitan city of international significance; work in partnership with citizens, communities, companies and government; and, ensure that all parts of the City benefit from economic growth (NCC, 2006). This strategy, whilst having been criticised for being "too gung-ho"[3], has resulted in a physically transformed city which "recognises the importance and value of the built heritage, whilst attracting high profile new development projects"[4].

Newcastle's built heritage reflects a long span of growth. There are approximately 1,730 Listed Buildings; a huge number, given the city's size compared to Liverpool, Manchester and Birmingham. Of these, 127 are Grade I and 196 are Grade II★. Furthermore, there are 11 Conservation Areas and 14 Scheduled Ancient Monuments (SAMs) in the city (EH, 2005). There are seven entries on the national register of parks and gardens in Newcastle. Part of the Hadrian's Wall World Heritage Site lies within the boundary of Newcastle; this designation offers no further protection, although the elements within the city are on the list of SAMs.

A number of tall buildings were developed in the post-war period, which impact upon the Tyne Gorge skyline. At present, several of these buildings are being refurbished through creative re-cladding. Australia House/Swan House (from 1968), the former British Telecommunication building, has been redesigned as luxury apartments with a health spa and bar (and renamed 55 Degrees North) and the 18-storey Cale Cross House (from 1969) opposite the Tyne Bridge has had some internal reordering and has been re-clad in silver. The multi-storey car park in Gateshead (from 1969), popularised in the film "Get Carter", which dominates the skyline of this side of the Tyne, was demolished in summer 2010, due to the expanding area of regeneration along the south bank of the Tyne.

More recently, five tall building proposals have reached the stage of going through the planning process in Newcastle (all of which have been withdrawn). One building of 16-storeys has been constructed to the rear of the Baltic Arts Centre in Gateshead. All of the buildings proposed have been either entirely residential, or residential with a small amount of retail use. It is somewhat surprising that the level of tall building is significantly below the volume of other large regional cities; heritage organisations and the City Council view this as a reflection of the strength that heritage plays in decision-making about development, whereas others see it more as a reflection of the weakness of the economy, and lower land values, in the north east. The idea that there is a consensus over the built heritage in Newcastle is reflected in policy and guidance documents, as well as in decision-making about particular proposals, with the result that inappropriate development proposals appear to be regulated out of the townscape.

Decisions about development in Newcastle rely on a number of key actors, who interact in informal and formal planning processes. These include the City Council, local communities, businesses, government and its agencies, statutory bodies and non-statutory pressure groups. In the context of the Northern Light Tower planning application, a number of groups were involved in the planning process: Newcastle City Council, Gateshead Metropolitan Borough Council, CABE, EH, Ouseburn Trust and Nathaniel Lichfield and Partners (NLP) on behalf of the developers, Wimpey Homes. Table 10.1 outlines the purpose of each of these. Newcastle's local conservation planning regime can, in summary, be characterised by a number of distinct elements which permeate the ways in which these bodies interact: consensus about what is of value to the townscape; consensus about what is particularly sensitive to change in the townscape; the role of new development in complementing the existing built heritage; and the role of new development in positively improving the townscape in particular places[5].

TABLE 10.1 Key actors involved in tall building proposals in Newcastle–Gateshead

Name	Tier	Focus
Newcastle City Council	Local	Planning within Department of Environment, Enterprise and Culture within Regeneration Directorate.
		Conservation Area Advisory Panel made up of representatives from amenity, professional and community bodies at local, regional and national level and provides specialist advice and local knowledge to City Council to assist it in determination of planning and other applications affecting Listed Buildings and Conservation Areas.
		Complements City Council's *Conservation Advisory Committee*, a quarterly committee dealing with conservation policy, projects and strategic matters.
		City centre Panel comprises personnel drawn from City centre Development Group which manages development of key sites in the City centre.
Gateshead Metropolitan Borough Council (GMBC)		Planning lies within Planning and Environmental Strategy Service within Directorate of Development and Enterprise.
		Conservation advice is given to other parts of the Council, developers and members of the public through this service.
		Tyne and Wear Specialist Conservation Team assists Gateshead in providing high quality advice to these groups.
CABE	National–regional	Of ten projects that have been reviewed in north-east region since their founding in 2000, two have been in Newcastle and one in Gateshead. One of these relates to the Northern Light proposal.
EH	National–regional	In Newcastle the north-east regional office carries out this function under the leadership of the Director of Planning and Development North.
Ouseburn Trust	Local	Registered charity and development trust founded in 1996 through efforts of local activists to recognise unique character of Ouseburn Valley.
		Aims to preserve heritage of valley and support sustainable development in it.

The regulatory framework forms the basis against which tall building proposals are assessed; these are summarised in Table 10.2. In summary, whilst a tall buildings policy for the city was yet to be commenced at the time of this study, a framework for their assessment was provided by a range of documents which attracted the support of the afore-mentioned key actors. The non-statutory characterisation study outlined, in particular, how the built heritage contributes to Newcastle's distinctive form, and how development can either improve or detract from the existing townscape.

TABLE 10.2 Regulatory framework for tall building proposals in Newcastle–Gateshead

Planning policy	Level	Tall buildings mentioned?	Key planning principles	Other comments
Regional Planning Guidance for the North East (RPG11) June 2002 (now RSS)	Regional	No	Growth in region be managed according to four main themes: to deliver economic prosperity and growth; to create sustainable communities; to conserve, enhance and capitalise on region's diverse environment, heritage and culture.	
Newcastle Plan (1998)	Local	No	SD02 seeks to protect city's natural and built heritage assets. EN02 identifies number of strategic approaches to city which it seeks to enhance by encouraging imaginative and high quality design on important sites and avoidance of developments which would harm views of historic buildings, skyline or other distinctive landmarks. Quayside regeneration area under Policy ED02 encourages regeneration of underused sites.	Document is currently in draft form and endorses previous approach of Plan in seeking to protect skyline of city, individual landmark buildings and a design quality agenda and asks whether these should be carried forward under the new regime.
Lower Ouseburn Urban Design Framework (2004)	Local	No	Principles include: larger structures and large development footprints should be avoided; there should be a legible river frontage and access to	Appendix to the Conservation Area Management Plan for the Lower Ouseburn Valley.

riverside walkway defined by public uses; and, new development should be of high quality.

Quayside Master Plan (Farrell and Partners, 1991)	Local	No	Envisages mixed use area incorporating residential, offices and leisure uses – application site forming end of Quayside.	City Council used master plan as guide to decision-making process not adopted.
Tall Buildings Discussion Paper (NCC) (2005)	Local	Yes	Relate mainly to need to ensure that tall buildings are appropriately located, that they assist in meeting regeneration goals and are of high design quality.	Not formally adopted by 2005 Consultees both supported and objected; supporters suggested that it was excellent starting point for a comprehensive discussion; detractors felt that document assumes that tall buildings can be appropriate and that paper should be rewritten to be more critical. Currently under review.
Tyne Gorge Study (Land Use Consultants (LUC), Gateshead MBC, NCC, EH, CABE, 2003)	Local	Yes	Study recognised sensitivity of particular view corridors: panoramic; contained/broad perspective; surprise; unfolding; and terminated vistas. Importance of views, topography, setting, bridges nd key monuments.	Charts view cones for each of views.

Adopted by Gateshead MBC; NCC had not adopted it by 2005.

The Northern Light Tower

The twin applications for the Northern Light Tower were submitted in two stages (see Table 10.3). This section covers the issues involved in the second of the two applications (Figures 10.4 and 10.5 show some of the visualisations of the proposed tower).

The site (see Figure 10.6) lies at the confluence of the Rivers Tyne and Ouseburn, in Newcastle. It is partly taken up with a water pumping station that is owned by Northumbrian Water; it is also partly within the Ouseburn Conservation Area. The site is split into two parcels of land by Quayside Road, the northern boundary being formed by Glasshouse Bridge. The Ouseburn Valley runs from the east of the site northwards; it is steep, with wooded slopes. The mouth of the Ouseburn, immediately to the east, is a harbour for many fishing boats allied to the St Ann's and St Lawrence quays. To the south lies the River Tyne, and to the west the land gradually rises to the north immediately adjacent to the site. The surrounding area reflects a mixture of uses, with new residential buildings adjacent to the site along the Tyne to the east and west, lower rise residential buildings along the Ouseburn to the north, and open space along the Ouseburn Valley.

The Development Control Section of NCC were responsible for assessing the Tower proposal. The revised application constituted the following elements: planning application forms and relevant certificates; detailed plans; Design Statement; Planning Statement; Transportation Assessment Report; and, Environmental Statement (ES) – comprising a non-technical summary, the statement itself, and a book of photo montages.

TABLE 10.3 Northern Light Tower planning applications

Application	Detail
2001/2133/01//DET (September 2001)	Erection of a 32-storey building for residential use comprising 154 dwellings, including parking for 158 cars at ground, first and second floors, unit for retail use (Class A1) or bar/restaurant use (Class A3) at ground floor, creation of a landscaped public space, relocation of existing pumping station, formation of new access and ancillary accommodation.
	Application remained undetermined during the following 3 years.
2004/0010/01/DET (March 2004)	Wimpey Homes decided to submit an identical application but utilised NLP and submitted far more comprehensive supporting information – approach would both allay previous concerns of NCC and make sure applicant had a number of options should applications remain undetermined.
	On 27th July 2004 both applications withdrawn.

Using the CABE–EH guidance as a base, NLP commissioned and undertook comprehensive documentation to accompany the planning application, with the understanding and consent of the City Council. The discussions which took place as part of the original planning application (2001/2133/01/DET) were referred to as pre-application discussions by the City Council, and were therefore directly

FIGURE 10.4 Proposed Northern Light Tower from the east

FIGURE 10.5 View of proposed Northern Light Tower location from the west

FIGURE 10.6 Site of the Northern Light Tower looking west

relevant to the determination of the later application. The main issues involved were not documented in any comprehensive way by the City Council, due to the application being withdrawn. A picture of the relevant issues was, however, compiled by interviewing key actors involved with the application. Table 10.4 outlines the issues.

Table 10.5 outlines the methods used in the submitted documentation for assessing the impact of the tower on Newcastle's built heritage. Again, these can be characterised by their comprehensiveness and reflected the importance of built heritage issues to the determination of the planning application.

TABLE 10.4 Issues in the determination of the Northern Light Tower planning application

i) Impact upon the Ouseburn Conservation Area.
ii) Impact upon the setting of the Grade II★ listed Ouseburn School.
iii) Development would affect the setting of the Tyne Gorge – Grade II listed Tyne Bridge, Scheduled and Grade I listed Swing Bridge and the Grade I High Level Bridge as well as the Central Conservation Area in Newcastle and Bridges Conservation Area in Gateshead.
iv) Development would affect the wider historical townscapes of Newcastle and Gateshead, and views from and to these.
v) Height, scale and massing of the building in this location.
vi) Public realm, car parking and permeability issues.

TABLE 10.5 Summary of decision support mechanisms in Northern Light Tower planning
         application

Assessment or study	Submitted	Comments
Characterisation study		
Urban Design statement	■	Demonstrates quality of proposal in urban design terms and how proposal related to existing regeneration strategies in city. Relates proposal to other towers in Core Cities.
PPG15 statement		
Planning statement	■	Outlines the planning policy context for determination of the proposal.
Tall building statement		
Traffic study	■	Assessment provided mainly looking at vehicular transport generation rather than the public realm.
Housing Market study		
Shadow study		
Cumulative impact study		
EIA/ Environment Statement	■	
Photo montage (digital or manual renderings)	■	Paper-based photo montages provided from a large number of views.
Night time study	■	Visualisations of the tower at night were provided as part of the photo montages against Tyne Gorge baseline. Comprehensive cumulative impacts of other proposals.
GIS model of building/area	☐	
Card model of building	☐	
Card model of area	☐	
CAD model of building	☐	
CAD model of area	☐	
Archaeological assessment	☐	
Options/Alternatives	☐	
Bat study	☐	
Acoustic study	☐	

KEY
■   Submitted as part of planning application
◻   Requested by planning authority for planning application to be validated
▲   Required as a result of consultation response or objection
☐   Not submitted or requested

Table 10.6 indicates which internal City Council departments, as well as external
bodies, were consulted as part of the planning application. This comprehensive
consultation, a hallmark of NCC, elicited a large number of responses – mainly
objecting to the proposal. EH had major concerns about the proposal, due to the

TABLE 10.6 Consultations undertaken for Northern Light Tower planning application

Internal consultations	Consulted	Outcome	External consultations	Consulted	Outcome
Conservation/Historic Environment	■	□	Local airport/Civil Aviation Authority	■	
Environmental Health	■		Countryside Commission	▣	
Housing	■		Environment Agency	■	
Operational Services	■		English Nature	■	
Traffic and transport	■		Passenger Transport	▣	
Members	■		Police	▣	
Individual residents	■	□	CABE	■	□
Local residents (groups)	■	□	EH	■	□
Local businesses	▣		Georgian Society	▣	
Local business individuals	▣	□	Victorian Society	▣	
City centre Manager	▣		20th Century Society	▣	
Conservation Area Advisory Committee	■	□	Local civic society	■ *	□
Design Review	■		Council for British Archaeology	▣	
			Adjoining local authorities	■	
			Friends of the Earth	▣	
			British Telecom	▣	
			Port of Tyne	▣	
			Nexus	■	
			Northern Electric	■	
			Transco	■	
			Northumbria Water	■	
			British Gas	■	
			Members of Parliament	■	□

■ Consulted by local planning authority
▣ Support planning application with comments
◄ No comment or response on planning application
□ Object to planning application
▣ Not consulted

* four were consulted: Friends of St Ann's, Newcastle and Northumberland Society, North of England Civic Trust and Ouseburn Trust.

impact of the building on the built heritage of the Tyne Gorge. Indeed, even though the proposals were presented in a comprehensive way, EH believed that the assertions stating that impacts would be minimal were misguided, at best[6]. EH had significant misgivings about the proposal, due to the inappropriateness of a building of this height, massing and detail, in this location. The fear of a precedent being set through the approval of such a tower also appears to have been a concern[7].

In determining the second application, Gateshead Council also reiterated its original objections to the first proposal tower on a number of grounds: the Council was concerned about the height of the tower, as a result of the majority of the buildings along the Gorge being between three and six storeys; the feeling was that the Tower would be isolated and dwarf the surrounding area; the consideration of such a Tower in the absence of a tall buildings policy by Newcastle Council prejudges its proper consideration; and it was argued that the Gorge is of international significance and, as such, any development should positively enhance this character, but this proposal was not presented within this context (Cousins, 2004; GMBC, 2002).

In terms of local opposition, a number of parties were involved, forming a coalition determined to protect the "integrity of the . . . [character] . . . of the Gorge"[8]. The local MP for Newcastle Central, Jim Cousins (Labour), was key to coordinating and articulating objections to the proposal and, in a sense, supported the main opposition group, the Ouseburn Trust. Uniquely amongst the tall building cases undertaken for the thesis, an MP was involved, and this is perhaps a reflection of the "importance with which the future of Newcastle–Gateshead is viewed" (Northumberland and Newcastle Society (NNS), 2004) by those in power. The Ouseburn Trust was instrumental in galvanising opposition to the proposal amongst local community groups and professional organisations. It headed a campaign entitled "Northern Blight", which sought to focus concern on the impacts of the proposal on the Tyne Gorge's built heritage. Again, the issue of precedent was of major concern to the local population. Both the Trust and the Northumberland and Newcastle Society recommended in their objections that the City Council reactivate its work on producing a tall buildings policy (NNS, 2004).

Having submitted detailed comments on the original proposal, CABE welcomed the revised proposals, which addressed many of its original concerns: the proposal did not refer to the faults in the original Farrell master plan, which supposed this site would visually "terminate" the Quayside, more specifically, the potential for the site to finish off the Quayside at its easternmost edge was addressed, and CABE appreciated that reference; the relationship to the wider context was not adequately articulated, more specifically, the role of existing tall buildings in the townscape was not analysed; the relationship to transport infrastructure needed to be illustrated; and the relationship between the ground plane and the landscape proposals should have been analysed and illustrated. CABE retained some uneasiness with the proposal, however; mainly as a result of EH's concerns over the impacts of the proposal, and the vocal local opposition to the Tower (CABE, 2002).

Assessment of the Northern Light Tower proposal

Both the planning application from 2001 and that from 2004 (which is the main subject of this chapter) were withdrawn by the applicant. The City Council indicated that if the applications were not withdrawn, they would be refused on the grounds of: impact upon the Tyne Gorge in general terms; the scale, height and massing of the building in relation to the surrounding townscape; and the City Council's intended development of a tall buildings policy in 2005[9].

There are three main areas in the management of this planning application, which are of particular interest: firstly, the quality of supporting information and the treatment of built heritage issues; secondly, the successful mobilisation and campaigning of an anti-tower coalition, in terms of resisting inappropriate tall building development; and finally, questions about the role of iconic buildings in Newcastle–Gateshead's regeneration, in terms of good quality and appropriate architecture and urban design. Each of these areas is discussed in turn, below.

The quality of supporting information and the treatment of built heritage issues, in contrast with the other case studies in Birmingham and Manchester, was acknowledged as being comprehensive, of high quality, and providing a robust background to the proposals. It would appear that, in the absence of a tall buildings policy, both Newcastle and Gateshead Councils have been able to rely on the detailed work undertaken as part of the Tyne Gorge Study, to inform their decision-making in different ways. In particular, Gateshead has produced draft guidance based on the report, whilst Newcastle has used it as a background supporting document in planning decision-making. As such, both the Councils have been able to request specific elements in planning applications, which would assist in the decision-making process, such as the impact of proposals on particular landmark buildings, on view cones, and on character. In other words, the study has provided a framework and a language, both of which can be used to challenge proposals effectively.

Whilst recognising that the supporting information was of a high standard, it is also evident that the documentation (particularly in the ES) was biased in favour of the proposal; whilst this is unsurprising, it was commented on by a number of interviewees, because of the political nature of such documentations,. For instance, the analysis of the impacts of the Tower (in visual terms) on the built heritage of the city was dealt with in an entirely subjective way; in instances where there may be a moderate to high impact on a Listed Building for example, the answer (in the ES) was to say that the quality of the development mitigated these impacts. No justification was provided for these assertions. There is also no evidence that the LPA critically reviewed the ES at any stage; although, after the election of the Liberal Democrat majority Council in May 2004, there appeared to be even less support for tall buildings in the city than under the previous administration.

It is evident that Newcastle is willing and able to resist inappropriate tall building developments in particular locations (in this case in the sensitive Quayside location) when it chooses, despite pressure for growth. The strength of this approach has meant that (in this case) the developers have shied away from challenging the local planning authority by seeking a refusal and appealing, instead seeking a more acceptable development for the site, working in partnership with the City Council. As a result of the many years of work in recognising and protecting the significance and value of the city's built heritage – in many instances, in conjunction with Gateshead – culminating in the production of the LUC report in 2003, Newcastle appears to be in a strong position to resist what it considers to be inappropriate development.

This view is shared by a number of other actors in the city, particularly in the heritage and community sectors. As such, a consensus about the character of the city is strongly evident. It certainly appears that the characterisation of the city as part of the LUC Tyne Gorge Study has assisted in articulating the strong visual identity of Newcastle–Gateshead, to the benefit of decision-making in planning. Cumulatively, therefore, importance is attached to rigorous studies, statutory heritage control, and the power of local heritage organisations, in creating a framework for appropriate development control.

The visual dominance of historic iconic buildings, and of new, high quality iconic architectural interventions in the Tyne Gorge, characterise the new Newcastle–Gateshead (Miles, 2005). Internationally, flagship regeneration projects in the last ten years have sought to reconfigure the image of Newcastle–Gateshead on the world stage (Miles, 2005). In particular, the Quayside (in general), the Baltic Arts Centre, Sage music venue, and Gateshead Millennium Bridge have all attracted a great deal of commentary, focusing attention on the rapid regeneration of the "twin cities". It has been recognised that the development of these good quality architectural icons adds new landmark buildings to those that already dot the valley (LUC et al., 2003). In this sense, these new additions are continuing the local tradition of creating a varied, attractive and "melodramatic landscape" (LUC et al., 2003: 306). Interestingly, the Northern Light Tower was presented by the developers as the next logical stage in the development of an architecturally iconic Newcastle–Gateshead style. However, neither NCC nor Gateshead Council subscribed to this vision; indeed, they viewed the connection of the Northern Light with the success of other regeneration projects as misguided, at best[10]. In particular, the Tower was seen as "clumsy, ugly and featureless"[11], and as representing a departure from the other redevelopment projects which "accentuate the horizontal"[12], and therefore the character, of the Gorge. The tower's verticality, combined with a perception of poor quality design was therefore the reason for withdrawal.

The design of the proposed Tower can be characterised by its height and little else, even though the developers brand the building as "high quality". The assessment of that quality is intrinsically difficult and subjective. Commentators such as Punter suggest that the elusive nature of design quality (Punter, 1999) requires a more sophisticated, efficient, inter-professional, transparent and participatory system of building regulation and control. He further suggests that better controls do not improve design quality in themselves. Instead, initiatives that are designed to promote architectural patronage, to encourage innovative design, architecture and urban design (nationally), and to support genuine environmental consciousness, offer more direct routes to improvements in quality than do mere regulation and control. Certainly, this appears to be the case in Newcastle, where a strong conception of local distinctiveness is reflected in a variety of planning and conservation tools, all of which feed into a desire to see architecture that is both beautiful and thought-provoking. Furthermore, the development of iconic projects in Newcastle–Gateshead has been centred around culture-led projects which, of course, Northern Light does not fit into, as it is a commercial scheme, offering residential and small-scale mixed uses.

The local conservation regime in Newcastle, together with an evolving understanding of the unique attributes of the townscape as a whole (through such studies as the characterisation undertaken by LUC) can go some way to explaining the success that NCC has had in managing tall buildings, with the built heritage as a core concern. This context has provided NCC with a robust and informative basis upon which to make decisions about individual planning applications, and plan effectively for the future. Indeed, Pendlebury (1999) has suggested that, "in mediating conflicts which have arisen, the City Council has had to achieve solutions that can be represented as both conservation and regeneration successes" (p.432).

As part of this approach, the policy basis for tall buildings in the city has continued to evolve from the *Tall Buildings Discussion Paper* (from 2002) into the more recent *Policy and Design Guidance for Tall Buildings in Newcastle*, which was adopted in late 2006. This policy document has taken the discussion paper further, by suggesting explicit assessment criteria on which all tall building proposals will be assessed. Furthermore, tall buildings should be sited in areas of the city that have minimal visual impact on sensitive historic environments, and they should retain and enhance key strategic views through careful siting. Interestingly, the City Council places the onus on the developer, by requiring the undertaking of a townscape study to outline the potential impacts of any proposed tall building on the character of the city. It remains to be seen how robust this policy document is in dealing effectively with tall building proposals, but it is certainly true to say that the document is a sound basis for decision-making, which attracts a great deal of consensus in dealing with a difficult issue.

11

TALL BUILDINGS IN VANCOUVER: CELEBRATING THE "CULT OF THE VIEW"[1]

Vancouver is, in many ways, one of the best planned cities in North America (Punter, 2003b) and a "poster-child of urbanism" (Berelowitz, 2005: 1). It has won innumerable awards for its particular style of urbanism that is a distinctive response to a particular topography and morphology, what Punter (2003b) describes as "the particular juxtaposition of its high-rise dominated downtown peninsula and dark forests of Stanley Park against a backdrop of the heavily rain-forested and often snow-capped Coast Range". This undeniable achievement is, in no great measure, down to the engagement of the city's planners and urban designers with the tall building typology: ways of promoting them in appropriate locations, limiting them where views of the surrounding mountains and water might be affected, and increasing urban densities to attract particular forms of living.

In 1997 the City of Vancouver (COV) adopted the *General Policy for Higher Buildings* (COV, 1997c) that sought to frame discussions about tall buildings in the downtown area that might exceed the height limits allowed by the Downtown District Official Development Plan (1975). This policy document emerged from a comprehensive piece of work undertaken by the city entitled *Downtown Vancouver Skyline Study – Recommended Option* (COV, 1997b) that sought to define a preferred profile for the Downtown Vancouver skyline. This new policy framework has been instrumental in promoting a positive engagement with the tall building typology, and in using building height to protect and enhance key views of and through the townscape, promote design quality and create a townscape of interest that enhances the natural environment.

This chapter will seek to explore the way in which Vancouver has sought to engage with building height through positive planning and urban design using the example of the recently built tower at 1120 West Georgia Street (the Shangri-La tower). It will start by outlining the context for development in Vancouver including an examination of the character of the city and existing tall building development. This will then be followed by an analysis of the development plan and policy framework. The construction of the Shangri-La tower will be used to illustrate the city's recent undertaking of a special review process for higher buildings and the subsequent establishment of Vancouver's Higher Building Advisory Panel (HBAP). This will be used as an example of the positive engagement with tall buildings as part of the city's character. Finally, the chapter will conclude with some reflections on the unique approach to tall building control exhibited in the city, and why Vancouver has achieved so much when other cities have struggled to plan for them effectively.

Context for development in Vancouver

Vancouver is a city of some 580,000 people on the south-west coast of Canada lying at the heart of a metropolitan region of 2.1 million people (Canada, 2006). Founded in the 1870s, the city was incorporated in 1886 and steadily grew as the transcontinental railways reached it from the east. The city is one of the fastest growing metropolitan regions in North America and has a booming population. Indeed, the city has witnessed huge immigration over its life, with many of its new citizens arriving from outside the country in the last 20 years[2]. The city is the largest in British Columbia, one of Canada's ten provinces. Canada is a federation of those ten provinces with three territories, and is a constitutional monarchy (with Queen Elizabeth II of the UK as head of state). Each of the ten provinces has a unicameral legislature that is sovereign, and exhibits a high degree of autonomy from the federal government.

Berelowitz (2005) defines Vancouver's *genius loci* as springing from its geography: the city's mild, temperate climate, its location beside the moderating influence of the ocean, and the presence of the mountain barrier along the coast. The city's natural environment comprises a low rise, undulating peninsula of land surrounded by a "wild farrago of steep slopes, jagged peninsulas and deep fjords" (Berelowitz, 2005: 11). The city's dramatic setting, with mountains rising steeply to the north, the sea from the west, and the plains of the Fraser River to the south, contribute to a unique environment which has encouraged a particular form of development. This "geography of constraint"[3] has led to a particular response to city-building that we can see in Vancouver today: topography has shaped the city's form.

The street grid has been the quintessential vehicle for Vancouver's growth and expansion since the British Empire's Royal Engineers built a path from the colonial capital of New Westminster to the sea, called the King's Way (now the Kingsway). From it, large tracts of land called District Lots were carved out to create the basis of a series of grids that form the basis for the character of the city to this day. Urban form is therefore concentrated on the flat lands of Burrard peninsula and the area to the south along the Fraser River. We can see, therefore, that the city itself was shaped by both the natural environment and a "relentless grid" (Berelowitz, 2005: 46), each affecting the way in which development evolved.

One of the other defining features of the city is the near absence of the eponymous North American highway: Vancouver, at a very early stage, recognised the potential for urban highways to destroy the essential character of place, and blocked development and regeneration from certain neighbourhoods. Having observed its sister city Seattle across the Canadian–US border suffer the ravages of the pro-highway movement, it did not repeat those mistakes. It was helped by there not being a natural need for highways: Berelowitz (2005) indicates that this is mainly as a result of manufacturing transportation resting on the use of the regional and national railways, and on shipping. Furthermore however, the city, during the 1960s, exhibited both relatively low population density and the feeling that Vancouver was somehow culturally inappropriate for such infrastructure. The city's citizenry did not tolerate proposals for highways being forced through downtown neighbourhoods (Stewart, 2006).

Vancouver's experience of the 1970s and 80s was one that was typical of most large cities in the west: out-migration of the wealthy from the central city, economic stagnation and little resourcing of infrastructure. Having said that, the city was able to engage with the idea of encouraging regeneration through event attraction. Expo '86 was held along the southern edge of the Burrard peninsula in an area known as False Creek. It had a huge impact not only spatially on this part of the city, but on the psyche of the city, its planners and urban designers, and citizenry (Reza-Jessa, 2009). The physical regeneration of the site during Expo '86 and the subsequent purchase and redevelopment by billionaire developer Li Ka-Shing resulted in a successful, high density, high-rise residential focused regeneration project that has acted as a catalyst for the advancement of *Vancouverism*, a set of principles, outlined below, which have led to Vancouver's mantel as the premier planned North American city (Olds, 1998) (Figure 11.1).

Vancouverism as an ideology emerged from the 1980s onwards and could be said to have a number of distinct elements which, when given the particular natural and physical context, has resulted in the city as we now see it: ". . . tall, but widely separated, slender towers interspersed with low-rise buildings, public spaces, small parks and pedestrian-friendly streetscapes and façades to minimise the impact of a high density population" (Chamberlain, 2005). In addition, *Vancouverism* also incorporates mixed use development that seeks to create and retain a lively street scene through commercial uses at the ground floors of the towers. In essence therefore, the particular ideology of the city planners and urban designers has been to encourage densification of the central area to support services, including new and expanding public transport (such as the new Richmond–Airport skytrain link) as well shops, restaurants and other community facilities. The product of this ideology can be seen in Figures 11.2, 11.3 and 11.4: note the profusion of glass designed to maximise views. This planned densification has also allowed development pressures to be diverted away from heritage neighbourhoods in the West End and Gastown to the north-east[4].

The common characteristic, therefore, during the city's different periods of growth and expansion has been the continuing relationship between the urban and natural landscapes. Since the early days of settlement, the most sought after neighbourhoods for development of housing (and indeed commercial development) are those with an elevated setting, those with a view or those with the potential for a view.

FIGURE 11.1 False Creek, Vancouver

FIGURE 11.2 Vancouver's towers with the mountains as a backdrop

FIGURE 11.3 Aerial view of Downtown looking south

FIGURE 11.4 False Creek towers

The regulatory planning framework for tall buildings

The regulatory framework for tall buildings in Vancouver forms the basis against which proposals are assessed by the relevant agencies and departments of city government. Table 11.1 summarises this framework. The key principles underpinning this planning framework are designed to, amongst other things, protect view corridors, encourage higher densities at certain locations in the downtown, promote liveability and treat streets as public realm. Furthermore this framework accepts two additional principles: that appropriate new tall buildings can perform specific functions in particular locations in downtown ("announce a particular moment in the city"[5]); and, that tall buildings are not appropriate in all locations (such as the site of the Olympic Village).

The View Protection Guidelines 1989 were instrumental in adding protected view cones to the planning framework established by the Downtown District Official Development Plan 1975. These guidelines established 26 view cones to protect "threatened public views" (COV, 2010). The guidelines do not necessarily give the maximum heights allowed within them, rather staff at the city council calculate that height based upon the individual characteristics of the site taking into account location, topography, and distance of the site from the view point. Figure 11.5 shows view cone D from Heather Bay to the Lions. In addition to the protection afforded by view cones, the city's General Policy for Higher Buildings (1997) is the basis for reviewing specific tall building proposals and outlines a number of criteria for review (see Table 11.2). One of those criteria is that the proposed building be subject to the adopted Special Review Process for Higher Buildings in Downtown (2002). This report outlines the approach for establishing the Higher Building Advisory Panel (HBAP) and indicates the procedures under which it operates. In essence, the panel is an advisory body appointed by the City Council for each building that is considered. The panel should give impartial, professional advice to the Director of Planning, City Council and Development Permit Board and should supplement the more general review undertaken by the Urban Design Panel, focusing on the proposed building's architectural excellence. As such, the panel does not approve or refuse proposals, and has a purely advisory role and its meetings are public. It does, however, charge a fee for the review which was originally set at CAD$9,600 but now at CAD$25,000.

The Downtown Vancouver Skyline Study 1997 recommended a skyline that incorporates a number of principles: firstly, that the backdrop of the mountains to the north of the city remain the predominant element in the skyline; secondly, that any new tall buildings do not block "the Lions" from most vantage points south of False Creek; thirdly, that buildings which might significantly exceed current height limits are limited to the Central Business District, to minimise blockage of the mountains from locations south of False Creek; fourthly, building heights should step down as they approach the water; and finally, that there are enough sites for taller buildings to ensure that a small number of landowners will not have a monopoly on the opportunity to develop tall buildings exceeding current height limits (COV, 1997a). The recommended skyline involves allowing buildings in the

TABLE 11.1 The regulatory framework for tall buildings in Vancouver

Planning policy	Main purpose of plan document	Key planning principles in relation to tall buildings	Other comments
Downtown District Official Development Plan (DDODP) 1975	The Official Development Plan By-law provides the general framework for the preparation of development plans for all individual buildings or complexes of buildings.	Section 4 outlines policy in relation to building height. The plan delineates several numbered areas where different height limits apply. The tallest buildings are to be allowed in area(s) 8, a height of up to 137.2 metres.	To be read in conjunction with the view cones (after 1989).
View Protection Guidelines 1989	Establishing view cones to protect "threatened" public views.	If cone crosses a development site, the City Council will calculate a maximum building height.	Amended in 1990 and 2010.
Downtown Vancouver Skyline Study 1997	Examined a variety of building heights and the resulting skylines. Council resolved that some higher buildings could be considered in the central business district.	Opportunities for buildings significantly exceeding existing permitted heights. Suggested amending the DDODP 1975 to allow buildings of up to 600 feet in certain parts of the Central Business District (CBD) north of Robson Street.	The review of the development plan was instigated as a way of combating the view that the "skyline lacks visual interest" (Vancouver, 1997).
General Policy for Higher Buildings 1997	To be read in conjunction with the DDODP 1975. Instigated as a policy to be implemented when seeking approval for buildings significantly exceeding the height limits outlined in the plan.	Buildings significantly exceeding current height limits will only be permitted in specific areas of downtown (specific on a map); they should exhibit the highest order of architectural excellence; achieve community benefits; should not involve the demolition of heritage buildings; building should be subject to a special review process.	This is a tool which has been used relatively frequently. The chapter goes on to discuss this in greater detail.

TABLE 11.1 (contd.) The regulatory framework for tall buildings in Vancouver.

Planning policy	Main purpose of plan document	Key planning principles in relation to tall buildings	Other comments
Special Review Process for Higher Buildings in Downtown 2002	General Policy for Higher Buildings called for the establishment of the Higher Buildings Advisory Panel. To supplement the city's usual design review process.	Panel should be mandated to by Council to give advice on significant re-zoning or development permit applications which significantly exceed the height limits established (as outlined above).	Advisory body to the City Council. Composed of not less than seven members (four renowned architects, one member nominated by Downtown Vancouver Association, one community representative from Vancouver, chair of Urban Design Panel). Panel appointed for each proposal. Panel to give impartial, professional advice to the Director of Planning, City Council and Development Permit Board.
Downtown Capacity and View Corridors Study 2008	Review the adopted height limits and view corridors. Recommend changes and achieve additional development capacity in the downtown area.	Site specific re-zoning in Downtown South area.	The document was drafted in the spirit of reflection about what public benefits might accrue from allowing additional building height.

FIGURE 11.5 View cone D: Heather Bay to the Lions

TABLE 11.2 General Policy for Higher Buildings

The following should be considered when reviewing proposals for higher buildings (those that exceed current height limits):

- Buildings significantly exceeding current height limits will only be permitted in specific areas.
- The highest buildings should be on one of downtown's primary streets (West Georgia, Granville, Burrard).
- The building should exhibit the highest order of architectural excellence.
- The building should achieve other community benefits such as being a recipient site for density transfers or density bonusing relating to heritage retention.
- It should not involve the demolition of a Class A heritage building.
- The building, where possible, should include activities and uses of community significance such as a public observation deck or other public amenity.
- The development should provide on site open space that represents a significant addition to downtown green and plaza spaces.
- The building should not contribute to adverse microclimate effects.
- Signage on buildings should not be located at a height which exceeds the current height limits.
- The building should be the subject of a special review process which includes, in addition to the current review requirements, a review assessing architectural excellence with input from a special panel of respected community leaders and notable design experts, and approval by Council.

current 137 metre high zone to go up to 183 metres. The review indicated that there were probably only five or so opportunities in the entire downtown for buildings to exceed 137 metres.

Vancouver's Zoning and Development By-law (No. 3575; updated to 01 January 2011) forms the basis for decision-making about particular developments in the city. It divides the city into a number of distinct zones each of which has its own schedule: typically, they cover such things as a "statement about the City objectives for the district, a list of permitted land uses and regulations governing maximum height, site coverage, floor area and related aspects of any development which may be permitted on a site" (COV, 2011). In addition, the Comprehensive Development District (CD-1) outlines where over 400 sites are governed by individual, custom designed (CD-1) by-laws that generally regulate permitted land uses and development. City Council must also approve the form of development in a CD-1 district. Applicants for development may also apply for the re-zoning of a particular site thereby requiring an application to the City Council which needs to be heard at a public hearing. The Planning Department of the City Council recommends refusal or acceptance of the amendment to the City Council who has the power to make the decision.

Vancouver City Council is somewhat unique in British Columbia in that it exhibits a high degree of autonomy from the provincial legislature. The unique arrangements for governance of the city have meant that it has been able to undertake discretionary zoning for more than 30 years[6]. Under this regime, the city has "gained the power to relax certain zoning regulations and to create . . . incentives" (Punter, 2003b: 18) for developers and development. The result of this ability to weigh decisions about particular proposals has allowed the city to encourage planning and design excellence leading to "good urbanism behaviours"[7]. In other words, the culture of planning in Vancouver is somewhat unique in British Columbia in that the framework has evolved as a result of the discretionary zoning activities that take place, meaning that not only do planners see the value in the process, developers and third parties take value from the planning process[8]. It is clear that the culture of planning and design in the city is evolutionary, open and collegial, thereby allowing the city to learn from the experience of particular projects, apply that knowledge to particular issues and problems, and innovate where necessary: so-called "win-win" planning.

In terms of planning for tall buildings, it is interesting that this approach means that developers can "earn" additional height with their developments, as the increase in performativity of development means an increase in community benefit[9].

In 1986, the City Council adopted the Vancouver Heritage Inventory, which was subsequently adopted as the Vancouver Heritage Register in 1994. The register is a list of buildings and structures, streetscapes, landscape resources and archaeological sites which have architectural or historical value. It is a planning tool that provides a record of Vancouver's heritage and which is augmented by a number of regulations, policies and guidelines that affect buildings or sites listed on the register. Buildings are designated as A, B or C on the register. Table 11.3 indicates the criteria for protection under each of these categories.

TABLE 11.3 Heritage register building categories

"A" building	*"B" building*	*"C" building*
Primary Significance Represents the best examples of a style or type of building; may be associated with a person or event of significance.	**Significant** Represents good examples of a particular style or type, either individually or collectively; may have some documented historical or cultural significance in a neighbourhood.	**Contextual Or Character** Represents those buildings that contribute to the historic character of an area or streetscape, usually found in groupings of more than one building but may also be of individual importance.

In 1974, Vancouver City Council adopted By-law No. 4800 to establish the Vancouver Heritage Advisory Committee, and in 1994, adopted the new name of Vancouver Heritage Commission. The Commission's mandate is to advise Council on: the need for preserving heritage buildings, structures and lands which collectively represent a cross section of all periods and styles in the City's historic and cultural evolution; the costs and benefits of preservation; the compatibility of preservation with other lawful uses of buildings, structures or lands; and, recommendation to the Council respecting the designation of heritage buildings, structures and lands and the demolition, preservation, alteration or renovation of these buildings, structures and lands.

Vancouver's Downtown contains a number of different character areas that give the city a sense of time, place, diversity, and individuality. These areas should be preserved, enhanced or developed appropriately (COV, 2011). Georgia Street, on the Downtown Peninsula, is "Vancouver's most important prestigious and ceremonial street" (COV, 2003a: 22). Both the west end and the east end of the street form gateways to the downtown. The street is a wide, major traffic route along its whole length. Prestigious buildings, significant public institutions, major public open spaces and cultural facilities are located along the street. A number of development objectives are set out in a supplement to the zoning by-law to provide guidance and directions for the development of the character area, the most relevant of which are outlined below:

- Reinforce the existing dominant processional and formal character of the whole of Georgia Street.
- The significant views obtainable from much of Georgia Street are an important component of the image of Downtown. It is important to preserve and enhance all existing views from the street ends by ensuring that physical elements do not protrude into the view cones.
- Create a strong unified image for the whole of Georgia Street.
- Ensure that all developments contribute to defining the street edge along Georgia Street through building elements and/or landscaping.
- Create a coherent high quality environment within the public realm. Ensure that all new developments contribute to creating this high quality street environment (COV, 2003a).

It is within this planning and conservation context that proposals for development are assessed by the City Council. The following section outlines the core details of the proposed Shangri-La Tower at 1120 West Georgia Street.

The Shangri-La Tower

An application for the re-zoning of 1120 West Georgia Street from Downtown District to Comprehensive Development District (CD-1) including the addition of dwelling units and general office live–work as permitted uses, and allowing an increase in building height from 137.2m. (450 ft.) to 183m. (600 ft.) and an increase in floor space ratio from 9.0 to 12.81, was received by the City of Vancouver on 22 April 2003. The development proposed was a mixed use, 57-storey tower designed to be the tallest in the city including residential, retail and hotel representing a total area of 62,779 sq.m., and an increase of approximately 30% over the permitted floor area (Figures 11.6 and 11.7). In addition a package of community

FIGURE 11.6
Shangri-La tower, West Georgia Street, looking south–east

benefits were proposed: the signing of a Heritage Revitalisation Agreement for the conservation of the nearby Church of Christ, Scientist building at 1160 West Georgia Street (representing CAD$4.4m worth of benefits), the provision of a sculpture garden, and a CAD$1m contribution to the city's Affordable Housing Fund. This investment was required as a reflection of the increase in value of the site as a result of the re-zoning.

FIGURE 11.7 Shangri-La tower, West Georgia Street, looking north-west

The site of the tower is situated on the eastern part of a long block at the corner of West Georgia Street and Thurlow Street. Immediately adjacent to the west of the site is the former First Church of Christ, Scientist, a "B" heritage register building at 1160 West Georgia Street. Alberni Street forms the southern boundary of sub-area A in the Downtown District in which residential use is not permitted, the floor space ration maximum is 9.0 and building height is limited to 137.2m. (450 ft.).

The site is identified in the General Policy for Higher Buildings as a probable site for the development of a higher building, to a height of 183m. (600 ft.) although the western part of the site is limited by False Creek View Cone D (Heather Bay to the Lions; see Figure 11.5) to 91.4m. (300 ft.).

The approval of the project followed a long process and two separate re-zoning applications. The first stage of the approval was the passing of the change in zoning with this application, and its assessment by the HBAP. During the initial assessment of the application, the re-zoning planner took the application to this panel for their views regarding the suitability of the proposal (on 20 June 2003). This panel was asked to reflect upon a number of specific areas: whether the proposal achieves "architectural excellence given it will likely become a Vancouver icon" (COV, 2003b); whether the building responds appropriately to its existing neighbours and to the existing skyline; the proposed building character and materials; and, its relationship with the surrounding streets and public realm connections. The Panel was convened especially to review this proposal and it was stated clearly at the outset that there were "very high expectations" (COV, 2003b: 4) for this project.

The Panel was made up of a number of invited guests and also included Ken Yeang, Adrian Smith, James Hancock and Paul Merrick reflecting the "high status of the proposal and its impact upon the city"[10]. In terms of the debate at the panel, a number of issues were accepted with little debate: the increase in density from 9.0 to 11.0 floor space ratio (FSR); the community benefits of the project; and, its sustainability. The interesting debate, in relation to the debates raised in this book about height regulation, related to the increase in height of the building, its relationship to other buildings in the immediate vicinity, and the impact upon the skyline of the city.

As the role of the Panel is advisory, the applicant was encouraged to reflect upon the significance of the increase in height for the skyline of the city, its impact upon the idea of a domed skyline, how the building's iconic status might be articulated, and how the building might reflect architectural excellence. As a result of negotiation of the re-zoning, the City Council recommended that the application be referred to a public hearing with the recommendation that it be approved. The subsequent Public Hearing approved the application for re-zoning on 10 December 2003. A Development Permit was issued on 17 February 2005 for the proposed tower following unanimous support from HBAP on 26 May 2004, and Development Permit Board on 5 July 2004.

A second application for re-zoning was submitted to amend the previous application in late 2004. In essence, it became apparent during discussions to approve the original re-zoning application, that a tower at 1133 West Georgia, nearby, was proposed which led the developers to review the viability of the original proposal. The applicant proposed an additional live–work floor with seven units for a total of 11,100 sq.ft. of additional floor space, and an increase in height of 1.83m. (6 ft.), and a raising of the top of the uppermost habitable floor by 8.8m. (29 ft.). This would increase the maximum building height from 183m. (600 ft.) established by the original re-zoning application, to 191.7m. (629 ft.). This was approved by the City Council on 19 July 2005 to be reviewed by HBAP and a Public Hearing. The meeting and hearing were particularly interested in the changes to the roof form that accrued from the changes in height proposed, and were convinced of its architectural and design merit. The final development permit for the changed detail at the crown of the tower was issued on 13 June 1006. Construction of the tower commenced in mid 2005 and was completed at the beginning of 2009.

Assessment of the Shangri-La proposal

The negotiation of both re-zoning applications centred around the proposed building height (amongst other issues not relevant to this chapter), and its relationship to the D view corridor. The increase in density and its effect on the form (particularly height) of development was the first issue considered by both the planners and the HBAP, and centred on the request for an increase (from the original zoning ordinance) of 30% floor area on the site, or 18,369 sq.m. This was a significant increase in the level of development that the site might accommodate, and the debate was therefore framed within the need to provide community benefits which would be equal to ". . . at least 91% of the increased land value of the site after re-zoning approval" (COV, 2003b: 5). There is, as such, a clear principle encouraged through the administration of the zoning ordinances that any increased value that comes from a proposed change to that ordinance, is somehow reflected in benefits to the immediate and wider community.

The benefits of the scheme have briefly been outlined above, yet the interesting element from the perspective of heritage protection, a theme running throughout this book, is the requirement that residential re-zoning in the core CBD only be considered if this will facilitate the retention of a heritage building. The former First Church of Christ, Scientist, "is an important part of Vancouver's heritage, and is notable for being a rare example of a building from the First World War era. Architecturally, it is a finely executed example of the Colonial Revival Style, uncommon in Vancouver" (COV, 2003b: 28). The church was added to the heritage register in 1986 in the "B" category but did not recognise, explicitly, the value of the interiors. The Vancouver Heritage Commission supported the project to restore and rehabilitate the building, and recognised that these works would encourage the conservation of the wider Georgia Street Character Area particularly as it attracted more than CAD$4m for the project. As such the negotiation of a Heritage Revitalisation Agreement was a relatively uncontested and simple process[11].

Perhaps the most important issue dealt with by the planners and the HBAP was in relation to the height of the building and its relationship to the D view corridor, as outlined previously. The site, as has been indicated, was identified in the General Policy For Higher Buildings as a probable site for a tower of up to 183m. (600 ft.). A higher building can only be considered on the eastern part of the site, adjacent to Thurlow Street, as the western part is limited by a False Creek View Cone to 92m. (300 ft.). The first point of note, is that the view cone remained sacrosanct throughout the discussions for the new tower's design, height and form. There was no hint at all from the developers that they would challenge the protection afforded by this designation. Indeed the HBAP welcomed the "axial slash" (COV, 2005: Appendix D, page 2) across the site that the design proposed (see Figure 11.5). This, in itself, is an interesting element in Vancouver's complex and rich planning framework. Indeed, it can be said to contribute to the city's good "urbanism behaviour"[12] that encourages a positive engagement with the zoning ordinance and supporting regulations that are the result of a high degree of consensus. In other words, there is added value in the processes of planning in Vancouver that come from that consensus[13]. Secondly, the HBAP (which met on 19 and 20 June 2003) recognised that there were, in fact, very few possibilities in Downtown for a tall building to punch above the general building height and thereby create a skyline of interest. Furthermore, there was a recognition that due to these limited possibilities, the aspiration to create a domed skyline hinged on the decisions about a small number of existing and future proposals (COV, 2003c).

Planning policy allows for a tower on this site that not only respects the view cone envelope, but which should exhibit the "highest order of architectural excellence" (COV, 1997c) to be determined, through consensus, by the City Council, HBAP and the community. The concern amongst the HBAP was that not only were there huge expectations about the significance of this proposal, but that it should become a "Vancouver icon" (COV, 2003c: 19; COV, 2003b). A large part of the discussion, aside from the issue of height, was around the "skin" of the building and how it might relate to the sensitive façade on West Georgia Street; indeed, the panel took up a large amount of its time trying to come to a coherent view about the skin detail. This level of detail had yet to be worked out by the architect and, as a result, the views of the panel became crucial in feeding back into the working out of the detail of the building[14]. The applicant's response to this feedback was interesting: ". . . the reserved, taught glass skin expression on both West Georgia and Thurlow . . . reflects the business nature of the CBD. The simplicity of the façades speaks to the flexibility of uses rather than emphasising their differences . . . In contrast, the animated expression of the angled view cone façade reveals more of the mixed nature of the tower to the emerging residential character on Alberni Street" (COV, 2003c: 25). Figures 11.6 and 11.7 show each of these points.

Conclusions

We can see, therefore, that the use of the proposed tower at 1120 West Georgia Street assists us in reflecting on the success of the planning regime in Vancouver;

indeed, one can suggest that this regime encourages a positive engagement with design outcomes in the city, irrespective of whether the building in question is viewed positively, encouraged by the autonomy that the city is able to practise (uniquely in BC). In other words, the city's "urbanism behaviour" is such that it encourages a particular type of planning culture in which there is positive engagement with zoning and the issuing of development permits[15]. This is not, of course, to say that there are not conflicts about particular development proposals on particular sites, but there is a feeling that there is certainly some element of the system which encourages "peer review" (Punter, 2003a: 133). In other words, it is precisely Vancouver's particular "urbanism behaviour" that means that developers strive for excellence in their designs, and in terms of the HBAP, it appears to have become ". . . a matter of professional pride for many developers/designers to seek a unanimous endorsement of their proposals when only a majority in favour [at panel] is actually required" (Punter, 2003a: 132).

As such we can reflect upon the factors that Punter indicates how it has been possible for Vancouver to create and sustain such a multi-faceted, elaborate and demanding planning system. Firstly, it is the very environmental quality of the city's site, setting, and location, recognised through the planning regime, which frames all debates about development. Indeed, it is the shared public and political beliefs in this quality that drives the City Council and the development planners, in seeking quality outcomes from the processes of planning. The autonomy that Vancouver can exercise from the normal zoning regulation acceptable to BC, and the delegated powers to "establish technical excellence and incentives for design" is particularly noticeable. Finally, the system of planning encourages and enforces a planning and design community where there is substantial peer pressure to "conform and perform" (Punter, 2003a: 132).

Finally it is interesting to reflect upon the significance of the "cult of the view" exhibited by the processes of planning in the city. As Berelowitz notes, "both Vancouver's urban form and its public spaces have been profoundly informed by the view imperative" (2005: 173). It is the views out of the city towards the city's natural setting, however, that is promoted through the city's zoning and planning regulations. The view cones and the consensus around their protection and management are a defining feature of the city's planning system. In Vancouver these are not contested, rather they are accepted as a frame from which innovative design solutions might emerge[16].

12

CONCLUSIONS

The use of the seven case cities in this book has shown that the effectiveness of techniques in regulating and assessing tall building proposals is dependent upon the local context for decision-making in each city, reflecting the multi-scaled nature of urban planning and the trade-offs which occur during the negotiation of planning consents, particularly in relation to built heritage issues. In all of the cities there was evidence that the possibility of tall buildings in some locations was regulated out as a result of heritage concerns, and that these concerns were taken seriously in all cases, often resulting in modifications to those designs that were given approval. As such, the conservation of built heritage was a central issue across all of the cities presented in this book, and conservation concerns had to be negotiated in the decision-making process. That said, the effectiveness of specific regulatory frameworks and assessment techniques in the cities has reflected the tensions and trade-offs that occur around development in each location.

The conclusions will seek to examine what techniques in tall building assessment were the most effective in decision support and why, drawing on the experiences of each of the cities explored. Secondly, it will look at how differences in approach to tall building decision-making might be explained looking at how the local political and regulatory contexts for decision-making impacted upon the use of specific techniques for assessment. The chapter will conclude with some reflections on the state of tall building assessment regimes, and make some suggestions about how cities might approach such assessment in the future.

Tall building assessment techniques

A range of regulatory and assessment methods were utilised across the seven case studies which give a clear picture of what might work in effectively managing proposals for tall buildings and which do not. Table 12.1 outlines the regulatory framework for tall buildings in each location. Whilst the cases exhibit some com-

TABLE 12.1 Regulatory framework and assessment methods utilised in the case studies

	Liver-pool	Man-chester	Birming-ham	Newcastle–Gateshead	Oslo	Dublin	Vancouver
National guidance	■			■			
Development plan			■		■	■	■
Local tall building guidance	■		■			■	■
Management of key views	■		■ partly	■	■	■	■
Clustering	■		■		■	■	■
Characterisation	■		■	■		■	■
Impact assessment	■	■		■		■	■
Design review	■	■	■	■		■	■
Visualisation	■	■	■	■	■	■	■
EIA	■	■		■		■	■

monality in the use of regulatory frameworks and assessment methods for proposals for tall buildings, particularly in the management of key views and the use of EIA in project assessment for example, one salient feature of the table is the local differentiation in methods deployed. In particular there are gaps in the regulatory frameworks and methods of assessment used by all of the case study planning authorities. In Liverpool a local framework reflecting national guidance was used as the basis for regulation and assessment, in Newcastle the national guidance with a supporting characterisation study, and in Birmingham, Oslo and Dublin locally instituted regulatory frameworks were employed. In Vancouver, the autonomy granted the city in zoning regulation terms (from British Columbia) has allowed the city to generate a sophisticated system which respects and enhances morphology of place.

Decisions about the Beetham Tower in Manchester however did not utilise any specific city-wide strategic approach designed to manage tall buildings. As such, given that there is widespread concern in Manchester about the impact of cumulative tall building proposals, the lack of political will in implementing a tall building regulatory framework reflects two points:

1 that a framework covering national and local approaches might suggest ways of finding local solutions to tall building management. Such frameworks appear to assist planning authorities make difficult decisions not just about the impacts of specific buildings, but the location of proposals including whether a cluster of tall buildings might be appropriate, and what the cumulative impact of proposals upon the city might be; and

2   that the status of any frameworks are important in determining specific tall building proposals. In other words how the national framework for tall buildings and conservation planning is interpreted and implemented at the local level.

In terms of assessment methods, a range were used across the cases, yet in Manchester and Oslo, and to a lesser extent Birmingham, the limited range of methods utilised was in stark contrast to the employment of multi-methods in the remaining cities. In Manchester for example, the lack of a deployment of a national–local regulatory framework for tall building assessment allied with the more limited use of individual assessment methods has meant that the basis for regulation and assessment is insufficient for the complex requirements of tall building decision-making. In contrast, a range of methods were used in the other case study cities which reflected a more robust approach to tall building management.

Few of the methods outlined in Chapter 3, particularly those pioneered and still used in North America – such as set-backs or transferable development rights – were used in any of the case studies, apart from in Vancouver. This is somewhat surprising given the huge amount of experience that has accrued in that country over time and that there is relatively little experience in dealing with tall buildings in the regional English cities particularly. Other methods used in the USA and Europe however, such as the clustering of tall buildings in particular locations, appear to have been used as part of a framework for decision-making in Liverpool, Birmingham, Oslo and Dublin. There is, however, a lack of dissemination of the utility of techniques for tall building management which are being developed, and pioneered, in London at this time to the regional cities. Advances in GIS and CAD technology do not appear to have been used outside London; the usefulness of the City of London's computer model which can appraise the impacts of tall building impacts, for example, does not appear to have been explored in any of the cities. It would appear that the more sophisticated approach in London reflects a number of factors, including the importance of particular sites for tall building development in the city, the large amount of financial investment required by LPAs to assess tall building planning applications, particularly if they refuse an application and are required to fight an appeal, and the pressures on London from politicians for tangible symbols of London's status and prestige on the world stage. As such, London could be said to be driving the advancement of methods for regulation and assessment of tall buildings due to its unique circumstances, but that experience is not necessarily reflected in the approaches of other cities in England. Interestingly, EH is concerned about its approach in assessing tall building proposals because it has lost so many appeals and public inquiries as a result of regeneration and economic arguments holding a greater status than heritage concerns[1].

Conservation planning concerns could be said to have prevented – or at least mitigated – the worst excesses of tall buildings on the built heritage in the case study localities primarily because it has led to the identification of built heritage elements upon which the direct impacts of tall buildings can be determined with relative ease. In none of the cases was there a tall building free-for-all. However, the indirect impacts of tall buildings on the wider townscape or character of a place remain difficult to ascertain in locations where the essentially preservationist view of conservation planning holds true. The result is that decision-making for tall buildings in pro-growth environments that do not have a robust understanding of townscape value or quality lead to more tall buildings in more locations. As such, for regulatory frameworks and assessment methods to be effective this research has shown that a view of conservation planning as a way of managing urban change needs to be prevalent. For this to hold true however, particularly as all cases exhibited pro-growth and development agendas, some sort of detailed characterisation of place would appear to need to be undertaken for the basis of decision-making to be robust. The theme of characterisation has permeated much of the empirical work in the case studies. In Newcastle–Gateshead, Birmingham, Liverpool, Dublin and Vancouver attempts at characterising the townscape were used to underpin the identification of built heritage elements. In Newcastle–Gateshead the Tyne Gorge Study suggested a way of positively managing tall buildings which recognises the importance of elements of the townscape such as views, landmarks and topography, where enhancement through new building could occur and what is particularly sensitive to change. In this way the City Council was able to systematically examine the Northern Light proposals against a detailed understanding of the constraints and opportunities within the townscape.

There is also evidence that in the absence of such robust frameworks for managing tall building proposals, decision-making processes favour certain heritages over others, reflecting the dynamics of local politics. In Manchester for example, the Victorian elements of the townscape have particular importance to debates about built heritage in the impact of new development (While and Short, 2011) whilst in Dublin, the Georgian fabric of the central city plays a significant part in debates about growth and development. In Birmingham the relatively few Victorian buildings (compared to Manchester, Liverpool and Newcastle–Gateshead) that remained after bombing from the Second World War and redevelopment in the post-war period have a hugely important status in debates about development. The city's post-war townscape appears to be of negligible value, particularly in the development process which gives little status to concerns about impacts upon locally protected elements of that townscape. In Newcastle–Gateshead however, the recognition of all elements of the townscape in conjunction with their setting in the Tyne Gorge appears to suggest that planning decisions can be made which reflect a desire to develop whilst recognising the importance of the townscape to the character of the city. That some heritage is of more importance than others is an interesting element of the research. The notion of "hybrid heritage" assists in understanding why there is little consensus over the type and value of the built heritage. As was described earlier, hybridity can be used to explain the fluidity and multiplicity of "space-times generated in/by the movements and rhythms of heterogeneous associations" (Whatmore, 2002: 6), in other words, that the form of cities reflect a palimpsest of development over time (While, 2006). In this way particular elements of the heritage are valued over others reflecting willingness to trade conservation off against change. The determination of tall building proposals within hybrid heritage cities therefore reflects the values attributed to different elements of the townscape, to political struggles over the future of elements of the built heritage, and its value to economic and physical growth.

In particular, post-war buildings and townscapes appeared to have little weight during the assessment process. In Manchester for example, the impact of the Beetham Hilton Tower on the Listed CIS Tower and the skyline of the city was not examined. Likewise in Birmingham, the Beetham Holloway Circus Tower proposal was related to the existing post-war townscape as a new landmark building in the same vain as the Listed post-war Rotunda and also the BT Tower but no assessment on the impacts of this building on these elements was undertaken. Conversely in Newcastle–Gateshead, elements of post-war heritage are recognised as contributing to the legibility of the city and represent a particular period of development in the city (such as Swan House and Cale Cross House) through the Tyne Gorge Study. Whilst post-war buildings and townscapes are highly visible in the townscape, they are not necessarily part of negotiations and discussions about impacts of particular tall building proposals, reflecting the political will of the cities in promoting and demoting elements of the townscape.

Approaches to tall building decision-making

Understanding how the regulatory frameworks and assessment methods deployed in each of the case studies were effective or not is crucial. Firstly, the distinctiveness evident in each case was a reflection of a number of elements; the regulatory and assessment context, the attributes of the tall building proposal under investigation, the range of potential impacts identified and the role of built heritage in discussions about the appropriateness of the proposals. Secondly however, it was recognised that the impact of local conservation politics, the distinctive and unique built form of each place and the involvement of local and non-local actors in the assessment process was crucial in understanding the dynamics of each case study. This section will analyse the distinctiveness of local conservation regimes and how the politics of tall building decisions reflect the ways in which those regimes operate.

In each of the case studies, the local authority was involved in the promotion of a pro-growth agenda to attract inward investment, provide jobs, re-image and re-brand. The reasons for this varied between cases. In Liverpool, Manchester, Birmingham and Newcastle–Gateshead the pro-growth agenda was advanced by city councils eager to address major weaknesses in the local economy and physical decay through pro-active regeneration strategies. Concern about the implications for the built heritage therefore related to the impact of new development on the existing built heritage in these cities and how particular built heritage designations could be utilised as part of regeneration strategies. More specifically in Liverpool attempts to regenerate, re-brand and re-image go hand in hand with a pro-growth agenda that seeks to exploit the city's heritage for marketing and tourism purposes whilst attracting development projects in specific places. In Manchester, the City Council likewise is seeking the creative re-imaging of place but within a more aggressively pro-growth context. The physical transformation of the city has been astounding and has been fuelled by relatively weak control over the form and direction of development as the Council seeks to attract as much development as it can. Elements of the built heritage are recognised as being important to the form of the city yet there is little understanding of what the character of the city is and how development control decisions affect that character. In Birmingham, the pro-growth agenda of the city is leading to tangible re-imaging of the city centre in particular. Combined with a planning framework which recognises the unique features of the city and how development can enhance or improve it, the character of the city is central to decision-making processes about development. In Newcastle–Gateshead, a "Going for Growth" agenda for development has seen parts of the central city in particular physically transform with signature buildings anchoring more widespread renewal. The built heritage of the city is central to its character and decision-making about development.

In Dublin and Oslo, the focus reflected the position in England even though, in both locations, pressure for redevelopment and regeneration reflected the economic power of each city and their status as capitals. The generally pro-development ethos of the local authority and the nature of the development pressure was similar to the English case studies. In Dublin, years of economic stagnation has recently been replaced by huge economic growth leading to land supply shortages, particularly in housing, as the population rapidly expands. Here, the City Council has attempted to regenerate the fabric of the city after years of neglect whilst simultaneously absorbing massive amounts of development in the city. This is leading to suburban sprawl, pressure to redevelop in the immediate area around the historic centre of the city and the creative re-use of some built heritage elements. In Oslo, where the economy of the city has been relatively robust for a long period of time by comparison, the kommune is keen to attract development to signify its wish to become a city on the world stage whilst managing population growth. This is leading to tensions around changes to the character of the city and the way that planning decisions are made. In Vancouver, there is a slightly different focus as the city has had to absorb large waves of immigrants and create places and spaces of quality to house them. As such, one might suggest that it is because the city is under huge pressure to grow that it has had to engage with difficult questions of character, place and the ways in which that growth might be planned for effectively.

It would appear therefore, that the form of the local regulatory regime for assessing tall buildings selects tools and techniques for assessment that reflect the distinctive political realities of each place. All of the tall building cases were proposed in cities with a pro-growth and pro-development agenda. The differences in approach to assessment therefore reflect the wider impact of local dynamics in decision-making and what the sense of local heritage might be. In Manchester, the lack of any coherent strategy for tall building regulation reflects the city's entrepreneurial approach to planning and conservation which is rooted in the city's desire to attract as much development to further regeneration and its benefits for as long as possible. At the other end of the spectrum in Dublin, the use of a detailed framework for tall building management allied with a clear sense of the cultural importance of the historic centre of the city has meant that the regulatory framework for tall buildings has more solid foundations. In both instances the decision to approve the towers was the same, yet the framework in each place is entirely different reflecting different norms and rationalities in the local conservation planning culture. Furthermore, the extent to which the use of specific methods is reflected in decision-making depends upon the weight given to the information within the supporting documents. In all instances the evidence of the case studies points to a lack of critical assessment of the information except in Newcastle–Gateshead where planners appear to have been able to use the characterisation study to counteract the claims of the planning application about the quality of the Northern Light Tower and its potential role in the townscape.

Within a context of strong pro-growth and pro-development discourses in the case studies and the politics of local conservation planning regimes, the problem of tall buildings is particularly interesting. Remembering that the development process relies on a wide range of regulatory frameworks and assessment techniques to ensure that decisions about tall buildings are in line with prevailing rationalities, the following section will reflect on the regulation and assessment of the seven case studies.

The built heritage and tall building assessment

It is clear from the case studies that politics matter in the decisions about tall build-ings, reflecting the pro-growth agendas of the cities examined. It is also clear that some built heritage elements have a more important status than others and that in these instances, tall buildings are regulated out of the most contentious spaces. Thus we can see the waterfront of Liverpool, the Tyne Gorge in Newcastle–Gateshead and the historic core of Dublin free from tall buildings precisely because there is consensus about the value of that heritage to a sense of character and place. Methods such as characterisation assist in the recognition of the value of these townscape elements and provide a robust framework for decision-making. Thus, both the direct impacts of proposed tall buildings on particular built heritage elements and the indirect impacts upon the townscape as a whole are contextualised. The flip side to this is that tall buildings were welcomed in other locations and their impact upon other heritages which do not reflect such a consensus is apparent. For example the Locally Listed Buildings in Birmingham or the centre of Manchester in general appear not be considered as part of tall building assessments. The direct impacts of tall buildings on built heritage elements are therefore difficult to quantify and the indirect impacts upon the wider townscape not considered.

Conservation planning therefore can prevent the worst excesses of tall buildings and in none of the cases, even Manchester, was there a tall building free-for-all. The direct impacts of tall buildings upon the character of universally recognised built heritage elements in Dublin, Liverpool and Newcastle–Gateshead can be determined with relative ease, although in those instances where there is no contextual basis for decision-making, in Manchester for example, the direct heritage impacts of tall buildings are harder to pinpoint. Indirect impacts on the wider townscape or character of place remain difficult to ascertain in such locations with the result that decision-making for tall buildings in pro-growth environments which do not have a robust understanding of townscape value or quality lead to more tall buildings in more locations.

As such it could be said that there is variety in the local commitment to conservation planning that reflects differentiation in approach to protecting buildings and areas, managing urban change, using regulatory and assessment frameworks and the dynamics of actors involved. One final element of the cases is that it can be said that there is a heritage dividend to many of the tall building proposals. Development projects offer opportunities for developer contributions that may mitigate some of the impacts of their development. In the case studies examined there were clear heritage related benefits to tall building proposals: in Liverpool the public realm works to the front of Lime Street station could be said to improve the context of a number of Listed Buildings; in Manchester the approval of Beetham Hilton Tower should lead to the reinvigoration of the bottom of Deansgate in economic terms, giving many Listed Buildings a new lease of life; in Dublin, the construction of the Heuston Gate Tower will offer an opportunity to restore a number of monuments and Protected Structures; and in Oslo, the development of Bjørvika will open up the waterfront to the people of the city and a medieval park created to interpret the ruins of the medieval city. As such large and complex building projects offer major opportunities for the improvement of built heritage elements in the townscape and of the townscape in general. Furthermore, the benefits of particular tall buildings can be recognised as part of a tall building strategy. In Dublin for example the DEGW report highlighted the specific improvements to the townscape of the Heuston area that a tower might bring. The ability however of contributions from development to lead to demonstrable improvement to particular built heritage elements, is improved through the use of a strong regulatory framework (Cullingworth and Nadin, 2002). The inference for tall building management is that in instances where there is a strong regulatory framework for tall buildings, the ability to explicitly recognise the contribution that large development projects can make to the public realm and to the conservation of particular built heritage elements is articulated. In Vancouver, the benefits of the Shangri-La scheme in terms of the protection of the former First Church of Christ, Scientist, is interesting in that it was a relatively uncontested and simple process, hinting at the importance of the negotiation of the impact of such towers on the built heritage at an early stage, in an open and transparent manner.

Priorities for improving practice

This section is designed to address the shortcomings of existing assessment of proposals for tall buildings on the built heritage outlined in the previous chapters. It will seek to achieve this by outlining what priorities for practice would improve the assessment of proposals for tall buildings on the built heritage.

One of the main themes of the book is the idea that tall buildings can contribute to the evolution of the city if they are planned for effectively. For this to be achieved, a top down change in planning policy would be required from national to local level. As such, as a first priority, there needs to be a clear *national policy* to frame tall building decision-making. As the House of Commons committee report stated in 2002, "a general national framework is required, setting down criteria on which tall building applications should be judged" (HoC, 2002: 5). Such a policy regime would require the unequivocal support of the full range of stakeholders in each country. The CABE–EH guidance (as amended in 2007) could be said to be a useful example of such a policy although confusion about its status means that there is uncertainty about the weight LPAs should attach to it in decision-making. At the local level, development plans (of whichever type) should promote a proactive approach to managing development, thereby interpreting national policy and guidance in a local, sensitive and distinctive way. Development plans offer an opportunity for tall building regulation and assessment in that: the broad strategy could offer the possibility for strong statements of intent regarding tall building location, potentially in clusters or at specific transport nodes; and more detailed policies within the plan could provide a method for townscape analysis reflected in detailed policies about tall building location, the potential impacts in particular local contexts and design issues. Each element of the plan could therefore reflect both the conservation planning imperative of the LPA and the ability to plan for tall buildings effectively. McPherson (2006) suggests that the involvement of local communities and key stakeholders in the evolution of such documents will reflect positively on the management of the built heritage, though it might be said that this is an optimistic perspective given the evidence in the case studies about public involvement in planning policy formation and decision-making. The adoption of specific policies and guidance documents in support of the development plans should allow locally-based tall building solutions to evolve which reflect local concerns, and offer greater scope for them to be both appropriately sited and reflective of community and stakeholders opinions. Recognition of the range of impacts that tall buildings may present, allied with the potential for characterising the existing townscape, could offer opportunities to plan for tall buildings effectively. However, local planning cultures and the politics of development in each place will no doubt have an impact upon the effectiveness of development plans to manage tall buildings in particular places. As such, the requirement for characterisation for all of our major city centres could strengthen the basis for development plans.

Above all, the use of characterisation studies such as the one in Newcastle–Gateshead appears to improve the possibility of tall buildings being managed effectively, allowing a greater understanding of all elements of the townscape and thereby leading to potential for areas where tall buildings may be appropriate to be identified. The use of such studies allows for the acceptance of the importance of townscape and morphology in conservation planning decisions. Particularly, it appears to be a useful mechanism in hybrid heritage cities where layers of history intertwine and compete in the determination of tall building proposals. Such studies recognise the intrinsic value of all of the elements of a townscape, as well as an appreciation of the townscape as a composition. Thus, the impacts of a particular development appear to be more likely to be recognised and addressed where a characterisations study has been undertaken, and the distinctiveness of that place recognised as a result.

The design review of tall building proposals utilising various methods of decision support mechanisms was a feature of the cases analysed. Whilst built heritage issues formed the basis of the discussions about the tall building proposals, the use of these mechanisms and the discussions elicited were not necessarily reflected in the planning decision. As any decision-making process is one of learning and negotiations between multiple stakeholders at multiple scales, the design review of proposals utilising such tools as visualisations and EIA must be reflected on. The first stage in this process is to instigate the monitoring and review of decisions made by the LPA. This would require some investment from LPAs in terms of staff time and expertise but would allow for the establishment of a clear picture of which planning conditions are being met, which aren't and the successful implementation of planning consents. Furthermore, in this period of regulatory search for tall building assessment methods, it offers the opportunity to reflect on how and why certain decisions are made so that practice can be improved in the future. In this way a robust basis for advising developers and their consultants on the information required for design review can be established.

The ways in which tall building proposals are presented also needs some consideration. Particularly in the visualisation of tall building proposals, methods need to be established which command the trust and respect not only of those stakeholders directly involved in the planning process but those which are either marginalised from that process or not part of it at all. A role for frameworks such as CABE–EH guidance is apparent here; suggested methodologies for visualising proposals would be useful to LPAs and interest groups in particular. To reflect the need to inspire confidence in the planning system generally and in reflecting the actual form of the building in reality, visualisations therefore need to reflect a consensus in methodological approach including how the visualisations are represented (CAD, GIS, paper or other models). The Landscape Institute (LI) – Institute of Environmental Management and Assessment (IEMA) Guidelines for Landscape and Visual Impact Assessment (LI-IEMA, 2002) suggest a way of attracting consensus in producing such visualisations through the identification of viewpoints which reflect consensus amongst stakeholders. As such, the involvement of communities, heritage interested groups and the public should be reflected in this process. Furthermore, the guidance suggests that the cumulative impact of proposals should be undertaken. Decision-makers, consultees and stakeholders could therefore reflect on those permissions which have not yet been implemented as well as ones recently built or under construction in the determination of tall building proposals.

Conclusions

The cities presented in this book uncovered a number of key elements for further discussion and debate. Firstly, they have outlined the distinctive dynamics of local conservation regimes which reflect the pro-growth agenda of local authorities seeking to attract inward investment and high profile development projects to underpin regeneration and redevelopment. Secondly, built heritage concerns have clearly been an important part of the assessment of proposals and are reflected in decision-making about tall building proposals. This is particularly true when the value of built heritage elements is recognised as part of the wider townscape, through characterisation studies, for example, such as in Vancouver and Newcastle. Thirdly, there is evidence that the worst impacts of tall buildings are regulated out of the most sensitive locations but that the indirect impacts of tall buildings are much more ambiguous and therefore difficult to address, particularly in pro-growth environments. Finally, the cities uncovered that there can often be a heritage dividend to tall building development particularly in the improvement of particular elements of the townscape and public realm works. As such some of the impacts of tall buildings can be mitigated through thoughtful and planned improvements to the townscape.

The distinctive form of tall buildings, particularly their height, offer unique challenges to decision-makers although the cities in this book have shown that tall buildings and the built heritage can co-exist. This is particularly the result of built heritage concerns being integrated into the wider framework for urban planning policies (Negussie, 2006). Approaches to built heritage and tall building management are understandable only within their locally specific contexts reflecting the dynamics of place and actor–network relations. The capacity for different local conservation planning regimes to manage the built heritage is contingent upon a range of factors including the extent to which built heritage concerns are embedded within wider planning cultures in a particular locality, the breadth of understanding of the wider townscape and opportunities for enhancement and change, and the relationships between key organisations who have responsibilities for change in the built environment.

The case studies have shown that tall buildings are not necessarily a threat to the built heritage in particular locations particularly when they are managed in a positive way as part of a deep understanding of the character and distinctiveness of place. The cases have also shown that the worst excesses of tall buildings are regulated out of our cities but that the impacts of such buildings are felt in locations where there is a lack of strategic planning about their location.

It is also true to say that planning practice in England has been slow to absorb the lessons of the past in seeking to locate tall buildings in particular locations as part of clusters and nodes. The history of tall building regulation in places like Paris shows us that it is possible for tall buildings and built heritage to co-exist and complement each other. Practice in England is starting to recognise that the approach of cities from this period could teach some important lessons for tall building management. Likewise it was apparent in the research that the broad spectrum of tools for tall building management employed in North America were not utilised in any of the

European cities. The lack of sophistication in approaches to tall building management was a feature of these cities although there is evidence that practice is improving as planning authorities become more experienced in dealing with this type of development. In Dublin, for example, the use of a tall building study combined with consensus about the conservation of the historic core of the city has reflected the approach of cities such as Paris and Stockholm in practically planning for conservation and growth. In Oslo however the designation of a growth node for tall buildings has been slightly more controversial due to the potential for tall buildings in that location to impact upon the form and fabric of the city. Furthermore, the use of assessment methods such as the visualisation of new buildings in particular view frameworks or the use of EIA in presenting potential impacts does not necessarily add much value to the process of design review in the absence of a strong understanding and appreciation of the townscape.

This book has sought to demonstrate that despite the evolution of new regulatory and decision support mechanisms in tall building assessment, there are significant barriers to the effective management of tall buildings in our cities. These barriers relate to the identification of heritage assets through the development control process, the evolving nature of decision support tools for tall buildings, the influence of certain actors on the development process, the particularity of place and local conservation cultures and the contested nature of tall building regulatory systems, and the overriding interests of economic development. It has found that in instances where characterisation of the townscape is undertaken (such as in Vancouver and Newcastle), proposals for tall buildings can be managed in a way that respects the significance of that townscape and which contribute to a twenty-first century city. It also allows for the identification of areas where tall buildings may be appropriate as well as areas where they will be inappropriate.

It remains to be seen whether the evolution of characterisation as a basis for proactive urban planning can play an important role in the management of change in cities. Having said that, without particular commitment by LPAs and central government, decision-making about proposals for tall buildings are doomed to be ad-hoc and incremental with our townscapes and skylines, reflecting this lack of strategy.

> *"Legislation must be sufficiently robust to protect what is fragile and sufficiently flexible to allow change. It must enable us to sustain what we value from the past both for its own sake and as a stimulus to creative new architecture and good design. It must enable our heritage to be a force for regenerating our cities."*
>
> *(Tessa Jowell in DCMS, 2003: 2)*

NOTES

Introduction

1 Definitions from Oxford English Dictionary (2002) Oxford: OUP.

4 The conservation challenge of tall buildings

1 Planning (Listed Buildings and Conservation Areas) Act 1990, 1(i).
2 Planning (Listed Buildings and Conservation Areas) Act 1990, 69(i).
3 Ancient Monuments and Archaeological Areas Act 1979, 61(xii).
4 Wagner, C. (2006) Conversation (*English Heritage, London office*), 06 March 2006.
5 McCallum, D. (2003) Conversation (*English Heritage, London office*), 03 December 2003.
6 Cole, S. (2005) Interview (*English Heritage, London office*), 18 October 2005.
7 Van Bruggen, B. (2005) Interview (*CABE*), 26 January 2005.

5 Tall buildings in Liverpool: balancing conservation and change in the maritime mercantile city

1 Bennison, J. (2005) Interview (*Liverpool Vision*), 29 July 2005.
2 Ibid.
3 Hinchliffe, J. (2005) Interview (*Liverpool City Council*), 17 June 2005 and 29 July 2005.
4 Lee, N. (2005) Interview (*Liverpool City Council*), 07 July 2005.
5 From Liverpool interviews.
6 Ibid.
7 Bennison, J. (2005) Interview (*Liverpool Vision*), 29 July 2005.
8 Lee, N. (2005) Interview (*Liverpool City Council*), 07 July 2005.
9 Ibid.
10 Burns, R. (2005) Interview (*English Heritage, Manchester office*), 20 July 2005.
11 Burchnall, M. (2005) Interview (*Liverpool City Council*), 29 July 2005.
12 Denyer, S. (2005) Interview (*ICOMOS*), 29 April 2005.
13 Bennison, J. (2005) Interview (*Liverpool Vision*), 29 July 2005.
14 Douglas, J. (2005) Interview (*Liverpool Vision*), 29 July 2005.
15 Lee, N. (2005) Interview (*Liverpool City Council*), 07 July 2005.

16 Denyer, S. (2005) Interview (*ICOMOS*), 29 April 2005.
17 Lee, N. (2005) Interview (*Liverpool City Council*), 07 July 2005.
18 Ibid.
19 Burns, R. (2005) Interview (*English Heritage, Manchester office*), 20 July 2005.

6 Tall buildings in Manchester: while Liverpool thinks, Manchester constructs

1 Ward, D. (2006) While Liverpool thinks, Manchester constructs, *The Guardian*, 02 February 2006, p.1.
2 Roscoe, D. (2005) Interview (*Manchester City Council*), 24 January 2005.
3 Harvey, R. (2005) Interview (*Manchester Civic Society*), 15 February 2005.
4 Sidebottom, M. (2005) Interview (*Manchester City Council*), 31 March 2005.
5 Martindale, A. (2005) Interview (*former English Heritage, Manchester office*), 21 January 2005.
6 Cooper, M. (2005) Interview (*English Heritage, Manchester office*), 28 January 2005.
7 Roscoe, D. (2005) Interview (*Manchester City Council*), 24 January 2005.
8 Roscoe, D. (2005) Interview (*Manchester City Council*), 24 January 2005.
9 Cooper, J. (2005) Interview (*Drivers Jonas*), 18 January 2005.
10 Martindale, A. (2005) Interview (*former English Heritage, Manchester office*), 21 January 2005.
11 Roscoe, D. (2005) Interview (*Manchester City Council*), 24 January 2005.
12 Harvey, R. (2005) Interview (*Manchester Civic Society*), 15 February 2005.
13 Shearn, M. (2005) Interview (*Manchester Civic Society*), 15 February 2005.
14 Harvey, R. (2005) Interview (*Manchester Civic Society*), 15 February 2005.
15 Ibid.
16 Roscoe, D. (2005) Interview (*Manchester City Council*), 24 January 2005.
17 Denyer, S. (2005) Interview (*ICOMOS*), 29 April 2005.
18 Roscoe, D. (2005) Interview (*Manchester City Council*), 24 January 2005.
19 Ibid.
20 Van Bruggen, B. (2005) Interview (*CABE*), 26 January 2005.
21 Roscoe, D. (2005) Interview (*Manchester City Council*), 24 January 2005.
22 Sidebottom, M. (2005) Interview (*Manchester City Council*), 31 March 2005.

7 Tall buildings in Birmingham: the new image of the city?

1 Parker, D. and Long, P. (2004) "The mistakes of the past?" Visual narratives of urban decline and regeneration, *Visual Culture* 5 (1), p.51.
2 Brown, M. (2005) Interview (*Birmingham City Council*), 21 February 2005.
3 Ling, E. (2005) Telephone conversation (*Twentieth Century Society*), 26 March 2005.
4 Powell, A. (2005) Interview (*Birmingham City Council*), 14 March 2005.
5 Ling, E. (2005) Telephone conversation (*Twentieth Century Society*), 26 March 2005.
6 Brown, M. (2005) Interview (*Birmingham City Council*), 21 February 2005.
7 Powell, A. (2005) Interview (*Birmingham City Council*), 14 March 2005.

8 "The blue, the creen and the city in between": tensions between conservation and tall building development in Oslo

1 Gallagher, K. (2005) Interview (*Oslo Teknopol*), 25 October 2005.
2 Horntvedt, G. (2005) Interview (Oslo kommune), 25 October 2005.
3 Karlberg, I. (2005) Interview (*Riksantikvaren*), 02 November 2005.
4 Sjaastad, M. (2005) Interview (*Arkitektur-og designhøgskoken i Oslo*), 27 October 2005.
5 Langset, H. (2005) Interview (*Riksantikvaren*), 02 November 2005.
6 Sjaastad, M. (2005) Interview (*Arkitektur-og designhøgskoken i Oslo*), 27 October 2005.

7 Sødal, A. (2005) Interview (*Stiftelsen Byens Fornyelse*), 28 October 2005.
8 Sjaastad, M. (2005) Interview (*Arkitektur-og designhøgskoken i Oslo*), 27 October 2005.
9 Sødal, A. (2005) Interview (*Stiftelsen Byens Fornyelse*), 28 October 2005.
10 Langset, H. (2005) Interview (*Riksantikvaren*), 02 November 2005.
11 Langset, H. (2005) Interview (*Riksantikvaren*), 02 November 2005.
12 Olaisen, S. (2005) Interview (*Byantikvaren*), 03 November 2003.
13 Sjaastad, M. (2005) Interview (*Arkitektur-og designhøgskoken i Oslo*), 27 October 2005.
14 Horntvedt, G. (2005) Interview (*Byrådsavdeling for byutvikling*), 25 October 2005.

9 Tall buildings in Dublin: property-led regeneration within an evolving conservation planning framework

1 Shaw, G. (2005) Interview (*Dublin Civic Trust*), 17 November 2005.
2 Central Statistics Office Ireland, www.cso.ie [accessed 15 September 2006].
3 Ibid.
4 Oifig Régiún na hÉireann, www.iro.ie [accessed 15 September 2006].
5 Greene, S. (2005) Interview (*Carrig Conservation*), 23 November 2005.
6 Shaw, G. (2005) Interview (*Dublin Civic Trust*), 17 November 2005.
7 Skeen, C. (2005) Interview (*Dublin Institute of Technology*), 17 November 2005.
8 Ibid.
9 Cahill, D. (2005) Interview (*Irish Georgian Society*), 15 November 2005.
10 Rose, K. (2005) Interview (*Dublin City Council*), 22 November 2005.
11 Ibid.
12 Lumley, I. (2005) Interview (*An Taisce*), 22 November 2005.
13 Rose, K. (2005) Interview (*Dublin City Council*), 22 November 2005.
14 Greene, S. (2005) Interview (*Carrig Conservation*), 23 November 2005.
15 Cahill, D. (2005) Interview (*Irish Georgian Society*), 15 November 2005.
16 Rose, K. (2005) Interview (*Dublin City Council*), 22 November 2005.

10 Tall buildings in Newcastle-Upon-Tyne: reconciling the past with the present?

1 Buswell, R. J. (1984) Reconciling the past with the present: conservation policy in Newcastle-upon-Tyne, *Cities* 1 (5), p.500.
2 Dewar, C. (2005) Interview (*English Heritage*), 20 April 2005.
3 Wyatt, T. (2005) Interview (*Newcastle City Council*), 21 March 2005.
4 Dewar, C. (2005) Interview (*English Heritage, Newcastle office*), 20 April 2005.
5 Wyatt, T. (2005) Interview (*Newcastle City Council*), 21 March 2005.
6 Dewar, C. (2005) Interview (*English Heritage, Newcastle office*), 20 April 2005.
7 Ibid.
8 Charge, R. (2005) Interview (*Newcastle City Council*), 21 March 2005.
9 Charge, R. (2005) Interview (*Newcastle City Council*), 21 March 2005.
10 Wyatt, T. (2005) Interview (*Newcastle City Council*), 21 March 2005.
11 Ibid.
12 Dewar, C. (2005) Interview (*English Heritage, Newcastle office*), 20 April 2005.

11 Tall buildings in Vancouver: celebrating the "cult of the view"

1 Berelowitz, L. 2005. *Dream City: Vancouver and the Global Imagination*, Vancouver, Douglas and McIntyre.

2   52% of the city's residents do not speak English as a first language, and a third of the population is of Chinese origin.
3   In conversation with Gordon Price, 2 November 2010.
4   Interview with Sylvia Holland, 31 October 2010.
5   Interview with Scot Hein, Vancouver City Council, 2 November 2011.
6   Interview with Scot Hein, Vancouver City Council, 2 November 2011.
7   Ibid.
8   Ibid.
9   Interview with Michael Gordon, Vancouver City Council, 3 November 2011.
10 Interview with Michael Gordon, 3 November 2010.
11 Interview with Michael Gordon, 3 November 2010.
12 Interview with Scot Hein, 2 November 2010.
13 Interview with Sylvia Holland, 31 October 2010.
14 Interview with Michael Gordon, 3 November 2010.
15 Interview with Sylvia Holland, 31 October 2010.
16 Interview with Michael Gordon, 3 November 2010.

12 Conclusions

1   McCallum, D. (2006) Conversation (*English Heritage, London office*), 12 September 2006.

REFERENCES

Introduction

Abel, C. 2003. *Sky High: Vertical Architecture,* London, Thames and Hudson Ltd.

Beedle, L. 1986. High-Rise Building: Recent Progress. Bethlehem: Council on Tall Buildings and Urban Habitat, LeHigh University Publications.

Carmona, M., Carmona, S. and Gallent, N. 2003. *Delivering New Homes: Processes, Planners and Providers,* London, Routledge.

Cohen, N. 1999. *Urban Conservation,* Cambridge, Massachusetts, The MIT Press.

Höweler, E. 2003. *Skyscraper: Designs of the Recent Past and for the Near Future,* London, Thames and Hudson.

Huxtable, A. 1984. *The Tall Building Artistically Reconsidered: the Search for a Skyscraper Style,* New York, Pantheon Books.

Huxtable, A. 1992. *The Tall Building Artistically Reconsidered: the Search for a Skyscraper Style,* Berkeley; Oxford, University of California Press.

McNeill, D. 2005. Skyscraper Geography. *Progress in Human Geography,* 29, 41–55.

Namier, L. B. S. 1931. *Skyscrapers: and Other Essays,* London, Macmillan and Co. Ltd.

Pløger, J. 2010. Contested Urbanism: Struggles About Representation. *Space and Polity,* 14, 143–165.

Sklair, L. 2006. Iconic Architecture and Capitalist Globalisation. *City,* 10, 21–48.

Strelitz, Z. 2005. *Tall Buildings: A Strategic Design Guide,* London, British Council for Offices.

Whatmore, S. 2002. *Hybrid Geographies: Natures, Cultures, Spaces,* London, Sage.

While, A. and Short, M. 2006. Hybrid Heritage: Post-war Urbanism and the Design Identity of Post-industrial Manchester. In: *Global Places, Local Spaces,* 05–07 April 2006, Bartlett School of Planning, UCL, London.

1 The tall building typology

Abel, C. 2003. *Sky High: Vertical Architecture,* London, Thames and Hudson Ltd.

Bradford Landau, S. and Condit, C. W. 1996. *Rise of the New York Skyscraper 1865–1913,* New Haven, Yale University Press.

Cobb, H. 2003. The Skyscraper as Citizen: Reflections on the Public Life of Private Buildings. In: LSE (ed.) *Cities Programme: Discussion Paper Series*, London, LSE.

Dupré, J. (1996) Skyscrapers, New York, Black Dog & Leventhal.

Evenson, N. 1979. *Paris: A Century of Change, 1878–1978,* New Haven and London, Yale University Press.

Evenson, N. 1981. The City as an Artefact: Building Control in Modern Paris. In: Kain, R. (ed.) *Planning for Conservation*, London, Mansell.

Francis-Jones, R., Nield, L., Ruan, X. and Van Der Plaat, D. (eds.) 2009. *Skyplane: What Effect do Towers have on Urbanism, Sustainability, The Workplace and Historic City Centres?*, Sydney, UNSW Press.

Goldberger, P. 1981. *The Skyscraper,* London, Penguin Books.

Goldberger, P. 1983. *On the Rise: Architecture and Design in a Postmodern Age,* New York, Penguin Books.

Hall, P. 1998. *Cities in Civilization: Culture, Innovation, and Urban Order,* London, Weidenfeld & Nicolson.

Harwood, E., Barson, S. and Cole, E. 2002. Tall Buildings: Aspects of their Development and Character in England. In: EH (ed.) *Historical Analysis and Research Team Reports and Papers 59*, London, English Heritage.

House of Commons 2002. Tall Buildings: Sixteenth Report of the Urban Affairs Sub-committee. London, TSO.

Höweler, E. 2003. *Skyscraper: Designs of the Recent Past and for the Near Future,* London, Thames and Hudson.

Huxtable, A. 1984. *The Tall Building Artistically Reconsidered: the Search for a Skyscraper Style,* New York, Pantheon Books.

Kain, R. 1981. *Planning for Conservation: An International Perspective,* Oxford and London, Mansell Publishing.

Kitt-Chappell, S. A. 1990. A Reconsideration of the Equitable Building in New York. *The Journal of the Society of Architectural Historians,* 49, 90–95.

Kostoff, S. 2001. *The City Shaped: Urban Patterns and Meanings Through History,* London, Thames and Hudson Ltd.

Lampugnani, V. M. 1983. *20th Century Architecture,* New York, Thames and Hudson.

Lee, L. O. 1999. Shanghai Modern: Reflections on Urban Culture in China. *Public Culture* 11, 75–107.

LeGates, R. T. and Stout, F. 2003. *The City Reader,* New York, Routldege.

LSE 2002. Tall Buildings: Vision of the Future or Victims of the Past? London, London School of Economics.

Millard, R. (Director) 2010. *Towering Ambition: A Tale of Two Cities,* UK, BBC Radio 4.

ML 2010. Revised Supplementary Planning Guidance: London View Management Framework. London, Mayor of London.

Namier, L. B. S. 1931. *Skyscrapers: and Other Essays,* London, Macmillan and Co. Limited.

Oldfield, P. and Wood, A. 2009. Tall Buildings in the Global Recession: 2008, 2020 and beyond. *Council on Tall Buildings and Urban Habitat (CTBUH) Journal,* 1, 20–26.

Pickard, R. 2001. *Management of Historic Centres,* London, Spon.

Qian, Z. 2010. Without Zoning: Urban Development and Land Use Controls in Houston. *Cities,* 27, 31–41.

Shiling, Z. 2002. Shanghai as a Mega-City, under the Influence of Globalization. In: Shanghai Architectural Society Annual Conference, 17 June 2002, Shanghai.

Sudjic, D. 1993. *The 100 Mile City,* London, Flamingo.

Sudjic, D. 2005. *The Edifice Complex: How the Rich and Powerful Shape the World,* York, Allen Lane.

Tan, A. and Low, L. 1999. Shanghai World Financial Center: Love and Rockets in the Spree Economy. In: Moore, R. (ed.) *Vertigo: The Strange New World of the Contemporary City*, Glasgow, Laurence King Publishing.

Tung, A. M. 2001. *Preserving the World's Great Cities: the Destruction and Renewal of the Historic Metropolis*, New York, Clarkson Potter.

Vickers, G. 1999. *Key Moments in Architecture: the Evolution of the City*, London, Hamlyn.

Watkins, D. 2000. *A History of Western Architecture*, London, Laurence King Publishing.

Webster, J. C. 1959. The Skyscraper: Logical and Historical Considerations. *Journal of the Society of Architectural Historians*, 18, 126–139.

Wood, A. 2004. New Paradigms in High Rise design. *CTBUH annual conference*. Seoul, Korea.

Yeang, K. 2002. *Reinventing the Skyscraper: A Vertical Theory of Urban Design*, Chichester, Wiley-Academy.

2 The potential impacts of tall buildings

Ashworth, G. J. and Larkham, P. J. 1994. *Building a New Heritage: Tourism, Culture and Identity in the New Europe*, London and New York, Routledge.

Attoe, W. 1981. *Skylines: Understanding and Molding Urban Silhouettes*, Chichester, Wiley.

BCO 2002a. Tall Office Buildings in London: Guidance on Planning. London, British Council for Offices.

BCO 2002b. Tall Office Buildings in London: The Economic Realities. London, British Council for Offices.

CABE 2003. Design Review: Guidance on How CABE Evaluates Quality in Architecture and Urban Design. London: CABE

Cohen, N. 1999. *Urban Conservation*, Cambridge, Massachusetts, The MIT Press.

Cullingworth, B. and Caves, R. W. 2003. *Planning in the USA: Policies, Issues and Processes*, London, Routledge.

Cullingworth, B. and Nadin, V. 2002. *Town and Country Planning in the UK*, London and New York, Routledge.

DEGW 2002. London's Skyline, Views and High Buildings. *SDS Technical Reports, number 19*, London, Greater London Authority.

Heath, T., Smith, S. G. and Lim, B. 2000. Tall Buildings and the Urban Skyline: the Effect of Visual Complexity on Preferences. *Environment and Behavior*, 32, 541–556.

HoC 2002. Tall Buildings: Sixteenth Report of the Urban Affairs Sub-committee. London, TSO.

Höweler, E. 2003. *Skyscraper: Designs of the Recent Past and for the Near Future*, London, Thames and Hudson.

Jones, C. and Slinn, P. 2006. Cultural Heritage and Environmental Impact Assessment in the Planarch Area of North West Europe. Manchester, University of Manchester.

Kostoff, S. 2001. *The City Shaped: Urban Patterns and Meanings Through History*, London, Thames and Hudson Ltd.

Larkham, P. J. 1992. *Conservation and the Changing Urban Landscape*, Oxford, Pergamon Press.

LSE 2002. Tall Buildings: Vision of the Future or Victims of the Past? London, London School of Economics.

Lynch, K. 1960. *The Image of the City*, Cambridge, Mass. and London, MIT Press.

Strelitz, Z. 2005. *Tall Buildings: A Strategic Design Guide*, London, British Council for Offices.

3 The emergence of planning frameworks for tall buildings

Adams, D., Croudace, R. and Tiesdell, S. 2011. Design Codes, Opportunity Space, and the Marketability of New Housing. *Environment and Planning B: Planning and Design,* 38, 289–306.

Babcock, R. F., Siemon, C. L. and Lincoln Institute Of Land, P. 1985. *The Zoning Game Revisited,* Cambridge, Mass, Lincoln Institute of Land Policy.

Barden, J. 1999. Computer Visualization: the Coming Revolution. *Impact Assessment and Project Appraisal,* 17, 331–338.

Bartlett, R. V. and Kurian, P. A. 2003. The Theory of Environmental Impact Assessment: Implicit Models of Policy Making. *Policy and Politics,* 27, 415–432.

Carmona, M., Carmona, S. and Gallent, N. 2003. *Delivering New Homes: Processes, Planners and Providers,* London, Routledge.

Carmona, M., Marshall, S. and Stevens, Q. 2006. Design Codes: Their Use and Potential. *Progress in Planning,* 65, 209–289.

Cullingworth, B. and Nadin, V. 2002. *Town and Country Planning in the UK,* London and New York, Routledge.

Dankwa, E. T. 1996. *New York Skyscrapers; 100 Years of High-rises.* New York City. Online: www.greatgridlock.net/NYC/nyc.html [accessed 25 June 2006].

EH and CABE 2002. *Buildings in Context: New Development in Historic Areas,* London, English Heritage.

Faludi, A. 1987. *A Decision-centred View of Environmental Planning,* Oxford, Pergamon.

Forrester, J. 1989. *Planning in the Face of Power,* Berkeley and Los Angeles, University of California Press.

Healey, P. 1992. Planning Through Debate: the Communicative Turn in Planning Theory. *Town Planning Review,* 63, 143–162.

Healey, P., Cameron, S., Davoudi, S., Graham, S. and Madanipour, A. 1995. *Managing Change: the New Urban Context,* Chichester, John Wiley & Sons.

Kitt-Chappell, S. A. 1990. A Reconsideration of the Equitable Building in New York. *The Journal of the Society of Architectural Historians,* 49, 90–95.

Kørnøv, L. and Thissen, W. A. H. 2000. Rationality in Decision- and Policy-making: Implications for Strategic Environmental Assessment. *Impact Assessment and Project Appraisal,* 18, 191–200.

Kumar, S. 2003. Information in Design Review. *Planning, Practice & Research,* 18, 243–263.

Kwartler, M. 1989. Legislating Aesthetics: The Role of Zoning in Designing Cities. In: Kayden, C. M. H. A. J. S. (ed.) *Zoning and the American Dream: Promises Still to Keep,* Washington DC, Planners Press.

Lauria, M. and Soll, M. J. 1996. Communicative Action, Power, and Misinformation in a Site Selection Process. *Journal of Planning Education and Research,* 15, 199–211.

Malczewski, J. 2004. GIS-based Land-use Suitability Analysis: a Critical Overview. *Progress in Planning,* 62, 3–65.

March, J. 1994. *A Primer of Decision-making,* New York, Free Press.

Punter, J. 1999. *Design Guidelines in American Cities: a Review of Design Policies and Guidance in Five West Coast Cities,* Liverpool, Liverpool University Press.

Punter, J. 2000. Regulation and Control. In: Knox, P. and Ozolins, P. (eds.) *Design Professionals and the Built Environment: an Introduction.* Chichester; New York, Wiley.

Sager, T. 2001. A Planning Theory Perspective on Impact Assessment. *Nordregio Report,* 6, 197–222.

Smith, H. H. 1983. *The Citizen's Guide to Zoning,* Chicago, American Planning Association.

Sussna, S. 1967. Bulk Control and Zoning: The New York Experience. *Land Economics,* 43, 158–171.

Sussna, S. 1989. Another Look at Height Regulations and Air Rights. *The Appraisal Journal,* 109–117.

Thomas, R. M. 2004. Urban Characterisation: Improving Methodologies. *English Heritage Conservation Bulletin,* 11–17.

Wakeford, R. 1990. *American Development Control: Parallels and Paradoxes from An English Perspective,* London, H.M.S.O.

Watkins, D. 2000. *A History of Western Architecture,* London, Laurence King Publishing.

Weiss, A. 1992. Density and Intervention: New York's Planning Tradition. In: Zunz, W. A. (ed.) *The Landscape of Modernity: Essays in New York City 1900–1940,* New York: Russell Sage Foundation.

Wood, C. 2003. *Environmental Impact Assessment: a Comparative Review,* Harlow, Pearson Education Ltd.

4 The conservation challenge of tall buildings

Ashworth, G. J. 1997. Conservation as Preservation or as Heritage: Two Paradigms and Two Answers. *Built Environment,* 23, 92–110.

Ashworth, G. J. 2002. The Experience of Heritage Conservation: Outcomes and Futures. In: Phelps, A., Ashworth, G. J. and Johansson, B. O. H. (eds.) *The Construction of Built Heritage: A European Perspective on Policies, Practices and Outcomes,* Aldershot, Ashgate.

Ashworth, G. J. and Larkham, P. J. 1994. *Building a New Heritage: Tourism, Culture and Identity in the New Europe,* London and New York, Routledge.

Barden, J. 1999. Computer Visualization: the Coming Revolution. *Impact Assessment and Project Appraisal,* 17, 331–338.

Bartlett, R. V. and Kurian, P. A. 2003. The Theory of Environmental Impact Assessment: Implicit Models of Policy Making. *Policy and Politics,* 27, 415–432.

Brown, M. 2006. Turning the Guidance into Working Documents. *Context,* 94, 17–19.

CABE 2002. The Value of Good Design: How Buildings and Spaces Create Economic and Social Value. London, CABE, Bartlett School of Planning.

CABE 2003. Design Review: Guidance on How CABE Evaluates Quality in Architecture and Urban Design. London, CABE.

CABE and EH 2003. Guidance on Tall Buildings. London.

Cohen, N. 1999. *Urban Conservation,* Cambridge, Massachusetts, The MIT Press.

Cullingworth, B. and Nadin, V. 2002. *Town and Country Planning in the UK,* London and New York, Routledge.

DCLG 2010. PPS5: Planning for the Historic Environment. London, DCLG.

DETR (1994) Planning Policy Guidance 15: Planning and the Historic Environment, London, TSO.

EH 2000. Power of Place: The Future of the Historic Environment. London, English Heritage.

EH 2001. Public Attitudes Towards Tall Buildings in Cities. London, English Heritage.

EH 2005a. English Heritage: The First 21 Years. *Conservation Bulletin.* London, English Heritage.

EH 2005b. Guidance on Conservation Area Appraisals. London, English Heritage.

EH 2005c. Guidance on the Management of Conservation Areas. London, English Heritage.

Formby, J. 1989. The Politics of Environmental Impact Assessment. *Impact Assessment Bulletin,* 8, 191–196.

Forrester, J. 1989. *Planning in the Face of Power,* Berkeley and Los Angeles, University of California Press.

Forrester, J. 1993. *Critical Theory, Public Policy and Practice,* Albany, State University of New York Press.

Graham, B., Ashworth, G. J. and Tunbridge, J. E. 2000. *A Geography of Heritage: Power, Culture and Economy,* London, Arnold.

Healey, P. 1988. *Land Use Planning and the Mediation of Urban Change,* Cambridge, Cambridge University Press.

Healey, P. 1997. *Collaborative Planning: Shaping Places in Fragmented Societies,* London, MacMillan Press.

Hewison, R. 1987. *The Heritage Industry: Britain in a Climate of Decline,* London, Methuen.

Hobson, E. 2004. *Conservation and Planning: Changing Values in Policy and Practice,* New York, NY, Spon Press.

HoC 2002. Tall Buildings: Sixteenth Report of the Urban Affairs Sub-committee. London, TSO.

HoC 2005. Government Response to the ODPM Housing, Planning and Local Government and the Regions Committee Report on the Role and Effectiveness of CABE. London, TSO.

ICOMOS 2005. ICOMOS and the World Heritage. In: ICOMOS (ed.). Vienna, ICOMOS.

Jones, C. and Slinn, P. 2006. Cultural Heritage and Environmental Impact Assessment in the Planarch Area of North West Europe. Manchester, University of Manchester.

King, A. 1997. The Politics of Vision. In: Groth, P. and Bresler, T. (eds.) *Understanding Ordinary Landscapes,* London, Yale University Press.

Kørnøv, L. and Thissen, W. A. H. 2000. Rationality in Decision- and Policy-making: Implications for Strategic Environmental Assessment. *Impact Assessment and Project Appraisal,* 18, 191–200.

Kumar, S. 2003. Information in Design Review. *Planning, Practice & Research,* 18, 243–263.

Langstaff, L. and Bond, A. 2002. The Consideration of Cultural Heritage within EIA Practice Throughout Europe. In: SUIT (ed.) *SUIT Position Papers,* University of Wales, Aberystwyth.

Larkham, P. J. 1996. *Conservation and the City,* London, Routledge.

Madanipour, A. 2006. Roles and Challenges of Urban Design. *Journal of Urban Design,* 11, 173–193.

March, J. 1994. *A Primer of Decision-making,* New York, Free Press.

Mason, R. 2002. Assessing Values in Conservation Planning: Methodological Issues and Choices. In: GCI (ed.) *Assessing the Values of Cultural Heritage,* Los Angeles, GCI.

McPherson, A. 2006. The New English Heritage Guidance. *Context,* 94, 15–17.

Mourato, S. and Mazzanti, M. 2002. Economic Valuation of Cultural Heritage: Evidence and Prospects. In: GCI (ed.) *Assessing the Values of Cultural Heritage,* Los Angeles, GCI.

Murdoch, J. 2000. Space Against Time: Competing Rationalities in Planning for Housing. *Transactions of the Institute of British Geographers,* 25, 503–519.

ODPM 2000. Our Towns and Cities: The Future – Delivering an Urban Renaissance (The Urban White Paper). London, TSO.

ODPM 2004. *Planning Policy Statement 12: Local Development Frameworks,* London, TSO.

Phelps, A., Ashworth, G. J. and Johansson, B. O. H. 2002. *The Construction of Built Heritage: A European Perspective on Policies, Practices and Outcomes,* Aldershot, Ashgate.

Shaw, B. J. and Jones, R. 1997. *Contested Urban Heritage: Voices from the Periphery,* Aldershot, Ashgate.

Strange, I. 1999. Urban Sustainability, Blobalisation and the Pursuit of the Heritage Aesthetic. *Planning Practice and Research,* 14, 301–311.

Strange, I. and Whitney, D. 2003. The Changing Roles and Purposes of Heritage Conservation in the UK. *Planning, Practice & Research,* 18, 219–229.

Tait, M. and While, A. 2009. Ontology and the Conservation of Built Heritage. *Environment and Planning B,* 27, 721–737.

Tewdwr-Jones, M. 1995. Development Control and the Legitimacy of Planning Decisions. *Town Planning Review,* 66, 163–181.

Thomas, R. M. 2004. Urban Characterisation: Improving Methodologies. *English Heritage Conservation Bulletin,* 11–17.

Tunbridge, J. E. and Ashworth, G. J. 1996. *Dissonant Heritage: the Management of the Past as a Resource in Conflict,* Chicester, Wiley.

While, A. 2006. Modernism vs Urban Renaissance: Negotiating Post-War Heritage in English City Centres. *Urban Studies,* 43, 2399–2419.

While, A. and Short, M. 2006. Hybrid Heritage: Post-war Urbanism and the Design Identity of Post-industrial Manchester. In: Global Places, Local Spaces, 05–07 April 2006, Bartlett School of Planning, UCL, London.

Wood, C. 2003. *Environmental Impact Assessment: a Comparative Review,* Harlow, Pearson Education Ltd.

5 Tall buildings in Liverpool: balancing conservation and change in the maritime mercantile city

Allinson, J. 2010. Population Migration and Urban Renaissance. *Town and Country Planning,* April 2010, 174–177.

Ben-Tovim, G. 2003. Futures for Liverpool. In: Munck, R. (ed.) *Reinventing the City? Liverpool in Comparative Perspective,* Liverpool, Liverpool University Press.

Biddulph, M. 2010. Liverpool: Liverpool's vision and the decade of cranes. In: Punter, J. (ed.) *Urban Design and the British Urban Renaissance,* London, Routledge.

Cocks, M. 2009. Governance Arrangements from a Regulationst Perspective: the Case of Liverpool. *Local Economy,* 24, 456–472.

Couch, C. 2003. *City of Change and Challenge: Urban Planning and Regeneration in Liverpool,* Aldershot, Ashgate.

Davis, L. (2002) Why We Were Right to Ignore Public Opinion, Liverpool Daily Post, 09 December 2002, p.4.

Donald Insall Associates (DIA) 2005. Lime Street Gateway: Heritage Impact Assessment. London, DIA.

EH 2005. Lime Street Gateway, Letter to Liverpool City Council from English Heritage, 11th February 2005.

Fray, G. 2004. Fourth Grace is Axed, *Liverpool Echo,* 19 July 2004, p.1.

Hobson, E. 2004. *Conservation and Planning: Changing Values in Policy and Practice,* New York, NY, Spon Press.

Jones, P. and Wilks-Heeg, S. 2004. Capitalising Culture: Liverpool 2008. *Local Economy,* 19, 341–360.

LCC 2004. Tall Buildings: Consultation Draft Supplementary Planning Document. Liverpool, LCC.

LCC 2005a. Draft Tall Buildings SPD: Consultation Response Schedule. Liverpool, LCC.

LCC 2005b. Planning Committee Report Agenda Item 17: Lime Street Station and Concourse House. Liverpool, LCC.

LCC 2009. World Heritage Site Supplementary Planning Document. Liverpool, LCC.

LCC and DCMS 2003. Nomination of Liverpool Maritime Mercantile City for Inscription on the World Heritage List. Liverpool, LCC and DCMS.

Meegan, R. 2003. Urban Regeneration, Politics and Social Cohesion: the Liverpool Case. In: Munck, R. (ed.) *Reinventing the City? Liverpool in Comparative Perspective*, Liverpool, Liverpool University Press.

Munck, R. 2003. *Reinventing the City? Liverpool in Comparative Perspective,* Liverpool, Liverpool University Press.

ODPM 2003. Regional Planning Guidance for the North West: RPG13. London, TSO.

ONS 2008. *Mid-year Population Estimates.* London, ONS. Online: www.statistics.gov.uk/census2001 [accessed 21 June 2011].

Pemberton, S. and Winstanley, R. 2010. Moving Beyond the Limits of Joined-up Government? Meta-governance, Quality of Relations and Addressing the Politics of Joining-up. *Urban Research and Practice,* 3, 25–38.

Sharples, J. 2004. *Pevsner Architectural Guide: Liverpool,* New Haven and London, Yale University Press.

Short, M. 2008. Tall Building Management in England. *Urban Design,* 105.

UNESCO 2004. Liverpool – Mercantile Maritime City. Vienna, UNESCO.

UNESCO 2005. Draft Memorandum on World Heritage and Contemporary Architecture: Managing the Historic Urban Landscape. Vienna, UNESCO.

6 Tall buildings in Manchester: while Liverpool thinks, Manchester constructs

CABE and EH 2003. Guidance on Tall Buildings. London.

Hall, P. 1998. The First Industrial City: Manchester 1760–1830. *Cities in Civilization: Culture, Innovation, and Urban Order.* London, Weidenfeld & Nicolson.

Hartwell, C. 2002. *Pevsner Architectural Guides: Manchester,* New Haven and London, Yale University Press.

Hebbert, M. 2010. Manchester: Making it happen. In: Punter, J. (ed.) *Urban Design and the British Urban Renaissance*, London, Routledge.

Kitchen, T. 1997. *People, Politics, Policies and Plans; the City Planning Process in Contemporary Britain,* London, Paul Chapman Publishing Ltd.

Marshall, W. 1994. Urban Design in Manchester. *Urban Design Quarterly,* 50, 18–21.

MCC 2004a. A Guide to Development in Manchester 2: Consultation Draft Supplementary Planning Guidance December 2004. Manchester, MCC.

MCC 2004b. A Guide to Development in Manchester: City Centre Development Event April 2004. Manchester, MCC.

MCC 2005a. Manchester and Salford (Ancoats, Castlefield and Worsley) Tentative World Heritage Site. Manchester: MCC.

MCC 2005b. *Manchester Civic Society: Its Purpose and Vision.* Manchester: MCS.

ONS 2008. *Mid-year Population Estimates.* London, ONS. Online: www.statistics.gov.uk [accessed 21 June 2011].

Peck, J. and Ward, K. 2002. *City of Revolution: Restructuring Manchester,* Manchester, Manchester University Press.

Quilley, S. 2000. Manchester First: From Municipal Socialism to the Entrepreneurial City. *International Journal of Urban and Regional Research,* 24, 601–615.

Short, M. 2008. Tall Building Management in England. *Urban Design,* 105.

Ward, K. 2003. Entrepreneurial Urbanism, State Restructuring and Civilizing "New" East Manchester. *Area,* 35, 116–127.

Williams, G. 2002. City Building: Developing Manchester's Urban Core. In: Peck, J. and Wood, K. *City of Revolution: Restructuring Manchester*, Manchester, Manchester University Press, 155–175.

7 Tall buildings in Birmingham: the new image of the city?

BCC 1993. The Birmingham Plan. Birmingham, BCC.

BCC 2000a. 2–18 Holloway Circus Planning Application Memorandum to Principal Planning Officer from Assistant Director of Planning. Birmingham, BCC.

BCC 2000b. Issues Report, 2–18 Holloway Circus. Report of Acting Director of Planning and Architecture to Members. Birmingham, BCC.

BCC 2001. 20th Century Birmingham Buildings: 50s. Birmingham, BCC.

BCC 2002a. 2–18 Holloway Circus Committee Report: Report to Members of the Development Control Committee. BCC, Birmingham.

BCC 2002b. Minutes of the Conservation Area Advisory Committee. Birmingham, BCC.

BCC 2003. High Places: A Planning Policy Framework for Tall Buildings. Birmingham, BCC.

BCC 2005. *Conservation of the Historic Environment.* Online: www.birmingham.gov.uk/buildingconservation [accessed 25 June 2006].

CABE 2002. 2–18 Holloway Circus, Mixed Use Tower. Letter to Birmingham City Council, BCC.

Cherry, G. E. 1994. *Birmingham: A Study in Geography, History and Planning,* Chichester, John Wiley & Sons.

Foster, A. 2005. *Pevsner Architectural Guides: Birmingham,* New Haven and London, YUP.

Harwood, E. 1999. White Light/White Heat: Rebuilding England's Provincial Towns in the Sixties. In: TCS (ed.) *The Sixties,* London, Twentieth Century Society.

Higgott, A. 2000. Birmingham: Building the Modern City. In: Dekker, T. (ed.) *The Modern City Revisited,* London, Spon Press.

Holyoak, J. 2010. Birmingham: Translating Ambition into Quality. In: Punter, J. (ed.) *Urban Design and the British Urban Renaissance,* London, Routledge.

Jenkins, S. 2003. Brum Looks to a Giant Bottom to Save its Soul. *The Times,* 03 September 2003.

Jones, P. 2004. The City as Artwork: the Dismemberment of Modern Birmingham. City in Art Conference, 08–11 September 2004, Krakow, Polish Academy and Institute of Art History, Jagiellonian University.

Kennedy, L. 2004. *Remaking Birmingham: the Visual Culture of Urban Regeneration,* London, Routledge.

King, A. 1997. The Politics of Vision. In: Groth, P. and Bresler, T. (eds.) *Understanding Ordinary Landscapes,* London, Yale University Press.

King, M. 2001. 2–18 Holloway Circus. Note from Mary King to Michael Taylor. Birmingham: EH.

Miles, S. 2005. "Our Tyne": Iconic Regeneration and the Revitalisation of Identity in Newcastle–Gateshead. *Urban Studies,* 42, 913–926.

ONS 2003. *Census 2001.* London, ONS. Online: www.statistics.gov.uk/census2001 [accessed 21 June 2011].

Parker, D. and Long, P. 2004. "The Mistakes of the Past?" Visual Narratives of Urban Decline and Regeneration. *Visual Culture,* 5, 37–58.

Short, M. 2008. Tall Building Management in England. *Urban Design,* 105.

Slater, T. R. and Larkham, P. 1996. Whose Heritage? Conserving Historical Townscapes in Birmingham. In: Gerrard, A. J. and Slater, T. R. (eds.) *Managing a Conurbation: Birmingham and its Region,* Studley, Brewin Books.

8 "The blue, the green and the city in between": tensions between conservation and tall building development in Oslo

Amdam, R. 2002. Sectoral Versus Territorial Regional Planning and Development in Norway. *European Planning Studies,* 10, 99–111.

Felberg, K. 2005. Cultural Implementation Programme – A New Tool for Cultural Planning. In: 41st ISoCaRP Congress 2005, April 2005, Oslo, Directorate for Public Construction and Property.

Herbjørnsrud, D. 2004. Slutt på høyhus i Oslo [The End of Tall Buildings in Oslo]. *Aftenposten,* 10 November 2005.

Langset, H. 2005. The Seafront Development of Bjørvika and the Challenge of Maintaining and Strengthening the Integrity of the Old Port. In: Civvih Congress, Istanbul, 21–24 May 2005.

OK 2002. Høyhus i Oslo: vurdering av prinsipper for høyhussstrategi [Tall Buildings in Oslo: an Evaluation of Principles for a Tall Buildings Strategy]. Oslo, Avdeling for Byutvikling.

OK 2003. Byutvikling i Bjørvika–Bispevika–Lohavn: Reguleringsplan [Town Development in Bjørvika–Bispevika–Lohavn: Development plan]. Oslo, byrådet, byrådssak 138/03, 22 May 2003.

OK 2004a. Høyhus kun i Bjørvika-området [Tall Buildings Only in the Bjørvika Area]. Oslo, Oslo kommune press release 2583–7786.

OK 2004b. The Political and Administrative Systems of the City of Oslo. Oslo, Oslo Kommune.

OK 2005. Høyhus i Oslo – strategi for videre arbeid [Tall buildings in Oslo – A Strategy for Further Work]. Oslo: Oslo Kommune.

OK 2006a. Kommunedelplan for byutvikling og bevaring i indre Oslo 2005–2020 [District Plan for Town Development and Conservation in inner Oslo 2005–2020]. Oslo, Oslo Kommune.

OK 2006b. Oslo – the Fjordcity. Plan for Urban Development of the Waterfront. Oslo, Oslo Kommune.

Skjeggedal, T. 2005. Ambitions and Realities in Norwegian Regional Planning. *European Planning Studies,* 13, 731–748.

Statistics Norway 2010. Population Statistics by County. Online: www.ssb.no [accessed on 17 August 2010].

9 Tall buildings in Dublin: property-led regeneration within an evolving conservation planning framework

ABP 2005. Inspector's Report into the Appeal by the Irish Georgian Society and Others Against the Decision to Approve Development, ref. 1290/04. Dublin, ABP.

Bor, W. 1967. An environmental policy for Dublin. *Journal of the Town Planning Institute,* 53, 293–296.

DCC 2004a. Dublin City Development Plan 2005–2011. Dublin, DCC.

DCC 2004b. Report to Committee: Heuston Gate Tower. Dublin, DCC.

DCC 2008. A Review of the Discussion Document "Maximising the City's Potential: A Strategy for Intensification and Height" and Recommendations for Way Forward. Dublin, DCC.

DCC 2011. Dublin City Development Plan 2011–2017 Interim Document. Dublin, DCC.

DEGW 2000. Managing Intensification and Change: A Strategy for Dublin Building Height. London, DEGW.

DEHLG 2002. The National Spatial Strategy for Ireland. Dublin, DEHLG.

Green, P. 2005. Inspectors Report: Application for a Ten Year Planning Permission for Mixed Use Development on the Site at Military Road/St John's Road, Dublin 8. Report to An Bord Pleanála. Dublin: An Bord Pleanála.

Lane, P. R. 2011. The Irish Crisis. Dublin: Trinity College Dublin.

McDonald, F. and Nix, J. 2005. *Chaos at the Cross Roads,* Kinsale, Gandon Books.

McGuirk, P. M. 2000. Power and Policy Networks in Urban Governance: Local Government and Property-led Regeneration in Dublin. *Urban Studies,* 37, 651–672.

McWilliams, D. 2005. *The Pope's Children: Ireland's New Elite,* Dublin, Gill and MacMillan.

Negussie, E. 2001. Dublin, Ireland. In: Pickard, R. (ed.) *Management of Historic Centres,* London, Spon Press.

Negussie, E. 2006. Implications of Neo-liberalism for Built Heritage Management: Institutional and Ownership Structures in Ireland and Sweden, *Urban Studies,* 43 (10) 1803–1824.

O'Sullivan, J. 2005. Policy on High-rise Buildings in Dublin, *The Irish Times,* 08 February 2005, p. 5.

Stirling, N., Cunningham, D. and Norwood, G. 2008. Republic of Ireland. *Estates Gazette,* 0821, 99–109.

Waldron, R. 2011. "The Debt of the Irish": Insights from the "Boom and Bust" in the Greater Dublin Area's Residential Property Market. In: The Struggle to Belong: Dealing with Diversity in 21st Century Urban Settings, 07–09 July 2011, Amsterdam, The Netherlands.

10 Tall buildings in Newcastle-Upon-Tyne: reconciling the past with the present?

Buswell, R. J. 1984. Reconciling the Past with the Present: Conservation Policy in Newcastle-upon-Tyne. *Cities,* 1, 500–514.

CABE 2002. Newcastle: Residential Tower, Quayside. Letter to Newcastle City Council.

Cousins, J. 2004. Proposed Quayside Tower. Letter to EH.

EH 2005. *Buildings at Risk Register.* London, English Heritage. Online: www.english-heritage.org.uk/server/show/nav.1424 [Accessed 21 June 2011].

GMBC 2002. Erection of 32 Storey Tower at Quayside, Adjacent to Mouth of the Ouseburn. Re-issued letter to NCC, GMBC.

LUC, EH and CABE 2003. Urban Landscape Study of the Tyne Gorge. London, Land Use Consultants.

Miles, S. 2005. "Our Tyne": Iconic Regeneration and the Revitalisation of Identity in Newcastle–Gateshead. *Urban Studies,* 42, 913–926.

NCC 2000. Going for Growth. Newcastle, NCC.

NCC 2006. *Historic Environment: Your City, Your Heritage.* Newcastle, NCC. Online: www.newcastle.gov.uk [Accessed 21 June 2011].

NNS 2004. Wimpey Tower Update. *City and County: Journal of the Northumberland and Newcastle Society,* p.2.

Office for National Statistics (ONS) 2003 Census 2001, Online: www.statistics.gov.uk/census2001 [Accessed on 25 June 2006].

Pendlebury, J. 1999. The Conservation of Historic Areas in the UK: a Case Study of "Grainger Town", Newcastle-upon-Tyne, *Cities,* 16, 423–433.

Pendlebury, J. 2001. Grainger Town, Newcastle-upon-Tyne, United Kingdom. In: Pickard, R. (ed.) *Management of Historic Centres,* London, Spon Press.

Punter, J. 1999. Improving the Instruments, Processes and Products of Design Control in Europe. *Urban Design International,* 4, 79–100.

Soult, G. 2003. Re-Graingerising Brasilia. *Northern Review,* 12, 1–6.

Wilkinson, S. 1992. Towards a New City? A Case Study of Image Improvement Initiatives in Newcastle-upon-Tyne. In: Healey, P., Davoudi, S., Tavsanoglu, S., O'Toole, M. and Usher, D. (eds.) *Rebuilding the City: Property-led Urban Regeneration,* London, E&FN Spon.

11 Tall buildings in Vancouver: celebrating the "cult of the view"

Berelowitz, L. 2005. *Dream City: Vancouver and the Global Imagination,* Vancouver, Douglas and McIntyre.

Chamberlain, L. 2005. Trying to Build the Grand Central of the West. *The New York Times,* 28 December 2005.

COV 1997a. Downtown Vancouver Skyline Study. Vancouver, COV.

COV 1997b. Downtown Vancouver Skyline Study – Recommended Option. Vancouver, COV.

COV 1997c. General Policy for Higher Buildings. Vancouver, COV.

COV 2003a. DD (except Downtown South) C-5, C-6, HA-1 AND HA-2 Character Area Descriptions. Vancouver, COV.

COV 2003b. HBAP minutes. Vancouver, COV.

COV 2003c. Urban Structure Policy Report: CD-1 Re-zoning at 1120 West Georgia Street. Vancouver, Vancouver City Council.

COV 2005. 1120 West Georgia Street: CD-1 Text Amendment. Vancouver, COV.

COV 2010. View Protection Guidelines. Vancouver, City of Vancouver Community Services.

COV 2011. Zoning and Development By-law. In: Vancouver, C. O. (ed.). Vancouver, COV.

Olds, K. 1998. Globalisation and Urban Change: Tales from Vancouver via Hong Kong. *Urban Geography,* 19, 360–385.

Punter, J. 2003a. From Design Advice to Peer Review: the Role of the Urban Design Panel in Vancouver. *Journal of Urban Design,* 8, 113–135.

Punter, J. 2003b. *The Vancouver Achievement: Urban Planning and Design,* Vancouver, UBC Press.

Reza-Jessa, A. 2009. Place Image in Vancouver: Vancouverism, EcoDensity and the Resort City. Vancouver, URST 400.

Statistics Canada 2006. *Population and demography.* Ottawa, Statistics Canada. Online: www.statcan.gc.ca/start-debut-eng.html [Accessed 21 June 2011].

Stewart, K. 2006. Designing Good Urban Governance Indicators: the Importance of Citizen Participation and its Evaluation in Greater Vancouver. *Cities,* 23, 196–2004.

12 Conclusions

Cullingworth, B. and Nadin, V. 2002. *Town and Country Planning in the UK,* London and New York, Routledge.

DCMS 2003. Protecting Our Historic Environment: Making the System Work Better. London: DCMS.

HoC 2002. Tall Buildings: Sixteenth Report of the Urban Affairs Sub-committee. London, TSO.

LI-IEMA 2002. Guidelines for Landscape and Visual Impact Assessment. Lincoln, IEMA.

McPherson, A. 2006. The new English Heritage guidance, *Context* 94, 15–17.

Negussie, E. 2006. Implications of Neo-liberalism for Built Heritage Management: Institutional and Ownership Structures in Ireland and Sweden. *Urban Studies,* 43.

Whatmore, S. 2002. *Hybrid Geographies: Natures, Cultures, Spaces,* London, Sage.

While, A. 2006. Modernism vs Urban renaissance: Negotiating Post-war Heritage in English City Centres. *Urban Studies,* 43, 2399–2419.

While, A. and Short, M. 2011. Place Narratives and Heritage Management: the Modernist Legacy in Manchester. *Area,* 43, 4–13.

INDEX